Related Books of Interest

Viral Data in SOA
An Enterprise Pandemic

by Neal Fishman
ISBN: 0-13-700180-0

Leading IBM information forensics expert Neal Fishman helps you identify the unique challenges of data quality in your SOA environment—and implement solutions that deliver the best results for the long term at the lowest cost. Writing for both business and technical professionals, Fishman shows how to think about data quality on a risk/reward basis...establishing an effective data governance initiative...how to evaluate data quality and overcome its inevitable decay...and, last but not least, how to actually derive a data quality initiative that works.

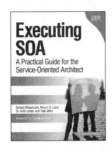

Executing SOA
A Practical Guide for the Service-Oriented Architect

by Norbert Bieberstein, Robert G. Laird, Dr. Keith Jones, and Tilak Mitra
ISBN: 0-13-235374-1

In *Executing SOA*, four experienced SOA implementers share realistic, proven, "from-the-trenches" guidance for successfully delivering on even the largest and most complex SOA initiative.

This book follows up where the authors' best-selling *Service-Oriented Architecture Compass* left off, showing how to overcome key obstacles to successful SOA implementation and identifying best practices for all facets of execution—technical, organizational, and human. Among the issues it addresses: introducing a services discipline that supports collaboration and information process sharing; integrating services with preexisting technology assets and strategies; choosing the right roles for new tools; shifting culture, governance, and architecture; and bringing greater agility to the entire organizational lifecycle, not just isolated projects.

 Listen to the author's podcast at:
ibmpressbooks.com/podcasts

Related Books of Interest

SOA Governance
Achieving and Sustaining
Business and IT Agility

by William A. Brown, Robert G. Laird, Clive Gee, and Tilak Mitra

ISBN: 0-13-714746-5

Inadequate governance might be the most widespread root cause of SOA failure. In *SOA Governance*, a team of IBM's leading SOA governance experts share hard-won best practices for governing IT in any service-oriented environment.

The authors begin by introducing a comprehensive SOA governance model that has worked in the field. They define what must be governed, identify key stakeholders, and review the relationship of SOA governance to existing governance bodies as well as governance frameworks like COBIT. Next, they walk you through SOA governance assessment and planning, identifying and fixing gaps, setting goals and objectives, and establishing workable roadmaps and governance deliverables. Finally, the authors detail the build-out of the SOA governance model with a case study.

The New Language
of Business
SOA & Web 2.0

by Sandy Carter

ISBN: 0-13-195654-X

In The New Language of Business, senior IBM executive Sandy Carter demonstrates how to leverage SOA, Web 2.0, and related technologies to drive new levels of operational excellence and business innovation.

Writing for executives and business leaders inside and outside IT, Carter explains why flexibility and responsiveness are now even more crucial to success—and why services-based strategies offer the greatest promise for achieving them.

You'll learn how to organize your business into reusable process components—and support them with cost-effective IT services that adapt quickly and easily to change. Then, using extensive examples—including a detailed case study describing IBM's own experience—Carter identifies best practices, pitfalls, and practical starting points for success.

Related Books of Interest

Dynamic SOA and BPM
Best Practices for Business Process Management and SOA Agility

by Marc Fiammante
ISBN: 0-13-701891-6

Thousands of enterprises have adopted Service Oriented Architecture (SOA) based on its promise to help them respond more rapidly to changing business requirements by composing new solutions from existing business services. To deliver on this promise, however, companies need to integrate solid but flexible Business Process Management (BPM) plans into their SOA initiatives. Dynamic SOA and BPM offers a pragmatic, efficient approach for doing so. Top IBM® SOA architect Marc Fiammante takes you step-by-step through combining BPM and SOA, and using them together to build a more flexible, dynamic enterprise. Throughout the book, he emphasizes hands-on solutions based on his experience supporting dozens of enterprise SOA implementations. Practical from start to finish, Dynamic SOA and BPM squarely addresses two of the most critical challenges today's IT executives, architects, and analysts face: implementing BPM as effectively as possible and deriving more value from their SOA investments.

Enterprise Master Data Management
Dreibelbis, Hechler, Milman, Oberhofer, van Run, Wolfson
ISBN: 0-13-236625-8

IBM WebSphere DataPower SOA Appliance Handbook
Hines, Rasmussen, Ryan, Kapadia, Brennan
ISBN: 0-13-714819-4

WebSphere Engineering
Ding
ISBN: 0-13-714225-0

Rapid Portlet Development with WebSphere Portlet Factory
Bowley
ISBN: 0-13-713446-0

The Greening of IT
Lamb
ISBN: 0-13-715083-0

Enterprise Java Programming with IBM WebSphere
Brown, Craig, Hester, Pitt, Stinehour, Weitzel, Amsden, Jakab, Berg
ISBN: 0-321-18579-X

Understanding IBM® SOA Foundation Suite

Learning Visually with Examples

Understanding IBM® SOA Foundation Suite

Learning Visually with Examples

Tinny Ng, Jane Fung, Laura Chan, and Vivian Mak

IBM Press
Pearson plc
Upper Saddle River, NJ • Boston • Indianapolis • San Francisco
New York • Toronto • Montreal • London • Munich • Paris • Madrid
Cape Town • Sydney • Tokyo • Singapore • Mexico City

Ibmpressbooks.com

IBM Press Program Managers: Tara Woodman, Ellice Uffer

Cover Design: IBM Corporation

Associate Publisher: Greg Wiegand

Marketing Manager: Kourtnaye Sturgeon

Publicist: Heather Fox

Acquisitions Editor: Bernard Goodwin

Managing Editor: Kristy Hart

Designer: Alan Clements

Project Editor: Andy Beaster

Copy Editor: Karen A. Gill

Indexer: Cheryl Lenser

Compositor: Jake McFarland

Proofreader: Jennifer Gallant

Manufacturing Buyer: Dan Uhrig

Published by Pearson plc

Publishing as IBM Press

The following terms are trademarks or registered trademarks of International Business Machines Corporation in the United States, other countries, or both: IBM, the IBM logo, IBM Press, CICS, Cloudscape, DataPower, DB2, DB2 Universal Database, developerWorks, FileNet, MQSeries, Rational, Tivoli, and WebSphere. Microsoft, Windows, and the Windows logo are trademarks of Microsoft Corporation in the United States, other countries, or both. Java and all Java-based trademarks are trademarks of Sun Microsystems, Inc. in the United States, other countries, or both. Other company, product, or service names may be trademarks or service marks of others.

Library of Congress Cataloging-in-Publication Data

Understanding IBM SOA foundation suite : learning visually with

examples / Tinny Ng ... [et al.].

   p. cm.

  ISBN 978-0-13-815040-2 (hardback : alk. paper) 1. Service-oriented

architecture (Computer science) I. Ng, Tinny, 1972-

 TK5105.5828.U54 2009

 004.6'54--dc22

                              2009023539

          Pearson Education, Inc.
          Rights and Contracts Department
          501 Boylston Street, Suite 900
          Boston, MA 02116
          Fax (617) 671 3447

          ISBN-13: 978-0-13-815040-2
          ISBN-10: 0-13-815040-0

Text printed in the United States on recycled paper at R.R. Donnelley in Crawfordsville, Indiana.
First printing August 2009

To my mother in heaven: Love you and miss you forever.
And to my father and my husband
Francis: Thank you for loving and standing by me all the time —Tinny Ng

To my beloved daughter Ashley and husband Ambrose. —Jane Fung

For Victoria, who reads about portlet at seven. For Claire, who just loves
reading. And for Dave, who is in every part of this journey. —Laura Chan

To my beloved parents, for always being there for me; my daughter Jasmine;
and my husband Xu. —Vivian Mak

Contents

Table of Contents

Preface

Without change, there is no innovation.

We all want to try new things, open the door, and step into the next exciting new space. But that first step is so overwhelming that it requires a huge amount of startup time and research. It is not easy. We often give ourselves excuses and resistance not to try.

There is no better time than the present. This book is intended to make it easy and effortless for you, as a software developer who wants to ramp up your skills for Service-Oriented Architecture (SOA), to try something new: the IBM SOA Foundation Suite.

The objective of *Understanding IBM SOA Foundation Suite: Learning Visually with Examples* is to build the skills you need for today and position you for the future. This book introduces you to ten IBM products in the IBM SOA Foundation (www-01.ibm.com/ software/solutions/soa/offerings.html) and gets you started with the basics quickly using a collection of hands-on tutorials. The target audience is assumed to have little or no skill for these products.

Each chapter has a product overview that talks about the significance of the product and some of the basic concepts related to the product space. Every chapter has a mini scenario that you will follow in the hands-on tutorial. These scenarios are designed to guide you through the basic navigations and usage of the products. Furthermore, the tutorials are accompanied by videos that allow you to watch and learn if you are under a deadline and do not have enough time to do the tutorials or set up the products.

IBM SOA Foundation is scalable. Companies who are interested in SOA can choose to begin with certain focus areas and progress through SOA gradually as requirements come. Being able to cover the fundamental concepts of ten different IBM SOA products in one book, *Understanding IBM SOA Foundation Suite: Learning Visually with Examples,* serves as a good reference for you. You, as a software developer for the company, can always come back to this book anytime to refresh your skills for various IBM SOA products when the company is ready to pull in different subsets. This book gives you a head start and positions you well in your company and in the job market. Being able to broaden your foundation across a spectrum of products will be an invaluable experience.

What Will Be Covered in the Tutorials?

This book contains eight chapters that represent a wide selection of products across the IBM SOA Foundation. The products can roughly be categorized into the following:

- Service Design
- Service Creation
- Service Governance
- Service Integration
- Service Connectivity
- Collaboration
- Service Security

Chapter 1: Introduction

This chapter expands above categories with more details and gives a brief overview of the IBM SOA Foundation.

Chapter 2: Service Design with IBM Rational Software Architect

The exercises in this chapter step you through how to design your service using Unified Modeling Language (UML) diagrams, share your design with peers as Hypertext Markup Language (HTML) files, and transform the UML design to and from Java using IBM Rational Software Architect.

- Tutorial 2.1—Use a UML Model to Capture a Service Design
- Tutorial 2.2—Capture the Use Cases for a Service Using a Use Case Diagram
- Tutorial 2.3—Design the Blueprint for a Service Using a Class Diagram
- Tutorial 2.4—Detail the Flow of a Service Using a Sequence Diagram
- Tutorial 2.5—Share the Service Design with Others
- Tutorial 2.6—Transform the Service Design to Implementation with Round-Trip Engineering

Chapter 3: Service Creation with IBM Rational Application Developer and IBM WebSphere Application Server

The tutorials that are featured in this chapter are separated into two parts: service creation in IBM Rational Application Developer and service deployment in IBM WebSphere Application Server. In IBM Rational Application Developer, you will create and invoke a Web service and access a database using Java Persistence API (JPA). In IBM WebSphere Application Server, you will deploy and configure the application after development is completed.

- Tutorial 3.1—Create, Deploy, and Test a Web Service
- Tutorial 3.2—Create a Database Table
- Tutorial 3.3—Invoke a Web Service and Persist the Data Using Java Persistence API
- Tutorial 3.4—Deploy an Application into a WebSphere Application Server

Chapter 4: Service Governance with IBM WebSphere Service Registry and Repository

The hands-on exercise for this chapter tells you a story about "A Day with WSRR," where you will explore many of the capabilities in IBM WebSphere Service Registry and Repository. The story has three users: an administrator, a service developer, and an application developer. As an administrator, you will set up the registry and repository with business model templates and a classification system. As a service developer, you will publish the developed service artifacts into the registry and repository, update them, and move them through the governance life cycle. As an application developer, you will perform a search for the right service and reuse it in your application.

- Tutorial 4.1—Set Up the Registry and Repository as an Administrator
- Tutorial 4.2—Publish a New Service as a Service Developer
- Tutorial 4.3—Reuse Services as an Application Developer
- Tutorial 4.4—Update Existing Services as a Service Developer

Chapter 5: Service Integration with IBM WebSphere Integration Developer and IBM WebSphere Process Server

In this chapter you will use existing services to create a new business process by assembling them. The scenario features an ordering process of a car manufacturing company. You will create a simple business process as well as other components in IBM WebSphere Integration Developer and then deploy them to IBM WebSphere Process Server.

- Tutorial 5.1—Create a Business Process
- Tutorial 5.2—Assemble and Execute the Module
- Tutorial 5.3—Deploy to a WebSphere Process Server

Chapter 6: Service Connectivity with IBM WebSphere Message Broker

This exercise lets you practice using IBM WebSphere Message Broker to implement a service that handles a library book search request. You will be writing Embedded Structured Query Language (ESQL) to implement a function that queries a library database for the book. You will also be using the Mapping node that is supplied with the product to create a search response message from the search request message.

- Tutorial 6.1—Configure Message Broker Toolkit with Predefined Databases and Runtime Artifacts
- Tutorial 6.2—Create the Message Flow and Message Set for the Library Book Search Service
- Tutorial 6.3—Deploy and Test the Library Book Search Service

Chapter 7: Collaboration with IBM WebSphere Portlet Factory and IBM WebSphere Portal

The tutorial in this chapter introduces you to IBM WebSphere Portlet Factory and IBM WebSphere Portal. It provides step-by-step instructions to give you a complete end-to-end experience from development to production. You will develop and test two portlets in a development environment using IBM WebSphere Portlet Factory, and then you will deploy/manage the portlets in a production environment using IBM WebSphere Portal. These portlets use the service provider and service consumer design.

- Tutorial 7.1—Create and Test a Simple Portlet
- Tutorial 7.2—Create and Test a Portlet That Accesses a Database
- Tutorial 7.3—Deploy a Portlet

Chapter 8: Service Security with IBM Tivoli Federated Identity Manager

The tutorials designed for this chapter illustrate both the token generator and token consumer functionalities of Tivoli Federated Identity Manager (TFIM). You will enable security for a service provider so that requesters must provide a valid Username security token for access. Then you will configure a service requester and enable its security so that it will generate a valid security token for accessing the service provider.

- Tutorial 8.1—Enable Security for a Service Provider
- Tutorial 8.2—Enable Security for a Service Requester
- Tutorial 8.3—Test the Service

What Is Included in the CD-ROM?

In the CD included in this book, you will find completed solutions for all the exercises discussed in this book. All of the tutorials have been recorded as videos so you can learn the operational concepts of the products.

The CD is organized as follows:

```
readme.html
chapter x
  readme.html
  /setup
  /tutorial x.y
    /solution
    /tutorial files
    /video
```

1. There is a readme file that can be opened in any browser. It provides a table of links to the readme file of each chapter.

2. Each chapter folder has the following structure:

   a. A readme file that can be opened in any browser. It gives you a brief introduction to what to expect in the folder underneath. It also provides a table of links to the videos that can be clicked and run directly.

   b. A setup folder that contains the files, if any, that are needed to set up the tutorials.

   c. A set of tutorial x.y folders. Each has:

      i. A solution folder that contains a completed solution, if any, for the subject tutorial.

      ii. A tutorial files folder that contains the files, if any, that are needed when exercising the subject tutorial.

      iii. A video folder that contains the video files for the subject tutorial allowing readers to watch the step-by-step instructions. Open the HTML file in any browser to watch the video.

Acknowledgments

We, the author team, would like to thank the following people who have contributed valuable input to our book:

Allen Chan
Anita Dave
David King
Eric Wood
Ian Shore
Julie King
Lawrence Mandel
Mike Diplock
Patrick R. Wardrop
Roke Jung
Suman Kalia

About the Authors

 **Tinny Ng** is a scenario architect at the Scenario Analysis Lab of IBM Software Group Strategy and Technology. Her primary focus is to improve the cross-brand integration capability and consumability of IBM SWG products. She architects solutions to address the identified integration issues and leads the team to bring the solution to delivery. Tinny has more than 15 years of experience in software development, from architectural design to implementation, including application building, packaging, testing, and support. She also has extensive publishing experience, including numerous IBM developerWorks articles with IBM developerWorks Contributing Author designation. In addition, she has a number of patent applications.

 Jane Fung is a senior IT specialist at IBM Canada Ltd. She has technical sales responsibility on WebSphere Service Registry and Repository. Previously, she was on the WebSphere Integration Developer development team responsible for developing the Business Process Execution Language (BPEL) and Business Rules debuggers. Jane received a bachelor in electrical engineering from the University of Waterloo. She has extensive publishing experience, including numerous developerWorks articles. Jane was the lead author of the IBM Press book, *An Introduction to Rational Application Developer, A Guided Tour*.

 Laura Chan is a senior software developer at IBM Software Group Strategy and Technology. She is currently responsible for providing scalable ways to solve major consumability issues experienced by the clients when combinations of IBM software are integrated to implement business scenarios. Laura has worked with a number of releases of the WebSphere Portal product and has published many developerWorks articles with this product. She has also worked in several aspects of software development, including development, testing, documentation, customer support, services, marketing, and project management.

 Vivian Mak is a software developer in the WebSphere Message Broker team and WebSphere Integration Developer team at the IBM Toronto Lab. She is responsible for developing the ESQL component in WebSphere Message Broker Toolkit and MQ adapter binding in WebSphere Integration Developer.

Introduction

Service-Oriented Architecture (SOA) has been around for years, and there is no doubt that its meaning, industry's interpretation, and approaches have evolved. No one will argue that the gist of SOA will continue to be true in the years to come.

What remains unchanged is the importance of possessing a good knowledge base for SOA. A solid foundation is essential for building any great structure. A pyramid without a wide base would shatter over time, and the Great Wall of China without strong groundwork would not last thousands of years. Similarly, for a SOA implementer, having a good knowledge foundation of SOA is crucial for building any information technology (IT) architecture or project.

This book, *Understanding IBM SOA Foundation Suite: Learning Visually with Examples*, intends to help developers build a good knowledge base of IBM SOA products. The products that comprise IBM SOA Foundation are complex, and the learning curve is large. Although product documentation, articles, and publications are available, it is challenging for a beginner to pick the right articles or tutorials. Often readers start doing a tutorial only to find out that it is not what they want to learn. With the abundance of information available, readers typically have to read thousands of pages just to get a glimpse of the products.

To simplify the learning process, this book selects ten products from IBM SOA Foundation and includes a number of useful and practical introductory-level tutorials that feature the fundamentals of IBM SOA products:

- Service Design with IBM Rational Software Architect
- Service Creation with IBM Rational Application Developer and IBM WebSphere Application Server
- Service Governance with IBM WebSphere Service Registry and Repository

- Service Integration with IBM WebSphere Integration Developer and IBM WebSphere Process Server
- Service Connectivity with IBM WebSphere Message Broker
- Collaboration with IBM WebSphere Portlet Factory and IBM WebSphere Portal
- Service Security with IBM Tivoli Federated Identity Manager

This book is designed for beginners who have basic Java skills and may or may not have knowledge of IBM products. As organizations advance through the SOA journey, educating the developers on SOA products becomes one of the main focus areas. Being able to learn ten IBM products quickly using one book and being able to broaden the skill set in a spectrum of products will be an invaluable experience.

IBM SOA Foundation

SOA is an architectural style for building systems that deliver capabilities as services. By modularizing business functions as services, SOA makes software easier to manage and maintain. Existing infrastructure may be complex and may contain many independent systems with multiple types of electronic data interchange. Transforming them all at once to be service oriented is neither feasible nor practical. Realizing SOA is a journey which should be planned with forethought and prudence.

IBM SOA Foundation (www-01.ibm.com/software/solutions/soa/offerings.html) is a set of offerings, technologies, and practices that address different SOA requirements. Companies can selectively deploy a subset of the suite according to their needs and progress through SOA gradually. IBM SOA Foundation is scalable; you can start small and grow as business requires. The following are various elements that you can consider for the SOA transformation journey.

Service Design and Service Creation

Services constitute the essential elements of SOA. What is a service? The Organization for the Advancement of Structured Information Standards (OASIS) defines service as "a mechanism to enable access to one or more capabilities, where the access is provided using a prescribed interface and is exercised consistent with constraints and policies as specified by the service description[1]". A service must fulfill a certain set of characteristics before it can be called a service. First, it must provide **access to capabilities**. For example, the weather network may provide a service for you to query the forecast temperature of a city. Second, the service interface that is the access point to the service must be **prescribed**, meaning that the interface must be clearly specified. For example, the input to the weather network service may be a city name, and the output may be the forecast temperature. The input and output of the services are well defined and prescribed.

---

[1] "Reference Model for Service Oriented Architecture 1.0," OASIS Standard, http://docs.oasis-open.org/soa-rm/v1.0/soa-rm.html

Finally, access must be **exercised consistently with constraints and policies**. If you provide a city name, the weather network service will return you with the forecast temperature. It will not return you with the name of its governor. The returned results must be consistent. Certain constraints and policies may be added on top; for example, access to the weather network service is restricted to registered members only.

So how do we expose system capabilities as services? What capability should a service provide? What is the prescribed access interface? What are the inputs and the outputs? What are the constraints and policies? A thorough and detailed analysis of the business and the major components and services in the infrastructure is critical for organizations to implement SOA successfully. Not all of the business capabilities need to be made into a service; the key is reusability. Therefore, strategic planning to identify which business capabilities ought to be made into reusable business services is important. It takes discipline to manage and maintain the reusable business services. IBM Rational Software Architect from IBM SOA Foundation is a design and development tool that allows IT analysts and software architects to perform **service design** using the open standard UML. It includes the full functionalities of IBM Rational Application Developer, which is a tool for developers to implement a service. SOA leverages open standards to represent business functions as services. One type of service is Web services. Rational Application Developer lets you do **service creation** and create Web services that can be used in a service-oriented architecture. IBM WebSphere Application Server provides a reliable, highly available, secure, and scalable platform for running services.

Service Integration

Once the services have been designed and created, we need to integrate them to form an application or a business process in SOA. **Service integration** helps organizations streamline their business processes such that they are more capable of responding to rapid market change. A business process engine is a service integration component that ties business services together into an executable form. Existing business processes are decomposed into discrete units of business function termed services. These services are then recombined into business processes in a more flexible manner. Such decomposition has led to the emergence of collaborative ecosystems, where the reconstructed processes often integrate services from partners, outsourced providers, and even customers.

For example, a travel booking business process can consist of the services illustrated in Figure 1.1. After booking air tickets, a customer is provided with a hotel reservation service and a car rental service. Once all the bookings are confirmed, any customer data—including his reward points—is updated at the end of the transaction. Such business process can be deployed onto a business process engine to streamline the travel booking process.

IBM SOA Foundation includes a comprehensive set of products to support the life cycle of a business process. It includes a modeling tool, IBM WebSphere Business Modeler, that business analysts use to model a business process based on business requirements; a development tool, IBM WebSphere Integration Developer, that integration specialists use to develop business processes; a business process engine, IBM WebSphere Process Server, that executes and manages business processes automatically; and a monitoring tool, IBM WebSphere Business Monitor, used by business users to monitor business performance through a dashboard user interface.

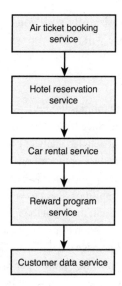

Figure 1.1   A travel booking business process

IBM WebSphere Business Modeler allows business analysts to model, simulate, and analyze key business processes for continuous process improvement. You can import business process modeling projects from IBM WebSphere Business Modeler to IBM Rational Software Architect and transform those business models into UML models, which can be used as starting points for architecting software services. IBM Rational Software Architect then supports the transformation of UML models into service artifacts such as Web Services Description Language (WSDL) documents, XML Schema Definition (XSD) files, and Service Component Definition Language (SCDL) artifacts, which can then be imported into IBM WebSphere Integration Developer for further development, testing, and deployment.

A major competency of IBM WebSphere Integration Developer is to assemble business services to create integration solutions that are SOA based. This allows organizations to quickly and easily bring people, applications, and information together to create streamlined business processes.

Providing complementary function, IBM Information Server is a revolutionary new data integration software platform that helps organizations derive more value from the complex, heterogeneous information spread across their systems. In addition, IBM FileNet P8 from IBM SOA Foundation delivers a comprehensive set of enterprise content management services that can be consumed and deployed in a service-oriented architecture.

In an on-demand business environment, efficient interaction between applications, customers, employees, and suppliers is critical. Interaction and collaboration support around business processes enables consistent human and process interaction, thus improving business productivity. Human tasks for automated business processes should be surfaced on the enterprise portal for users to interact with. This type of collaborative support around business processes is often referred to as a process portal, as illustrated in Figure 1.2.

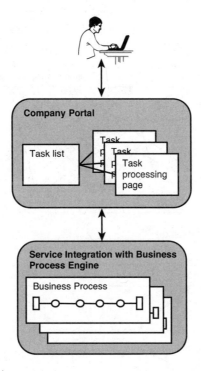

Figure 1.2 A process portal

IBM WebSphere Portal, with IBM WebSphere Portlet Factory being the development tool, provides interaction and collaboration services for the infrastructure. IBM WebSphere Portal can be integrated with IBM WebSphere Process Server to create a process portal and support for human tasks processing and task list query.

Service Connectivity

A key value proposition of SOA is the flexibility to make changes. The values of SOA diminish if services are being integrated point-to-point. Small changes can have large ripple effects when services are tightly coupled. Figure 1.3 displays a point-to-point integration whereby all services are tightly coupled, which makes changing anything difficult.

Enterprise service bus (ESB) eliminates point-to-point integration and enables loose coupling between services. When a service is being replaced, the consuming clients can remain unchanged and the bus will route the requests to a replaced service as appropriate. ESB enables users to increase the responsiveness and flexibility to make changes to application clients and providers independent of each other. In many cases an enterprise service bus not only provides loose coupling for services, it also provides connectivity and universal data transformation for both standard and nonstandard-based applications and services. Although each service has a pre-scribed access interface, its data format and message model may not necessarily be compatible. An ESB, as illustrated in Figure 1.4 below, provides **service connectivity** that ensures services are connected and exchanged with the correct data format and message model.

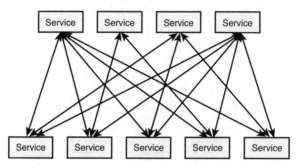

Figure 1.3   Point-to-point integration

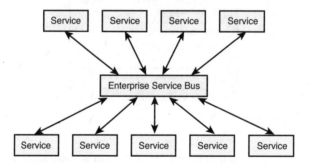

Figure 1.4   Enterprise service bus

IBM SOA Foundation offers three ESB products: IBM WebSphere Enterprise Service Bus provides Web services connectivity, JMS messaging, and service-oriented integration; IBM Web-Sphere Message Broker supports connectivity and universal data transformation for both stan-dard and nonstandard-based applications and services; IBM WebSphere DataPower Integration Appliance XI50 is a purpose-built hardware ESB for simplified deployment and hardened secu-rity. Users can implement one of them or all three of them in their SOA infrastructure depending on their requirements.

Besides ESB, the IBM WebSphere Business Service Fabric is a product that provides highly dynamic and flexible connectivity between services. It can perform dynamic service selections based on policies without coding. The policies that control the service selection can be reconfig-ured at runtime such that the business can adapt to any changes in the business requirements.

Service Security and Management

Besides data format and message model, security is a concern of service connectivity and integration. A critical asset that SOA brings to users is the ability to integrate with business partners effectively. It enables a loosely coupled way of linking applications within organizations, across enterprises, and across the Internet. However, the loose coupling of services and their operations across trust boundaries creates challenges in **service security**. A number of areas need to be considered regarding service security. One is transaction security. It is essential for services to provide a sufficient level of security to support business transactions. Ensuring the integrity, confidentiality, and security of services through the application of a comprehensive security model is critical, both for organizations and their customers. IBM WebSphere Application Server from IBM SOA Foundation provides the capability to enable Web Services messages to be sent asynchronously, reliably, and securely, focusing on interoperability with other vendors.

Another consideration for service security is identity. Establishing the trust relationship between the organizations is a key step in allowing interorganization cooperation. This involves establishing rules about the interaction, such as defining identity information that should be propagated between organizations. For example, when service Z of company C in Figure 1.5 receives a request from Tinny Ng, how does it know this Tinny Ng is the one it trusted? If the identity of Tinny Ng has changed, how can company A inform company B and company C about the change? Identity provisioning, identity propagation, identity authentication, and identity authorization are the four common considerations of service security around identity.

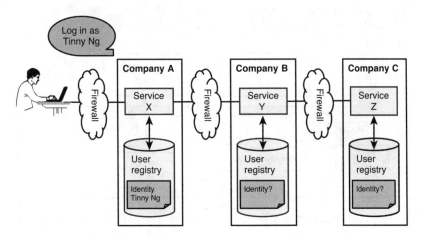

Figure 1.5 Identity propagation in SOA

Several types of electronic security tokens exist. In a heterogeneous environment, it is likely that different token types will be supported by different middleware infrastructure components, thus requiring the need to transform token types. For example, illustrated in Figure 1.6, service requester A, service requester B, and service requester C are making requests for a service from company A. Each of the service requests has associated with a different type of security token, including a Security Assertion Markup Language (SAML) token, a username token, and an X.509 token, respectively. However, the infrastructure of company A uses a security framework that can only accept Lightweight Third-Party Authentication (LTPA) security token. As a result, token transformation is required. An identity service can be integrated with an enterprise service bus so that services can be easily interconnected without worrying about how to map and propagate user identity from one service to the next. Mediation flows are to be developed to dynamically transform all these heterogeneous types of security tokens to the one expected by the service provider, which is an LTPA token in this case.

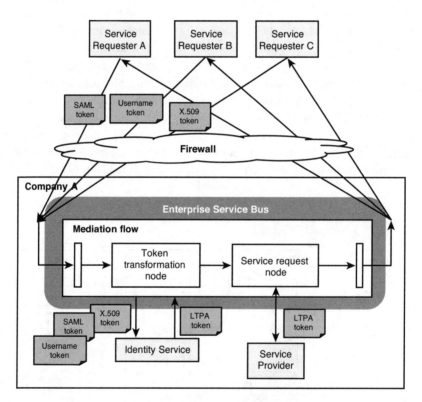

Figure 1.6   Heterogeneous types of security tokens being provided by various service requesters

IBM SOA Foundation includes various products to cover service security. IBM Tivoli Access Manager provides the needed authentication and authorization service to the infrastructure. And IBM Tivoli Federated Identity Manager can act as the service security component to ensure Web service security. In addition, IBM Tivoli Federated Identity Manager can be integrated with IBM ESB Offerings (WebSphere ESB, IBM WebSphere Message Broker, and DataPower) to support token transformation while connecting various services.

Traditional system management concerns such as continuous service delivery, service support, and service performance apply in the SOA world. Enabling operators and administrators to perform health monitoring for the system is critical in service management. Monitoring services during runtime and gaining an end-to-end view of the status and relationships for all of the services in the system is important. When one service among an integrated business process fails, how easy is it to diagnose the incident, analyze the root cause, and determine proper problem resolution? Besides, do we have a view of the performance of services, and are we able to measure their efficiency against key performance indicators? To manage the infrastructure and to aid life cycle availability and performance, IBM Tivoli Composite Application Manager for SOA from IBM SOA Foundation provides monitoring and management of services and mediations for the infrastructure.

Service Registry and Service Governance

Another value proposition of SOA is reusability. With so many services being created in a system, you may start wondering about the following: Is there a registry for managing a catalog of services and enabling reuse? What kind of metadata should be associated with the services so that it's easy to search for? How would one manage changes in a service such that it would not break other people's applications? What's the process involved? **Service governance** includes the processes, procedures, policies, and technologies used to manage the service development life cycle. It provides the control of reusable services in a SOA environment and ensures coherence.

The use of a **service registry** has two different aspects. As an asset management tool, a registry provides source control and governance. On the other hand, as a metadata management tool, a registry provides lookup service and allows users to search for the right service and enable reuse. During development of a service requester, a service registry needs to know what kind of services are available for it to call, what the prescribed interface is, and what the constraints and the policies are. A service registry maintains a catalog of services and its metadata that allow developers to search for the right service and implement the request. The provisioning of services can also be maintained during runtime. By integrating a service registry with an enterprise service bus, service requesters can dynamically look up for the right service and connect to the appropriate service provider for the needed capability using mediation flows, as illustrated in Figure 1.7.

IBM WebSphere Service Registry and Repository specializes in the support of the service metadata required to provision the runtime SOA environment. Once the service entities and metadata are published into the registry and repository, they can be used to do dynamic endpoint selection in an ESB. In the IBM ESB offerings, which include IBM WebSphere ESB and IBM WebSphere Message Broker, nodes are available to communicate with WebSphere Service Registry and Repository to obtain endpoints and metadata information to assist in the dynamic endpoint selections.

Although IBM WebSphere Service Registry and Repository is also capable of supporting the service creation of the service development process, IBM provides the IBM Rational Asset

Manager, which delivers the specialized capabilities required for an asset manager in an asset-based development environment. And to align IT infrastructure management with business priorities, IBM Tivoli Change and Configuration Management Database is available to automate data, workflows, and policies for managing changes.

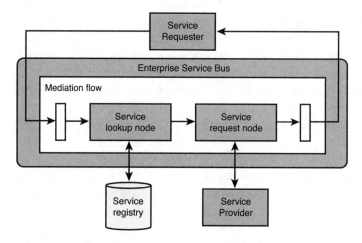

Figure 1.7   The use of a service registry with an enterprise service bus

How This Book Is Organized

The transformation to SOA is a journey. Companies that are interested in SOA do not need to convert the entire infrastructure to be service based all at once. It's also not necessary to address all the considerations mentioned earlier in one shot. IBM SOA Foundation is scalable. Depending on their needs and resource conditions, companies can choose to begin with certain focus areas and transform the system gradually as requirements come. Being able to cover the fundamental concepts of ten different IBM SOA products in one book, this book, *Understanding IBM SOA Foundation Suite: Learning Visually with Examples*, serves as a good reference for developers. They can always come back to this book to refresh their knowledge skills for different IBM SOA products when the company is ready to pull in different subsets bits by bits into its infrastructure at different point of times.

Chapter 2, "Service Design with IBM Rational Software Architect," leverages the design aspect of IBM Rational Software Architect and illustrates how to use various UML diagrams to design a service. Then Chapter 3, "Service Creation with IBM Rational Application Developer and IBM WebSphere Application Server," focuses on the development aspect and shows you how to use IBM Rational Application Developer for developing an application that is service based. It also covers how to deploy the application onto IBM WebSphere Application Server. Once a service has been designed and created, Chapter 4, "Service Governance with IBM WebSphere Service Registry and Repository," tells the story of using IBM WebSphere Service Registry and Repository in a typical development environment to manage and govern services.

To assemble business services, the competency of IBM WebSphere Integration Developer for creating integration solutions is demonstrated in Chapter 5, "Service Integration with IBM WebSphere Integration Developer and IBM WebSphere Process Server." IBM WebSphere Process Server, which acts as a business process engine, is also explained in this chapter.

This is then followed by Chapter 6, "Service Connectivity with IBM WebSphere Message Broker," which reveals the power of IBM WebSphere Message Broker in supporting connectivity and data transformation. Chapter 7, "Collaboration with IBM WebSphere Portlet Factory and IBM WebSphere Portal", gives you a different context and talks about collaboration. It goes over the details of developing a portlet using IBM WebSphere Portlet Factory and then hosting onto IBM WebSphere Portal.

Last but not least, Chapter 8, "Service Security with IBM Tivoli Federated Identity Manager," describes the fundamental concepts of IBM Tivoli Federated Identity Manager and discusses how to enable security for a service provider and how to enable a service requester to access a secured service provider.

Each chapter contains a product overview, which shows how the product fits into the SOA environment, and a collection of hands-on tutorials. The objective is to get you started with the basics quickly through interactive hands-on exercises. The tutorials are specially designed for teaching the essential elements of IBM SOA products such that you are well prepared for further deepening your skills in the future. The chapters are self-contained to allow maximum learning flexibility. Should you feel that you already know the material, you should simply skip that particular chapter and continue to the next.

Some of these products have a trial version available from IBM developerWorks (www.ibm.com/developerworks/downloads). Although having the IBM products installed and being able to try the tutorials hands-on are beneficial, there is value in simply reading our book and watching our videos. All the tutorials described in this book have been captured as videos for readers to watch the step-by-step hands-on. Watching our videos to understand the operational concepts of the products and to follow the tutorials visually is as effective as trying the exercises hands-on. You can find these videos on the CD that comes with this book.

Service Design with IBM Rational Software Architect

Product Overview

IBM Rational Software Architect (RSA) is an integrated design and development tool built on top of the Eclipse platform, an open and extensible development platform that leverages industry standards. It includes the full functionalities of IBM Rational Application Developer, which will be covered in more details in the next chapter. Developers who want to focus on development only can buy IBM Rational Application Developer and use it as a development tool to facilitate Java development, XML development, Web services development, and more. Software architects and senior developers who want to unify architecture, design, and development within one tool can use RSA to specify and maintain all aspects of an application's software architecture and perform model-driven development for Java, Web services, and others.

RSA supports an extensive list of features that uniquely differentiate it from its competitors. Support for Unified Modeling Language (UML) allows RSA to capture and communicate all aspects of an application architecture using a standard notation. Users can visually model systems and applications using UML notation and then transform the design to a skeleton application and continue the implementation development. RSA has included a number of transformations such as from UML to Java, UML to XML Schema (XSD), UML to Web Service Definition Language (WSDL), UML to Business Process Execution Language (BPEL), and others. Reverse engineering to transform Java back to UML, XSD to UML, and so on is also supported. To be able to share your design with people who do not have the modeling tool, RSA supports generation of Hypertext Markup Language (HTML), Portable Document Format (PDF), and XML reports from UML designs.

The tutorial in this chapter will step you through how to design your service using UML diagrams, share your design with peers as HTML files, and transform the UML design to and from Java using RSA.

What Is UML?

UML was released by the Object Management Group (OMG) in 1997. The current official version is UML 2.2 (as of February 2009). UML is designed to bring together the development community with a stable and common design language that can be used to develop and build applications. It is a modeling language that is independent of any programming language. Starting from UML 2, the UML specification is composed of two parts: Infrastructure and Superstructure. The Infrastructure part describes the foundational language constructs required for UML 2, and the Superstructure part specifies the user-level constructs required for UML 2. You can download the specification from OMG's website (www.omg.org/spec/UML/).

What Are UML Models and UML Diagrams?

A *UML model* is an abstract representation of a system. It consists of model elements such as actors, use cases, classes, components, activities, and others which are used to describe a system. *UML diagrams* are graphical representations of different parts of a UML model. Each of them groups different model elements to represent different aspects of a system. A UML model can contain one or a number of UML diagrams to describe different levels of details of a system. Some provide an abstract description of a system, whereas others show the system at a lower level; some illustrate the system outside-in from a user perspective, whereas others describe the system inside-out from system code perspective. These diagrams enable users to capture and communicate all aspects of an application architecture using a standard notation that many stakeholders recognize. There are 14 official UML 2.2 diagrams, each of which is a unique view that shows an aspect of the system.

As shown in Figure 2.1, UML diagrams can be divided into two categories: structure and behavior. Class diagrams, component diagrams, object diagrams, composite structure diagrams, deployment diagrams, package diagrams, and profile diagrams are classified as structure diagrams. They represent the static structure of a system and normally are independent of time. Activity diagrams, use case diagrams, state machine diagrams, sequence diagrams, interaction overview diagrams, communication diagrams, and timing diagrams are classified as behavior diagrams. They describe the dynamic behavior of a system and normally represent a series of changes over time.

The tutorial that is covered in this chapter shows you how to create a use case diagram, a class diagram, and a sequence diagram using RSA to design a time zone converter service.

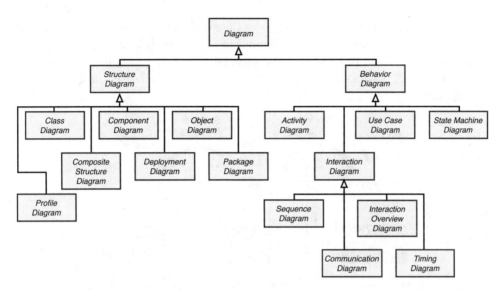

Figure 2.1 The taxonomy of structure and behavior diagram[1]

How Does It Support SOA?

RSA is part of the IBM SOA Foundation and gives companies the tools needed to perform **service design and model service-oriented applications**. It lets software architects visually model and design a flexible services architecture using the open standard UML.

You can use general UML modeling technique to design your services using RSA. Or you can start by using IBM WebSphere Business Modeler to model your business processes based on business requirements; then you can follow up by importing your business process modeling projects from IBM WebSphere Business Modeler to RSA to continue defining the specification of each service in details.

IBM WebSphere Business Modeler is normally used by business analysts, who understand customer and business needs, to model business processes and identify areas where business processes can be optimized to better serve those needs. IBM Rational Software Architect is normally used by IT analysts or software architects, who understand system requirements, to architect and design the details of a system. The system designed better aligns with the identified business requirements. Therefore, it is important for IT analysts and software architects to be able to understand the business models that business analysts put together in WebSphere Business Modeler using RSA.

RSA supports importing business process modeling projects from IBM WebSphere Business Modeler and transforming those business models into UML models. These UML service models can then be used as starting points for architecting software services and can be transformed into service artifacts such as Web Services Description Language (WSDL) documents,

---

[1]OMG Unified Modeling Language (OMG UML), Superstructure specification, Version 2.2, www. omg.org/spec/UML/2.0/Superstructure/PDF/

XML Schema Definition (XSD) files, and Service Component Definition Language (SCDL) arti-facts. These service artifacts can then be imported into IBM WebSphere Integration Developer for integration specialists performing further development, testing, and deployment as SOA solutions. Figure 2.2 illustrates this role-to-role interaction to model, design, and develop a ser-vice integration solution for SOA.

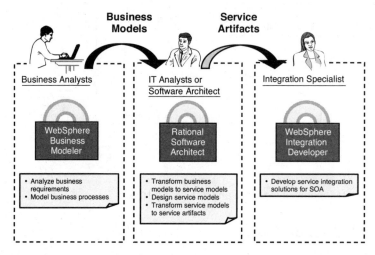

Figure 2.2   Role-to-role interaction to model, design, and develop a service integration solution for SOA

Tutorial Overview—Design a Time Zone Converter Service

In the following exercises, you'll use general UML techniques to design a time zone converter ser-vice using RSA. This service converts time from one time zone to another. UTC, Coordinated Uni-versal Time, is a worldwide standard for time and date. Time zones around the world are expressed as positive or negative offsets from UTC. Table 2.1 gives examples of various time zones.

Table 2.1   Examples of Various Time Zones

Abbreviation	Full Name	Location	Difference from UTC Time
CST	Central Standard Time	North America	–6
EST	Eastern Standard Time	North America	–5
PST	Pacific Standard Time	North America	–8
WST	Western Standard Time	Australia	+8

Service Specification

Each time zone is uniquely identified by its abbreviation and location. The time zone converter provides one service, `timeZoneConverter`, which takes the following parameters and returns the converted time in a string:

- **frTimeString**—String that represents the time that requires conversion
- **frTimeZoneAbbrev**—Abbreviation of the original time zone
- **frTimeZoneLoc**—Location of the original time zone
- **toTimeZoneAbbrev**—Abbreviation of the targeted time zone
- **toTimeZoneLoc**—Location of the targeted time zone

Table 2.2 shows a couple of sample inputs and outputs.

Table 2.2   A Couple of Sample Inputs and Outputs

frTime String	frTimeZone Abbrev	frTimeZone Loc	toTimeZone Abbrev	toTimeZone Loc	Return
4:30	EST	North America	CST	North America	3:30
4:30	EST	North America	PST	North America	1:30

The tutorials that are featured in this chapter illustrate how to utilize a use case diagram, a class diagram, and a sequence diagram to design a service. You can then convert the design to HTML format for ease of peer review. You'll also have the opportunity to use RSA's round-trip engineering to forward- and reverse-engineer the UML design to and from Java code. The tutorial will conclude with an implementation example.

- Tutorial 2.1: Use a UML Model to Capture a Service Design
- Tutorial 2.2: Capture the Use Cases for a Service Using a Use Case Diagram
- Tutorial 2.3: Design the Blueprint for a Service Using a Class Diagram
- Tutorial 2.4: Detail the Flow of a Service Using a Sequence Diagram
- Tutorial 2.5: Share the Service Design with Others
- Tutorial 2.6: Transform the Service Design to Implementation with Round-Trip Engineering

System Requirements

The tutorial has been developed with the following product:

- IBM Rational Software Architect for WebSphere Software 7.5

What Is Included in the CD-ROM?

In the CD included in this book, you will find a completed time zone converter service design and implementation. In addition, all of the tutorials covered in this chapter have been recorded as videos in the CD-ROM.

- **chapter 2/tutorial 2.1/solution/MyProject.zip**—A project interchange archive that contains a blank new model project called MyProject. To import a project interchange archive to RSA, select File, Import from the menu bar. Then expand Other and click Project Interchange. From there, click Next and follow the wizard's instructions.

- **chapter 2/tutorial 2.2/solution/UseCaseDiagram.zip**—A project interchange archive that contains a completed use case diagram stored in MyProject.

- **chapter 2/tutorial 2.3/solution/ClassDiagram.zip**—A project interchange archive that contains a completed class diagram stored in MyProject.

- **chapter 2/tutorial 2.4/solution/SequenceDiagram.zip**—A project interchange archive that contains a completed sequence diagram stored in MyProject.

- **chapter 2/tutorial 2.5/solution/PublishedHTMLFiles**—A folder of HTML files that are generated from the UML model stored in MyProject.

- **chapter 2/tutorial 2.6/solution/CompletedMyProject.zip**—A project interchange archive that contains a completed design of the time zone converter service.

- **chapter 2/tutorial 2.6/solution/Implementation_WebService.zip**—A project interchange archive that contains a completed time zone converter service with implementation and Web service created.

- **chapter 2/tutorial 2.x/video**—Contains the video files for all the tutorials discussed in this chapter. Open the HTML file in any browser to watch the video.

Tutorial 2.1: Use a UML Model to Capture a Service Design

A UML model describes an abstraction of a system. Different levels of details are captured using various model elements and are represented using one or more UML diagrams. To begin designing a service, you will need to create a UML model that will be used for the follow-up tutorials to store various UML diagrams. You can add a UML model to any type of project. A Model project is used in this tutorial. While creating a UML model, several templates are available for you to choose as a base. A template provides a default set of diagrams and elements for you to edit or add to. In this tutorial, you will choose the blank package template to start with. After completing this exercise, you will be able to create a new UML model.

1. Start RSA on your desktop.

    a. In the Windows taskbar, click Start, All Programs, IBM Software Delivery Platform, IBM Rational Software Architect for WebSphere 7.5, IBM Rational Software Architect for WebSphere.

   b. A dialog box appears asking for the workspace directory. Just click OK to accept the default one. A *workspace* is a directory that stores your work. The default workspace directory is used in this step.

   c. The first page is the Welcome page. Click the Workbench icon at the top of the Welcome page, or click the Close icon to close it.

2. Create a Model project to hold the UML model.

   a. Make sure you are in the Modeling perspective. If not, click Windows, Open Perspective, Other. Select Modeling (default) and click OK. Select the Show All check box if Modeling is not in the list. A *perspective* is a consolidation of tools and views that a user needs to perform a specific function. The default perspective of RSA is the Modeling perspective.

   b. From the workbench, click File, New, Model Project.

   c. In the Project Name field of the Create Model Project page, type `MyProject`.

   d. Leave other fields at their default, similar to Figure 2.3. Click Next.

Figure 2.3   Naming the new Model project

3. Create a UML model using the blank template package.

   a. Select General as the category and Blank Package as the template in the Create Model page.

b. In the File Name field, type `MyModel` as illustrated in Figure 2.4.

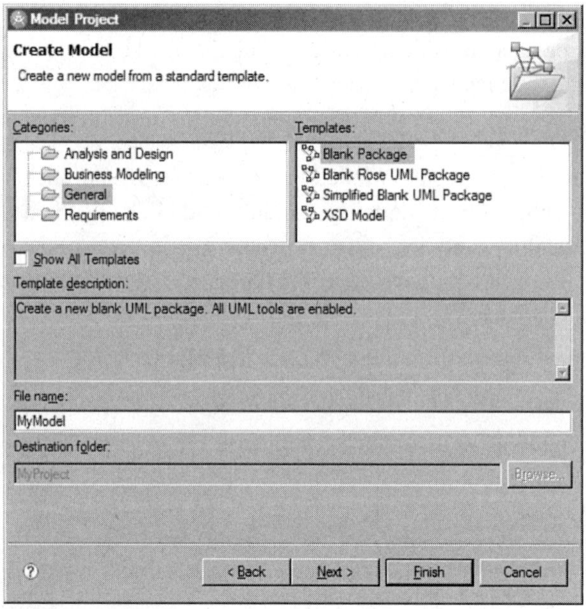

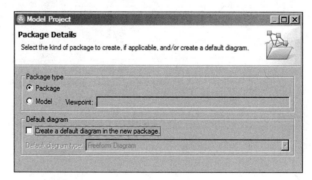

Figure 2.4   Selecting a template for the new Model project

c. Click Next.

d. Clear the Create a Default Diagram in the New Package check box in the Package Details page as shown in Figure 2.5. You will create the diagrams in the follow-up tutorials. Click Finish.

Figure 2.5   Specifying the package details

4. A Model project is now created on your workbench like Figure 2.6.

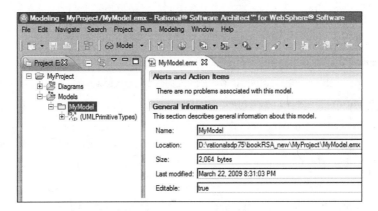

Figure 2.6   A UML model

You have created a UML model that you can use to store various model elements for the design.

Tutorial 2.2: Capture the Use Cases for a Service Using a Use Case Diagram

Use case diagrams model the behavior of a system and help capture the system requirements. They identify the interactions between a system and its actors, and they define the scope of a system. An *actor* represents a role of a user that interacts with the system. The user can be a human user, an organization, a machine, or another external system. A *use case* describes a function that a system performs to achieve the user's goal. A use case must yield an observable result that is of value to the user of the system. The use cases and actors shown in use case diagrams describe what the system does and how the actors use it, but not how the system operates internally. To relate an actor and a use case, you can create an association relationship indicating the connection between the two model elements.

For the time zone converter service design, you will use a use case diagram to capture the capability the service provides. `Service Requester` is our actor and `Convert time between time zones` is our use case. Gaining a clear view of what capabilities are being provided for service requesters is an important first step in designing services. As illustrated in Figure 2.7, the time zone converter service provides a capability for service requesters converting a time from one time zone to another.

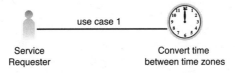

Service
Requester

Convert time
between time zones

Figure 2.7   Use case design for the time zone converter service

Follow the next steps to create a use case diagram for the time zone converter. After completing this exercise, you will be able to create a new use case diagram.

1. Create a use case diagram using the default name, `UsecaseDiagram1`.

   a. Expand the `Models` folder in the Project Explorer view.

   b. Right-click `MyModel` and click Add Diagram, Use Case Diagram on the pop-up menu.

   c. Press Enter to use the default diagram name, `UsecaseDiagram1`. Now you can draw a use case diagram by adding various model elements from the diagram editor palette to the diagram.

2. Create an actor called `Service Requester`.

   a. Double-click the UsecaseDiagram1 tab to maximize the diagram editor.

   b. Click Actor in the palette; then click anywhere in the diagram to create an actor. Name the actor `Service Requester`. The diagram should like Figure 2.8.

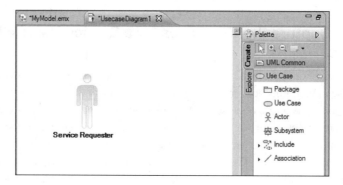

Figure 2.8   Adding an actor

3. Create a use case named `Convert time between time zones`.

   a. Click Use Case in the palette; then click anywhere in the diagram to create a use case. Name it `Convert time between time zones`. The diagram should be similar to Figure 2.9.

4. Associate the actor with the use case.

   a. Click Association in the palette.

   b. Click the actor `Service Requester`, hold the mouse, and drag to the use case `Convert time between time zones`. This draws an association relationship line from the actor `Service Requester` to the use case `Convert time between time zones` to initiate a relationship between the two model elements.

   c. Type `use case 1` as the relationship name.

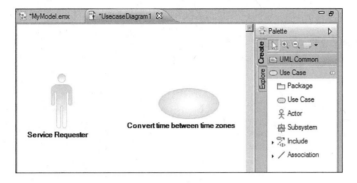

Figure 2.9   Adding a use case

5. The complete use case diagram should look similar to Figure 2.10.

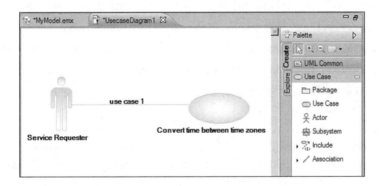

Figure 2.10   The complete use case diagram

6. Click File, Save All to save the changes.
7. Double-click the UseCaseDiagram1 tab to restore the size of the diagram editor.

   You have created a use case diagram to capture the requirements against the system.

Tutorial 2.3: Design the Blueprint for a Service Using a Class Diagram

Class diagrams define the structure of your system and are the blueprints of your design. You can use class diagrams to model the objects that make up the system, to display the relationships between the objects, and to describe what those objects do and what services they provide. A class diagram as illustrated in Figure 2.11 will be created in this tutorial to capture the internal details of our time zone converter service. It is made up of the following four classes:

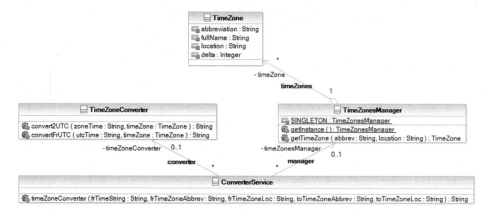

Figure 2.11   Class design for TimeZoneConverter

- **TimeZone**—Type that holds the time zone that contains the following attributes:
    - **abbreviation**—Abbreviation of the name; for example, CST.
    - **fullName**—Full name of the time zone; for example, Central Standard Time.
    - **location**—Location of the zone; for example, Australia.
    - **delta**—Difference in minutes from the UTC time; for example, +570, which represents +9:30 offset from the UTC.
- **TimeZonesManager**—A manager that manages a list of time zones. It uses abbreviation and location together to uniquely identify a time zone from the collection it manages. Design pattern "Singleton" is used in this design to ensure only one instance of the manager is instantiated in the system.
- **TimeZoneConverter**—A conversion engine that performs the calculation. Two operations are provided that convert time from one time zone to UTC and vice versa.
- **ConverterService**—A controller that retrieves time zone rules from TimeZonesManager and interacts with TimeZoneConverter to perform the conversion. It provides the timeZoneConverter service.

Classes are shown as rectangular boxes in a class diagram. The top section of the rectangle lists the attributes the class defines. The bottom section of the rectangle shows the list of functions the class supports. A different colored shape indicates the visibility of the attribute or operation. A green circle means the attribute or operation is public. A yellow diamond means the attribute or operation is protected, and a red rectangle means it is private. Underlining indicates that the attribute or operation has a static qualifier. For example, Figure 2.11 shows that the class TimeZonesManager has a private static attribute called SINGLETON.

When two classes need to share data, they have an association relationship that is represented as a connecting line in the diagram. A directed association relationship means the first class is aware of the second one, but not the other way around. For example, `ConverterService` has a directional line pointing to `TimeZonesConverter`. It may mean that `ConverterService` has a pointer to an instance of `TimeZonesConverter` and thus can access its attributes and operations. But `TimeZonesConverter` cannot access the data of `ConverterService`. Such a relationship is called *directed association*.

A directed arrow line with a diamond at one end represents a directed aggregation relationship. An *aggregation association* relationship represents a typical whole/part association. In our design, the class `TimeZonesManager` manages a collection of `TimeZone` that can be represented by a directed aggregation association relationship. The direction is important here because it represents `TimeZonesManager`, collects (that is, aggregates) for a group of `TimeZone` objects.

The purpose of this exercise is to show you how to use RSA when designing a service. The design itself is not the focus; you may proceed with a different design if you prefer. After completing this exercise, you will be able to create a new class diagram.

1. Create a class diagram using the default name, `ClassDiagram1`.

   a. Expand the `Models` folder in the Project Explorer view.

   b. Right-click `MyModel` in the Project Explorer view.

   c. Click Add Diagram, Class Diagram on the pop-up menu.

   d. Press Enter to use the default diagram name, `ClassDiagram1`. Now you can draw a class diagram by adding various model elements from the Diagram Editor palette to the diagram.

2. Create a class called `ConverterService`. This is the class that provides the `timeZoneConverter` service.

   a. Double-click the ClassDiagram1 tab to maximize the diagram editor.

   b. Click Class in the palette; then click anywhere in the diagram to create a class.

   c. Name the class `ConverterService` as illustrated in Figure 2.12.

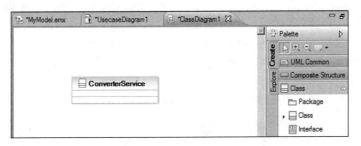

Figure 2.12   Creating the ConverterService class

3. Create an operation. The `timeZoneConverter` service is defined as an operation of `ConverterService`.

    a. Right-click the rectangular box of the created class `ConverterService`.

    b. Click Add UML, Operation on the pop-up menu to add an operation for this class.

    c. Name it `timeZoneConverter()`.

4. Add parameters to the `timeZoneConverter` operation. According to the service specification discussed earlier, the `timeZoneConverter` service accepts five parameters and returns the converted time as a string.

    a. Right-click the created operation `timeZoneConverter()` on the class diagram.

    b. Click Show Properties View on the pop-up menu to look at its properties.

    c. Click the Parameters tab.

    d. Click the Insert New Parameter icon on the right side of the Properties pane, as illustrated in Figure 2.13.

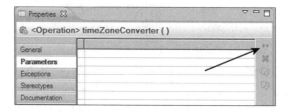

Figure 2.13 Adding a parameter

    e. Type `frTimeString` in the Name cell of the newly inserted row.

    f. Click the Type cell and click the ... button.

    g. Click the Browse tab of the Select Element for Type page.

    h. Expand the `MyModel` folder under MyProject, Models.

    i. Expand the (`UMLPrimitiveTypes`) folder and select String, as illustrated in Figure 2.14. Click OK.

    j. Repeat steps a to step i to create the other four input parameters and the return parameter as shown in Table 2.3.

Table 2.3 The Other Four Input Parameters and Return Parameters for timeZoneConverter

Direction	Name	Type
In	frTimeZoneAbbrev	String
In	frTimeZoneLoc	String
In	toTimeZoneAbbrev	String

Table 2.3 The Other Four Input Parameters and Return Parameters for timeZoneConverter

Direction	Name	Type
In	toTimeZoneLoc	String
Return	toTimeString	String

TIP The drop-down list to change the direction from the default value of In to the value of Return may not be easy to click. Extending the column width to give the cell more space may help.

Figure 2.14 Selecting a type

    k. The completed list should look similar to Figure 2.15.

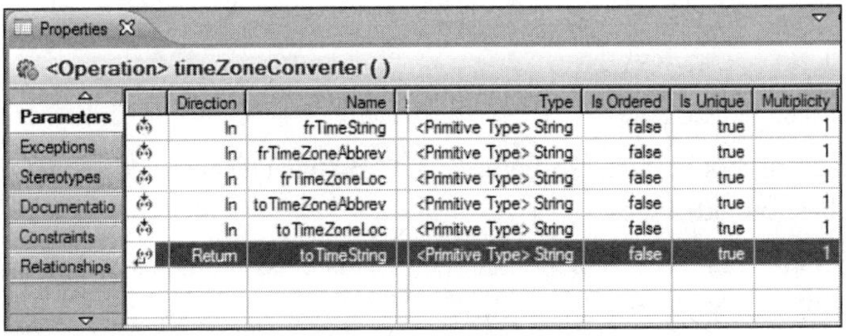

Figure 2.15 Defining parameters and return values of operation timeZoneConverter

5. Show signature of operations. The current class diagram does not show signature of operations by default. For ease of reviewing the design, you will change the view and display signature as well.

   a. Right-click the rectangular box of the created class ConverterService.

   b. Click Filters, Show Signature on the pop-up menu to display signature of operations for the selected class.

   c. The diagram should look like Figure 2.16. You have just created a class named ConverterService that has one operation named timeZoneConverter(). This operation has five input parameters of type String and one return parameter of type String.

Figure 2.16 The ConverterService class

6. Create a class called TimeZone. This class defines the time zone type.

   a. Click Class in the palette; then click anywhere in the diagram to create a class.

   b. Name the class TimeZone.

7. Create an attribute. According to the service specification discussed earlier, the TimeZone class has four attributes.

   a. Right-click the rectangular box of the created TimeZone class.

   b. Click Add UML, Attribute on the pop-up menu to add an attribute for this class.

   c. Name it abbreviation : String. This creates an attribute called abbreviation with a String type.

   d. Similarly, create three more attributes for this class:

      • fullName : String

      • location : String

      • delta : Integer

   The diagram should look like Figure 2.17. You have just created a class named TimeZone which has four attributes.

8. Create a class called TimeZonesManager. This class manages a collection of TimeZone objects.

   a. Click Class in the palette; then click anywhere in the diagram to create a class.

   b. Name the class TimeZonesManager.

Figure 2.17   The TimeZone class

9. Create a static attribute. As mentioned earlier, you will use the design pattern "Singleton" for the `TimeZonesManager` class to ensure only one instance of the manager is in the system.

   a. Right-click the rectangular box of the created `TimeZonesManager` class.

   b. Click Add UML, Attribute on the pop-up menu to add an attribute for this class.

   c. Name it `SINGLETON : TimeZonesManager`. This creates an attribute called `SINGLETON` with a `TimeZonesManager` type.

   d. Right-click the created attribute `SINGLETON` on the class diagram.

   e. Click Show Properties View on the pop-up menu to look at its Properties view.

   f. Select the Static Qualifiers check box for the singleton instance, as illustrated in Figure 2.18.

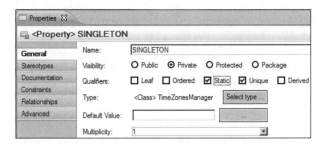

Figure 2.18   Setting the static qualifier for an attribute

10. Create two operations for this `TimeZonesManager` class as specified in Table 2.4.

Table 2.4   Operations Along with Parameter Information for TimeZonesManager

Static Operation	Parameter Direction	Parameter Name	Parameter Type
`getInstance()`	Return	`singleInstance`	`TimeZonesManager`

Operation	Parameter Direction	Parameter Name	Parameter Type
getTimeZone()	In	abbrev	String
	In	location	String
	Return	timeZone	TimeZone

NOTE   The getInstance() operation is static. Select the Static qualifier check box similar to the way you did it for an attribute in Step 9.

11. Create one more class, TimeZoneConverter, with two operations as specified in Table 2.5. This class is the engine that performs the time zone conversion calculation.

Table 2.5   Operations Along with Parameter Information for TimeZoneConverter

Operation	Parameter Direction	Parameter Name	Parameter Type
convert2UTC()	In	zoneTime	String
	In	timeZone	TimeZone
	Return	utcTime	String
convertFrUTC()	In	utcTime	String
	In	timeZone	TimeZone
	Return	zoneTime	String

12. The class diagram should look similar to Figure 2.19. Follow Step 5 to show signature for operations of the TimeZoneConverter class and the TimeZonesManager class. Note that static attribute and static operation are represented with an underline in UML notation.

13. Create a directed aggregation association relationship. In our design, the class TimeZonesManager manages a collection of TimeZone that can be represented by a directed aggregation association relationship.

    a. Expand the Association relationship in the Palette pane.

    b. Click Directed Aggregation Association, as shown in Figure 2.20.

    c. Click the TimeZonesManager class, hold the mouse click, and drag to the TimeZone class (the order is important) to draw a directed aggregation association relationship.

    d. Name this relationship timeZones.

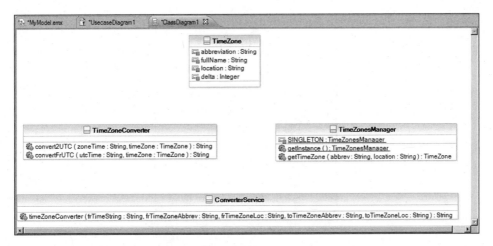

Figure 2.19   The class diagram with classes defined

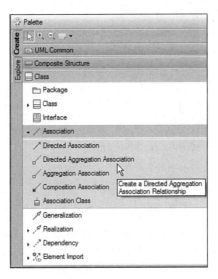

Figure 2.20   Directed Aggregation Association

14.   Create two directed association relationships. When two classes need to share data, they have an association relationship. A *directed association* relationship means the first class is aware of the second one, but not the other way around. In our design, the class ConverterService acting as the controller retrieves time zone rules from TimeZonesManager and interacts with TimeZoneConverter to perform the conversion.

    a. Expand the Directed Aggregation Association relationship in the Palette pane.

    b. Click Directed Association similar to Figure 2.21.

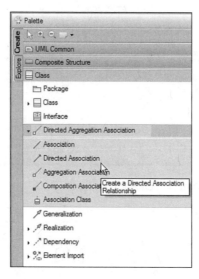

Figure 2.21   Directed Association

    c. Click the `ConverterService` class, hold the mouse click, and drag to the `TimeZones-Manager` class. (The order is important.)

    d. Name the class `manager`.

    e. Similarly, draw another directed association relationship between the `ConverterService` class and the `TimeZoneConverter` class. Name it `converter`.

15. The complete class diagram should look similar to Figure 2.22. Note that a directed aggregation association relationship looks different from a directed association relationship. The first one has a diamond shape at one end.

16. Click File, Save All to save the changes.

17. Double-click the ClassDiagram1 tab to restore the size of the diagram editor.

You have created a class diagram to describe the blueprint of the system.

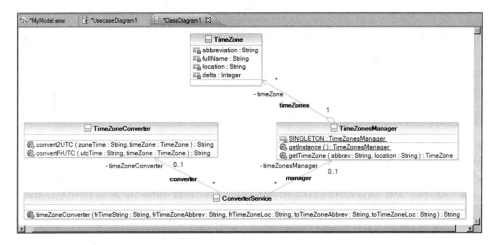

Figure 2.22   The complete class diagram

Tutorial 2.4: Detail the Flow of a Service Using a Sequence Diagram

Sequence diagrams model the flow of logic when interactions occur and belong to the behavior diagram in UML. They show the chronological sequence of messages exchanged between instances of various classes during interactions. In this section you will realize the Convert time between time zones use case and capture its interaction using a sequence diagram, as illustrated in Figure 2.23. The use case starts with the Service Requester actor, who sends a request for converting time from one time zone to another. The ConverterService receives the request. First it gets the singleton instance of TimeZonesManager to retrieve the source and the targeted time zones. Then it interacts with the TimeZoneConverter to convert the source time from the source time zone to UTC time; finally, it converts the UTC time to the time of the targeted time zone.

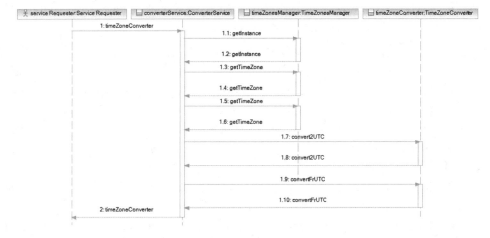

Figure 2.23   Use case realization using a sequence diagram

A *lifeline*, similar to the one shown in Figure 2.24, a sequence diagram represents an instance of a class that is involved in an interaction. The rectangular box is the head of a lifeline, which contains the name of the instance and the type of the instance. The vertical line below the rectangular box is the stem of the lifeline.

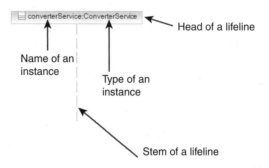

Figure 2.24   A lifeline

Messages that are exchanged between these instances are executed in a sequential order from top to bottom. There are different types of messages defined in UML. In this tutorial, interactions are presented as synchronous messages, in which the caller is blocked from other operations until he receives a response from the target instance. The information captured in a sequence diagram is useful for service design. It communicates the flow of logic and helps developers understand how the code should be implemented during the development phase.

After completing this exercise, you will be able to create a new sequence diagram.

1.   Create a sequence diagram using the default name, SequenceDiagram1.

   a.   Expand the Models folder in the Project Explorer view.

   b.   Right-click MyModel and click Add Diagram, Sequence Diagram on the pop-up menu.

   c.   Press Enter to use the default diagram name, SequenceDiagram1.

2.   Create lifelines to represent instances of various classes that participate in an interaction of getting time zone conversion (that is, the Convert time between time zones use case).

   a.   Drag the actor Service Requester from the Project Explorer view to the diagram editor to create an instance of the actor. An instance called serviceRequester:Service Requester is then created, as shown in Figure 2.25.

   b.   Create an instance of ConverterService by dragging it to the diagram editor, next to serviceRequester:Service Requester. Scroll the horizontal bar if necessary.

   c.   Similarly, drag TimeZonesManager to the space next to converterService: ConverterService.

   d.   Drag TimeZoneConverter to the space next to timeZonesManager:TimeZonesManager.

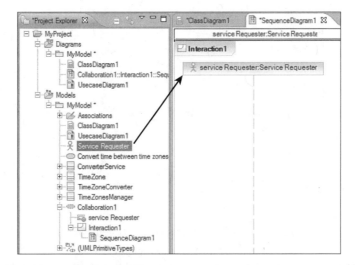

Figure 2.25   Dragging model elements to the sequence diagram

The sequence diagram should look like Figure 2.26.

Figure 2.26   Lifelines in a sequence diagram

3. Create the first synchronous message. The use case starts with `serviceRequester:Service Requester`, who sends `converterService:ConverterService` a request for converting time from one time zone to another.

   a. Double-click the SequenceDiagram1 tab to maximize the diagram view.

   b. Click Synchronous Message in the Palette.

   c. Click the stem of the lifeline of `serviceRequester:Service Requester`, hold the mouse click, and then release the mouse click at the stem of the lifeline of `converterService:ConverterService`.

   d. Click the operation `ConverterService::timeZoneConverter` from the drop-down list. When the actor `serviceRequester:Service Requester` requests time zone conversion, this is the first function that is called. The diagram should look similar to Figure 2.27

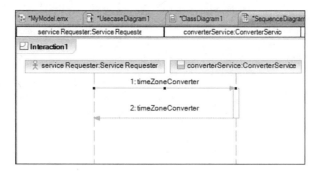

Figure 2.27   Calling timeZoneConverter

4. Create the next three synchronous messages between `converterService:Converter Service` and `timeZonesManager:TimeZonesManager`. The `converterService` first gets the singleton instance of `TimeZonesManager`, and then it works with it to get the source and the targeted time zones by calling the `getTimeZone` operation twice.

    a. Add three synchronous message lines as specified in Table 2.6. All these message lines are between `1:timeZoneConverter` and `2:timeZoneConverter` of `converter Service:ConverterService`.

TIP   To give room for more synchronous message lines, select the message line 2:timeZoneConverter and drag it downward to resize the vertical bar.

---

    b. The diagram should look like Figure 2.28.

Table 2.6   Other Synchronous Messages between converterService and timeZonesManager

From Instance	To Instance	Operation
converterService:Converter Service	timeZonesManager:TimeZones Manager	get Instance
converterService:Converter Service	timeZonesManager:TimeZones Manager	getTime Zone
converterService:Converter Service	timeZonesManager:TimeZones Manager	getTime Zone

5. Create the next two synchronous messages between `converterService:Converter Service` and `timeZoneConverter:TimeZoneConverter`. The `converterService` interacts with `timeZoneConverter` to convert the source time to UTC time by calling `convert2UTC`; then it converts the UTC time to the time of the targeted time zone by calling `convertFrUTC`.

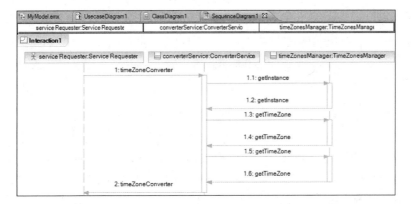

Figure 2.28   Calling timeZoneManager

   a. Add two synchronous message lines as specified in Table 2.7. All these message lines are between `1:timeZoneConverter` and `2:timeZoneConverter` of `converterService:ConverterService`, and they are after `1.6 getTimeZone`.

Table 2.7   Other Synchronous Messages between converterService and TimeZoneConverter

From Instance	To Instance	Operation
`converterService:Converter Service`	`timeZoneConverter:TimeZone Converter`	`convert 2UTC`
`converterService:Converter Service`	`timeZoneConverter:TimeZone Converter`	`convert FrUTC`

   6. The complete sequence diagram should look like Figure 2.29.

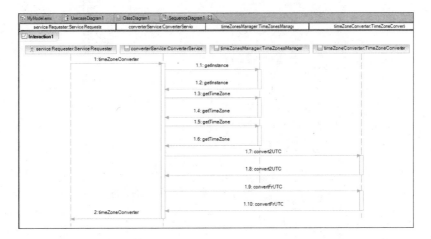

Figure 2.29   The complete sequence diagram

7. Click File, Save All to save the changes.

8. Double-click the SequenceDiagram1 tab to restore the size of the diagram editor.

You have created a sequence diagram that realizes the `Convert time between time zones` use case with its interaction.

Tutorial 2.5: Share the Service Design with Others

To share your design with people who do not have the modeling tool, RSA supports generation of HTML, PDF, and XML reports from UML designs. After completing this exercise, you will be able to generate HTML files for your design so that you can share them with others.

1. Publish the files as HTML files.

    a. Select `MyModel` in the Project Explorer view.

    b. From the workbench, click Modeling, Publish, Web. If you do not see Modeling in the menu, make sure you are in the Modeling perspective and that you have selected `MyModel`, not MyProject.

    c. Specify the target location of the generated HTML files; for example, `C:\Temp` as shown in Figure 2.30. The General tab also provides options that allow you to specify the level of details, navigation style, and other options to be used for the publication.

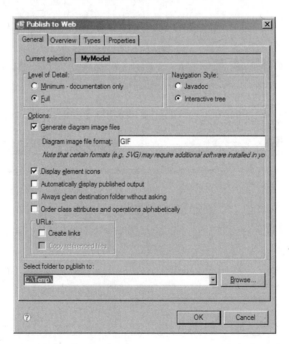

Figure 2.30   Publishing the design

    d. Click the Overview tab to review what other options offer. For example, you can enter your name as an author, enter your company name, and select your company logo to be used in the generated home page. Keep the defaults.

    e. Click the Types tab. This page allows you to select what model elements to be included in the published files. Keep the defaults.

    f. Click the Properties tab. This page allows you to specify whether empty properties should be removed from the published model elements. Keep the defaults.

    g. Click OK. The model will then be published to the specified location as HTML files.

2. Review the published files.

    a. Open the file `C:\Temp\index.html` using any Web browser.

    b. Click the link `MyModel`.

    c. The published model should look similar to Figure 2.31. Review the published model by clicking the various links. You can access all the diagrams and the model elements that you created earlier from this HTML page.

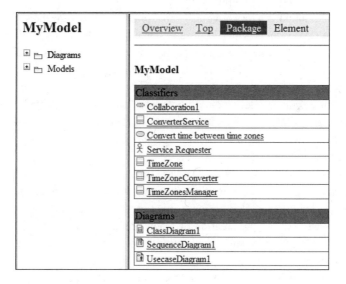

Figure 2.31 A published Web page

3. You can now share your design with your peers by sending them these HTML files.

The design has been transformed to HTML format and is now ready for sharing with your peers.

Tutorial 2.6: Transform the Service Design to Implementation with Round-Trip Engineering

Transformation is a key feature of RSA, allowing you to easily transform your designs from UML to various implementation skeletons such as Enterprise JavaBeans (EJB) components, WSDL, and Java code. Starting from version 7 of RSA, the transformation function has been extended to include support for round-trip engineering (RTE), giving you even more of a head start in implementing your designs.

Before you can run a transformation, you must create a transformation configuration. A *transformation configuration* is an instance of a transformation that includes properties that are specific to a given transformation such as a unique name, the source, and the target of the transformation. Three types of protocols are supported for a UML-to-Java transformation: conceptual, mixed, and reconciled.

Conceptual protocol supports a forward transformation in which the source is untouched after the transformation. Changing the generated Java files has no impact on the original UML model. To enable a reverse transformation, you need to create another Java-to-UML transformation configuration with a conceptual protocol.

Mixed protocol supports a forward transformation; at the same time, however, it also replaces the elements in the UML model with visual representations of the corresponding generated Java classes. This replacement enables you to change the Java code from the model and vice versa. The changes that you make to the model are reflected automatically in the corresponding Java file, and the changes that you make to the Java classes are reflected automatically in the corresponding model element. For example, deleting an attribute in a Java class is reflected immediately in the original UML model, and the corresponding attribute model element is deleted. Similarly, removing an attribute in the UML model is reflected immediately in the generated Java files, and the corresponding Java class no longer has the attribute.

Reconciled protocol supports both a forward transformation and a reverse transformation. The users consciously control when to run either transformation. Changes made to the source and to the target are being reconciled during a transformation. For example, adding a new attribute in a Java class will lead to the creation of a new attribute in the corresponding UML class after a reverse transformation. Similarly, inserting a new attribute in an UML class will add a new attribute to the corresponding Java class after a forward transformation. Reconciliation means compromising the differences between the source and target. As a result, only new additions are acknowledged. Deleting an attribute in a Java class is not reflected when running a reverse transformation, and the corresponding attribute model element still exists after a reverse transformation.

In this tutorial, the conceptual protocol is used. You'll transform the model into Java code, make a small change in the generated Java file, and then transform the Java class into another

UML model. The small change you made in the Java code will be reflected in the reverse-engineered UML model. You'll then compare the original UML model with the reverse-engineered UML model to see the difference.

Transform UML to Java

After completing this exercise, you will be able to create a new transformation configuration project for transforming UML to Java.

1. Create a Web project. Since the Java files that you are going to generate will serve as a service provider, you should create a Web project to hold these generated files.

   a. From the workbench, click File, New, Project.

   b. Click Web, Dynamic Web Project, and then click Next. Select the Show All Wizards check box if Web is not in the list. Click OK if prompted to enable the Web Development capability.

   c. In the Project Name field of the new dynamic Web project page, type `MyWebProject`. Leave the other fields at their default, as illustrated in Figure 2.32.

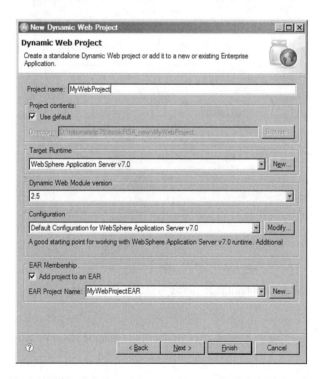

Figure 2.32   Creating a Web project

    d. Click Finish. Click No if you are prompted to switch to the Web perspective.

2. Create a transformation configuration for the UML-to-Java transformation.

    a. Make sure you are still in the Modeling perspective.

    b. Expand the `MyProject` > `Models` folder in the Project Explorer view.

    c. Select `MyModel`. Ensure that the model is opened. (Double-click `MyModel` to open it.)

    d. From the workbench, click Modeling, Transform, New Configuration.

    e. In the Name field of the new transformation configuration page, type `UML2Java`.

    f. Expand Java Transformations and select UML to Java, as shown in Figure 2.33. The conceptual protocol is used in this transformation. Click Next.

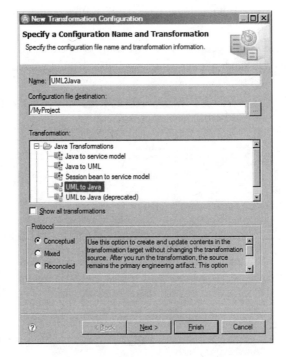

Figure 2.33   Specifying a configuration name and transformation

    g. Select MyProject, Models, MyModel in the Selected Source window.

NOTE   If you do not see MyModel, make sure the model is opened. Click Cancel and go back to step c above. Double-click MyModel to open it in a model editor first. Then continue to perform step d and onward again.

h. Select MyWebProject, Java Resources, src in the Selected Target window. The panel should look like Figure 2.34.

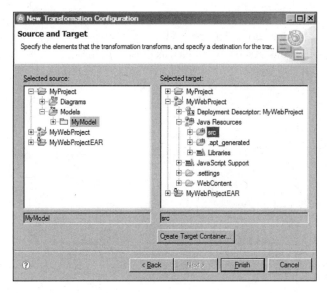

Figure 2.34   Selecting a source and target for transformation

i. Click Finish to create the transformation configuration.

3. Specify options for the transformation.

a. Click the UML to Java Options tab.

b. Clear the Generate Getter and Setter Methods check box like Figure 2.35. In this tutorial, you will not generate the getter and setter methods for the attributes defined in the UML model during the transformation.

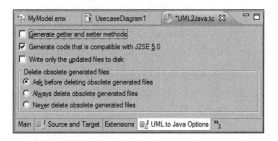

Figure 2.35   Setting transformation options

c. Click the Collections tab.

NOTE   If you do not see the Collection tab because of the screen size, click the >> icon
that is next to the UML to Java Options tab to see other available tabs.

    d. Review the selections. This page allows you map UML relationships with different
        Java collections. Keep the defaults, as illustrated in Figure 2.36.

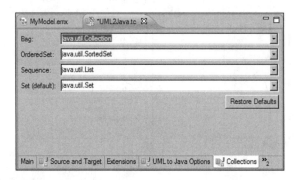

Figure 2.36   Reviewing the collections page

    e. Click File, Save All to save the file.

  4. Run the transformation.

    a. Click the Main tab.

    b. Click Run in the Forward Transformation panel to start the transformation.

  5. Review the generated Java files.

    a. Navigate to the newly generated Java files within `MyWebProject` to see how the UML
        model elements are being transformed. For example, look at `ConverterService.java`,
        shown in Figure 2.37. The generated class has one operation, `timeZoneConverter`,
        defined. This is the service that this service provider will provide.

    b. Also notice the two attributes, `timeZonesManager` and `timeZoneConverter`. These
        are created automatically because of the two directed association relationships.

  6. Make a change to the generated Java files by introducing a package called `sample` to
      group these Java classes. You will see later how this change is reflected in the reverse-
      engineered UML model.

    a. Right-click the `src` folder of Java Resources and click New, Package.

    b. Type `sample` as the package name, and click `Finish`. Use this Java package to hold
        the generated source instead of the default package.

    c. Select all four Java files (hold the Shift key) and right-click.

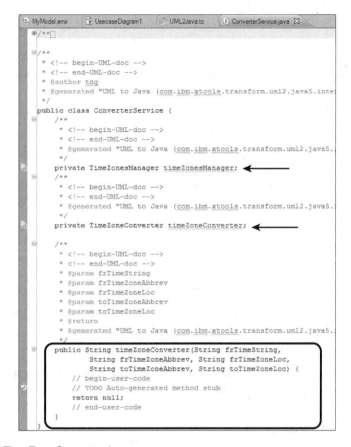

Figure 2.37   TimeZoneConverter.java

   d. Click Refactor, Move on the pop-up menu, as illustrated in Figure 2.38.

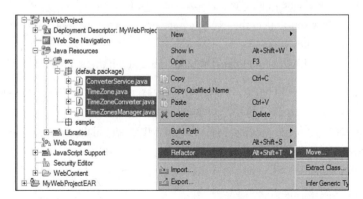

Figure 2.38   Refactoring the Java files into the sample package

> **NOTE**   If you do not see Refactor, Move, make sure all the classes' trees are collapsed.

    e. Select `sample` and click OK to move the four Java files under the `sample` package.

Transform Java to UML

Now create another transformation configuration to transform the Java files back to a UML model. For ease of comparison, you will place the transformed model into a new UML model instead of overwriting the existing UML model.

    After completing this exercise, you will be able to create a new transformation configuration file for transforming Java to UML.

  1. Create a transformation configuration for the Java-to-UML transformation.

    a. Make sure you are still in the Modeling perspective.

    b. Select `MyWebProject` in the Project Explorer view.

    c. From the workbench, click Modeling, Transform, New Configuration.

    d. In the Name field of the new transformation configuration page, type `Java2UML`.

    e. Expand Java Transformations and click Java to UML. The conceptual protocol is used in this transformation. Click Next.

    f. Click Create Target Container to create a new UML model for storing the generated files. For ease of comparison, you will place the transformed model into a new UML model.

  2. Create a new UML model.

    a. In the Create Model panel, make sure Standard Template is selected. Click Next.

    b. Select General under Categories and Blank Package under Templates.

    c. In the File Name field, type `MyReverseUMLModel`.

    d. Click Browse to select the existing `MyProject` as the location for the new model file. Then click OK.

    e. The Create UML Model panel should look like Figure 2.39. Click Finish.

  3. Select the source and target location for the Java2UML transformation configuration.

    a. Select `MyWebProject` in the Selected Source window.

    b. Select MyProject, Models, MyReverseUMLModel in the Selected Target window, as shown in Figure 2.40.

    c. Click Finish.

  4. Run the transformation.

    a. Click the Main tab.

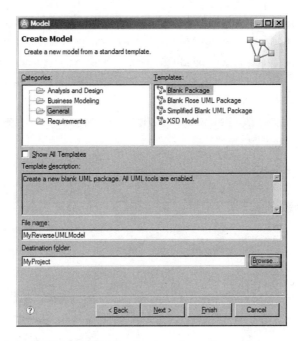

Figure 2.39   Creating a UML model for reverse transformation

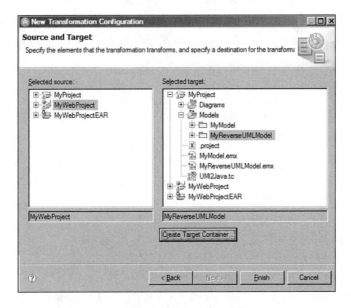

Figure 2.40   Selecting the source and target for transformation

b. Click Run in the Forward Transformation panel to transform the Java files to a UML model. Click OK if prompted to enable the Java modeling capability.

c. Click OK to accept any pending changes. This Merge Transformed Model panel. This page, similar to Figure 2.41, lists the changes that are going to be applied to the targeted project.

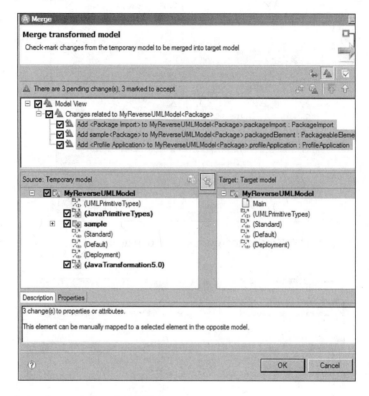

Figure 2.41   Accepting pending changes

d. The Java classes are now transformed to model elements and stored within MyReverseUMLModel.

5. Review the reverse-engineered model.

a. Take a look at the small change that you made earlier. In the project explorer view, expand MyProject, Models, MyReverseUMLModel, as shown in Figure 2.42. Note the new package sample that you have added.

6. Create a class diagram to validate the generated model elements.

a. Expand the Models folder in the Project Explorer view.

b. Right-click MyReverseUMLModel in the Project Explorer view as shown in Figure 2.42.

Figure 2.42   The generated UML model

d.   Click Add Diagram, Class Diagram on the pop-up menu.

e.   Press Enter to use the default diagram name, `ClassDiagram1`.

f.   Drag and drop the `sample` package from the Project Explorer view into the diagram.

g.   Right-click the `sample` model element on the diagram.

h.   Click Filters, Show Related Elements on the pop-up menu.

i.   Select `Show All Relationships [Default]` and click OK.

j.   The four classes are now shown in the diagram as related elements of the `sample` package, similar to Figure 2.43.

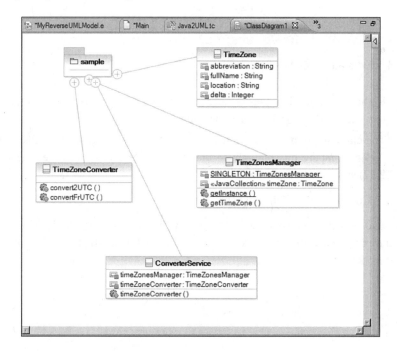

Figure 2.43   The reversed-engineered class diagram

7. Compare this class diagram with the class diagram you created earlier (see Figure 2.22).

a. The class ConverterService on this diagram has two extra attributes: timeZones Manager:TimeZonesManager and timeZoneConverted:TimeZoneConverter. Also, the class TimeZonesManager on this diagram has an extra attribute <<JavaCollection>> timeZone:TimeZone because the association relationships are shown as attributes on this diagram.

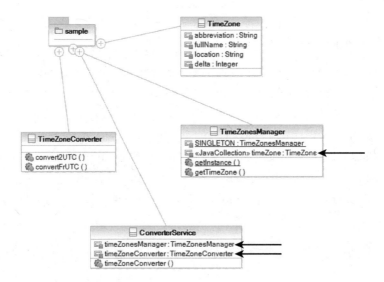

Figure 2.44   Extra attributes highlight

b. Right-click on each of these extra attributes and click Filters, Show As Association to turn each of them back to an association relationship.

c. The class diagram for your transformed UML model should look like Figure 2.45. Again, compare this diagram to the class diagram you created earlier (see Figure 2.22) and notice the similarity.

8. Press Ctrl+S to save all the changes.

You have transformed your design to a Java implementation skeleton, made a small change to the generated code, and then transformed it back to UML to see how the route trip engineering works.

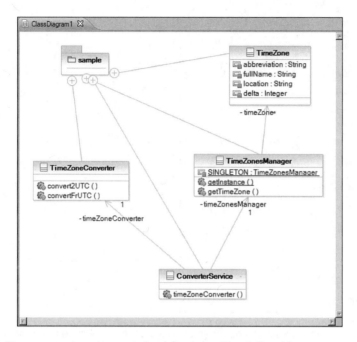

Figure 2.45   The reversed-engineered class diagram with relationships

Complete the Implementation

Once you have generated Java files from your UML diagram, you can modify the generated files to implement your design. Then you can turn this implementation to a Web service for deployment to a Web server. The next chapter about service creation using Rational Application Developer illustrates how to create a service from a Java implementation.

The CD included with this book contains a sample time zone converter service implementation with a Web service created. Run the provided sample implementation to validate that you can perform the application's use case, `Convert time between time zones`, similar to Figure 2.46. Remember: The purpose of use cases is to define the behavior of a system and capture the requirements. It is important that the implementation fulfills the requirements by working as expected.

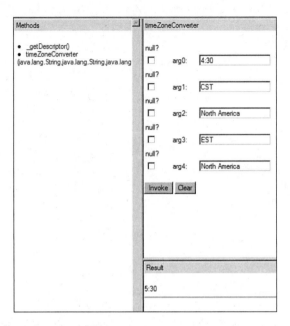

Figure 2.46   Running the sample implementation to convert time zone from one to another

Summary

This chapter provides a high-level hands-on introduction to RSA. You have followed step-by-step exercises and demonstrations to learn how to design an application using UML diagrams, generate HTML files from the UML model, transform your design to Java code, and then reverse-engineer the Java code back to a UML diagram using RSA.

Tutorial Summary:

- Tutorial 2.1: Use a UML Model to Capture a Service Design
  - Create a UML model and add it to a Model project
- Tutorial 2.2: Capture the Use Cases for a Service Using a Use Case Diagram
  - Create a use case diagram
  - Add a use case to a use case diagram
  - Add an actor to a use case diagram
- Tutorial 2.3: Design the Blueprint for a Service Using a Class Diagram
  - Create a class diagram
  - Add a class to a class diagram
  - Define details about a class (add a method, an attribute, and others)
  - Relate classes using relationships

- Tutorial 2.4: Detail the Flow of a Service Using a Sequence Diagram
  - Create a sequence diagram
  - Add lifeline onto a sequence diagram
  - Create messages to capture the interactions
- Tutorial 2.5: Share the Service Design with Others
  - Transform the design to HTML format
- Tutorial 2.6: Transform the Service Design to Implementation with Round-Trip Engineering
  - Create a transformation configuration
  - Transform the design from UML to Java
  - Transform the implementation from Java to UML

Service Creation with IBM Rational Application Developer and IBM WebSphere Application Server

Product Overview

Rational Application Developer V7.5 is an integrated development environment (IDE) that can be used for developing Java Platform, Enterprise Edition (Java EE) applications. WebSphere Application Server is a Web application server that can run and manage Java EE applications. It runs with IBM HTTP Server, which is based on the Apache HTTP Server developed by the Apache Software Foundation. WebSphere Application Server enables a computer that uses the HyperText Transfer Protocol (HTTP) to serve objects by responding to requests from the other programs, such as Web browsers.

Rational Application Developer is for developing Java EE applications, and WebSphere Application Server is for executing them. Rational Application Developer is based on the open-source Eclipse development platform. The Eclipse platform is an extensible development platform and application framework for building software. The Eclipse platform by itself comes with a Java IDE for Java application development. It provides some common tools and features for Java developers, like a Java editor and debugger, integrated JUnit support, and a compiler. Built on top of the Eclipse platform, Rational Application Developer adds a great number of capabilities including Java EE 5, Extensible Markup Language (XML), Web services, and database development.

When you start Rational Application Developer, you are prompted to select a workspace location, as shown in Figure 3.1. A workspace can be any directory location where your work is stored. If you are working on multiple projects at the same time, use different workspaces for each project to ensure a clear code separation.

When launched for the first time, Rational Application Developer displays a welcome page, as shown in Figure 3.2, which offers quick links to tutorials and samples. The Overview section provides a guided tour of Rational Application Developer, and the First Steps section contains step-by-step guides to some of the common features in Rational Application Developer.

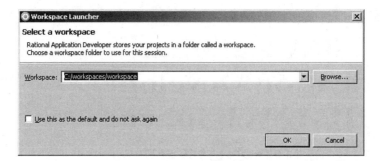

Figure 3.1   Selecting a workspace location

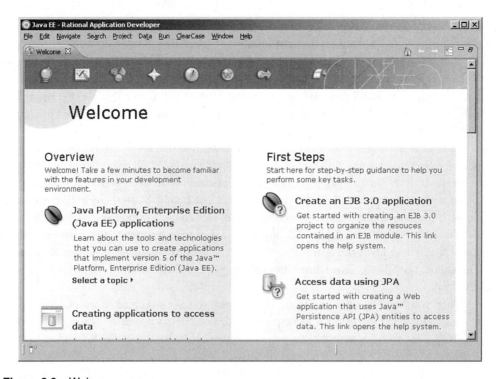

Figure 3.2   Welcome screen

The default perspective of Rational Application Developer is the Java Platform, Java EE perspective. A *perspective* is a consolidation of tools and views that a developer needs to perform a specific function, like developing a Java EE application. Rational Application Developer offers several perspectives tailored for different types of developers, such as Web, Data, Java EE, Debug, and Java.

Rational Application Developer supports the development of many types of applications, including:

- Java Platform, Enterprise Edition (Java EE)
- Web
- Enterprise JavaBeans (EJB)
- Database
- Web Service
- Java Message Service (JMS)
- SQLJ
- Portal
- Visual Modeling (allows you to visualize your source code in a Universal Markup Language (UML) diagram, topic diagram, and so forth)

You can develop, test, and debug any of the preceding applications right in Rational Application Developer. You can directly deploy and test Java enterprise applications on the embedded WebSphere Application Server, which is a Java EE–compliant application server. Rational Application Developer v7.5 comes bundled with an integrated WebSphere Application Server v7.0.

By default, Rational Application Developer ships with a WebSphere Application Server for unit testing. Figure 3.3 shows the Servers view, from which you can start and stop the integrated WebSphere Application Server.

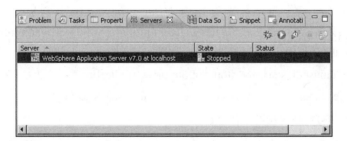

Figure 3.3   The server view

Rational Application Developer not only allows you to test with the integrated WebSphere Application Server, it can connect to servers that are on different machines.

After an application is unit tested and assembled in the Rational Application Developer, it can be packaged and deployed externally to staging and production WebSphere Application Servers.

WebSphere Application Server is administered through an integrated solutions console, which is a Web-based application. The *integrated solutions console*, which is also known as the *administrative console*, can deploy, manage, and configure enterprise applications that reside in a WebSphere Application Server. Figure 3.4 shows a Web browser loaded with the administrative console.

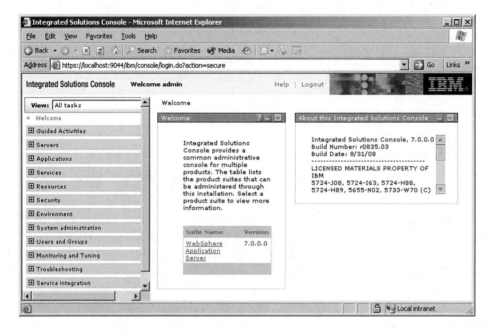

Figure 3.4   The integrated solutions console

The *integrated solutions console* has a URI of http://<host>:<port>/admin. An administrator can perform many activities in the administrative console, such as the following:

- Install, uninstall, start, and stop an Enterprise Application
- Manage resources such as datasource driver and mail session
- Manage server security

After development, a Java EE project is exported into a Java EE Enterprise Application (EAR) file. An EAR file is a Java Archive (JAR) file with an `.ear` extension that can be deployed to WebSphere Application Server. It consists of a META-INF directory, Web module, EJB module, Application Client module, and Resource Adapter module. The META-INF contains an optional deployment descriptor (`application.xml`). Most Java EE applications can be deployed without having a deployment descriptor. A Web module contains servlets, JavaServer Pages (JSP), Hypertext Markup Language (HTML), or any Web-related content. An EJB module contains Enterprise JavaBeans. An Application Client module contains class files of an application client. A Resource Adapter module is used to assemble resource adaptors that allow an application to access a resource such as data or an application on a remote server in a single deployable unit, called a *resource adapter archive* file (`.rar`).

There are several ways to start a WebSphere Application Server. The server can be installed as Windows services, which can be started automatically when Windows boots up. Alternatively, the application server can be started manually using the Windows menu or a command prompt.

When the server is installed, a default profile is created. A profile separates the runtime environments and JVM instances in the same server. You can have multiple profiles on the same server. Each profile can be configured uniquely with different applications deployed, and you can run multiple profiles at the same time. *Running multiple profiles* means running multiple server instances. The port number of each profile must be different. They are usually incremented by one in the order of creation. You can create additional profiles on top of the default one created during installation. The Profile Management Tool that comes with WebSphere Application Server allows users to easily create profiles as shown in Figure 3.5.

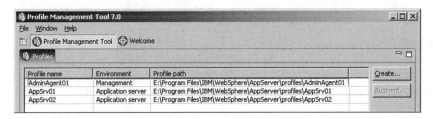

Figure 3.5　Profile Management Tool

Profiles are generally stored in the default directory `<WAS_INSTALL>\profiles`. However, you can create them outside of the WebSphere Application Server install directory. A profile directory has a structure as shown in Figure 3.6. It stores the XML configuration files, logs, installed applications, and more.

Administrators can manage server security on the administrative console. Fine-grained administrative authorization and role assignment allows a subset of the functions to be assigned to an administrator, as shown in Figure 3.7.

How Do They Support SOA?

Rational Application Developer is a robust and powerful development tool that fits well with the Service-Oriented Architecture (SOA). It enables customers to create sophisticated applications and solutions swiftly and easily by assembling them from new and existing services. Each business function in a company can be implemented as a service, which can then be integrated with other services to fulfill the company's business requirements.

SOA leverages open standards to represent business function as a service. Each service becomes a building block to create enterprise applications. Services in SOA can be implemented in multiple programming languages on various platforms. They can interact with each other because they are exposed using a common interface. One type of SOA service is Web services.

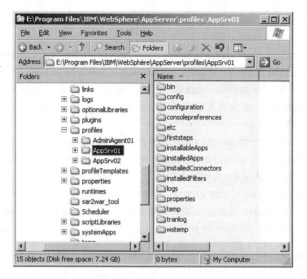

Figure 3.6   The file structure of a profile

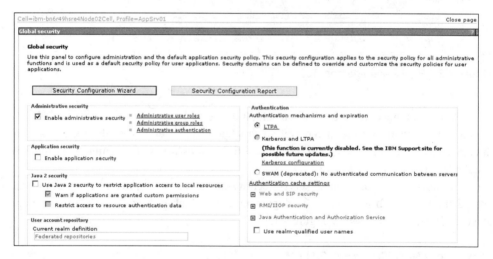

Figure 3.7   Global security page in the administrative console

Web services combine widespread technologies and open standards to help enable the integration of heterogeneous systems. Through Web services, an SOA can be implemented, with new and existing applications as functional building blocks accessible over standard Internet protocols that are independent from platforms and programming languages. Rational Application Developer lets you create Web services to use in a service-oriented architecture.

Rational Application Developer supports the creation of Web services using a top-down approach (starts with a Web Service Description Language (WSDL) file to generate the Web service implementation) or a bottom-up approach (starts with a JavaBeans or EJB implementation to generate a Web service). It provides wizards to quickly create Web services and Web services clients and to publish Web services externally.

IBM WebSphere Application Server is an important component of the IBM SOA Foundation. As the backbone of many SOA Foundation softwares, it is a crucial product to master. Applications and services can be deployed and executed on WebSphere Application Server. Many software products of the IBM SOA foundation are built on top of WebSphere Application Server. Some examples are WebSphere Process Server, WebSphere ESB, WebSphere Service Registry and Repository, WebSphere Portal, and WebSphere Services Business Fabric.

Tutorial Scenario

The tutorials that are featured in this chapter can be divided into two parts: service creation in Rational Application Developer and service deployment in WebSphere Application Server. In Rational Application Developer, we illustrate how to create and invoke a Web service and how to access a database using Java Persistence API (JPA). In WebSphere Application Server, we illustrate deploying and configuring an application after development is completed.

The application that is developed in Rational Application Developer is based on an auto insurance agency scenario. The scenario describes an auto insurance agent validating the risk of a new client by obtaining the person's driving record from a Web service. After the insurance agent has obtained the driving record, part of the information will be stored in a database for future reference.

An auto insurance agent receives a request from a new client to buy auto insurance. The insurance agent uses the Insurance Agent's Web Application to create a new auto insurance policy. The Web application obtains a driving record of the customer through the Driving Record Web Service. It then creates a new policy and stores the driving record and the policy in the database. In this chapter, you will create the Driving Record Web Service, the database table, and the Insurance Agent's Web Application. The Driving Record Web Service could be a third party or an in-house Web service that can be reused in other applications.

After the application is fully unit tested in Rational Application Developer using the embedded server, the application will be packaged as an EAR file and deployed to a staging or production server. In our scenario, we will also deploy the Driving Record Web Service to the WebSphere Application Server.

The chapter has four tutorials:

Service Creation in Rational Application Developer

Tutorial 3.1: Create, Deploy, and Test a Web Service

Tutorial 3.2: Create a Database Table

Tutorial 3.3: Invoke a Web Service and Persist the Data Using Java Persistence API

Service Deployment in WebSphere Application Server

Tutorial 3.4: Deploy an Application into a WebSphere Application Server

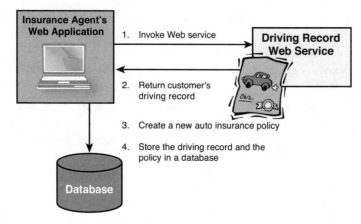

Figure 3.8   The auto insurance scenario

System Requirements

The tutorial has been developed with the following products and environments:

- Rational Application Developer 7.5
- Integrated WebSphere Application Server 7.0
- WebSphere Application Server 7.0

What Is Included in the CD-ROM?

The attached CD-ROM contains all tutorial solutions, which are Project Interchange files that can be imported into Rational Application Developer and run. They are located in the individual `tutorial` directory under the `solutions` folder. In addition, the CD-ROM includes step-by-step videos that illustrate the tutorials located in the individual `tutorial` directory under the `videos` folder.

1. **chapter3/tutorial 3.1/solution/solution3_1.zip**—A project interchange file that contains a completed Driving Record Web Service. To import it to Rational Application Developer, click File, Import from the workbench menu bar. Expand Other and select Project Interchange. Click Next and follow the wizard's instructions.

2. **chapter3/tutorial 3.2/solution/solution3_2.zip**—A project interchange file that contains the solutions from Tutorials 3.1 and 3.2.

3. **chapter3/tutorial 3.3/solution/solution3_3.zip**—A project interchange file that contains the solution for all tutorials.

4. **chapter3/tutorial 3.3/solution/DriversWebServiceProjectEAR.ear and InsuranceJPAProjectEAR.ear**—EAR files that contain the solutions for all tutorials ready to be deployed to the WebSphere Application Server.

5. **chapter3/tutorial 3.4/tutorial files/DerbyDatabases**—A folder that contains the Derby database that was created in Tutorial 3.2.

6. **chapter3/tutorial 3.4/tutorial files/DriversWebServiceProjectEAR.ear and InsuranceJPAProjectEAR.ear**—EAR files that are created from tutorial 3.3 and will be used to deploy to the WebSphere Application Server in Tutorial 3.4.

Tutorial 3.1: Create, Deploy, and Test a Web Service

This exercise demonstrates how to create a Web service and test it in Rational Application Developer. Web services help solve the interoperability problem between applications developed by different languages or on different platforms. A Web service uses open protocols such as XML, HTTP, or SOAP. A Web service is self-contained and self-describing. Each Web service is described by a Web Services Description Language (WSDL) interface. This interface contains the definitions for port types, operations, and message types for the Web service. The port type contains a collection of operations that this service supports. Each operation has input and output messages defined. In Java terms, a port type is like a class definition, an operation is like a method, and the input and output messages are like the input parameter or return types to a method.

Creating a Web service in Rational Application Developer is pretty straightforward. The Web Service Wizard automatically generates the Web service for you. In this example, you create a Java class that returns a mock-up driving record object, and then you use the Web Service Wizard to expose the Java class as a Web service.

After the Web service is created, you can deploy it to the WebSphere Application Server for other external applications to invoke. To invoke a Web service hosted on a local or remote server, obtain access to the WSDL file from the Web service provider either in the form of a URI or an actual file. The tooling can generate a Java proxy from the WSDL interface file. You can use the Java proxy to invoke the Web service from an external Java client such as a Java application or a JSP. In Java EE 5, an alternate way to invoke a Web service is to use Web service annotations. An `@WebServiceRef` annotation declares a reference to a Web service.

In the following listing, the annotation specifies that the variable `service` is initialized by looking up a Web service Java Naming Directory Interface (JNDI) reference named `DrivingRecordWS_Servlet`.

```
@WebServiceRef(name = "DrivingRecordWS_Servlet")
static DrivingRecordWebServiceService service;
```

This annotation is equivalent to declaring a Web service reference `<service-ref>` in the Web deployment descriptor and doing a JNDI lookup to get the `DrivingRecordWebServiceService` object through the JNDI reference. By using the `@WebServiceRef` annotation, developers no longer have to put in the service reference in the deployment descriptor or have to look up the service through JNDI. It saves developers time and makes coding simpler. The Web service annotations can only be used in certain Web components such as Servlet, Servlet filters, Event listeners,

Taglib tag handler, and JavaServer Faces managed beans. You can use the administrative console to augment or override the Web service endpoint location that is defined by a `@WebServiceRef` annotation.

Listing 3.1 The Web Service Reference Equivalence of the @WebServiceRef Annotation

```
<service-ref>
      <service-ref-name>DrivingRecordWS_Servlet</service-ref-name>
      <service-interface>
      com.drivers.webservice.DrivingRecordWebServiceService
      </service-interface>
      <service-ref-type>
      com.drivers.webservice.DrivingRecordWebServiceService
      </service-ref-type>
      <wsdl-file>
      WEB-INF/wsdl/DrivingRecordWebServiceService.wsdl
      </wsdl-file>
      <service-qname>
      http://webservice.drivers.com/:DrivingRecordWebServiceService
      </service-qname>
</service-ref>
```

Web service providers can advertise their Web services using Web Services Inspection Language (WSIL). A WSIL file typically lists all the Web services provided by the service provider. It contains service descriptions and the WSDL file access information. A requester can use the WSIL file to discover what Web services are available from the service provider. A WSIL file is normally placed in a common Web entry point. A hypothetical example would be www.ibm.com/inspection.wsil.

Listing 3.2 Example of an inspection.wsil File

```
<?xml version="1.0" encoding="UTF-8"?>
<inspection xmlns="http://schemas.xmlsoap.org/ws/2001/10/inspection/">
    <abstract>The drivers services API</abstract>
    <service>
      <abstract>Getting Driving Records</abstract>
      <description referencedNamespace="http://schemas.xmlsoap.org/wsdl/"
location="http://localhost:9080/DriversWebServiceProject/DrivingRecordWebService
Service?WSDL"/>
    </service>
</inspection>
```

In this tutorial, you will create a Web service, Driving Record Web Service, to provide the record for a given driver. The Web service is generated from a Java class that generates a mock-up driving record Java object. The Web service resides in a Web project, which you will test using the Web Services Explorer test client. The Insurance Agent's Web Application to be created in Tutorial 3.3 will invoke this Web service.

1. Start Rational Application Developer if it's not already started.

   a. From the Windows Start menu, select All Programs, IBM Software Delivery Platform, IBM Rational Application Developer 7.5, Rational Application Developer.

   b. A dialog will appear asking for the workspace directory. Just click OK to accept the default one.

   c. The first page is the Welcome page. If security was enabled in the embedded WebSphere Application Server when Rational Application Developer was installed, a dialog would appear to prompt for the user ID and password as shown in Figure 3.9. Enter the password and click Finish.

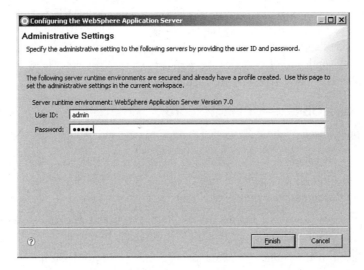

Figure 3.9   Administrative settings dialog for the embedded WebSphere Application Server

   d. Click the Workbench icon on the top of the Welcome page, and you will be in the Java EE perspective.

Creating a Web Project

Web projects can be created in the Web or Java EE perspective. All Web elements, such as JSP and Java servlets, are stored in Web projects. A Java EE application consists of three components: Application clients, Web, and EJB modules. You will work with the Web module in this example where the Web service resides.

1. Make sure you are in the Java EE perspective. If not, click Windows, Open Perspective, Other. Select Java EE (default) and click OK.

2. From the workbench, click File, New, Dynamic Web Project.

3. Enter `DriversWebServiceProject` as the project name. Click Finish.

4. When you are prompted to change to the Web perspective, click No.

A Web project in Rational Application Developer is set up in compliance with the Java EE 5 standard and can be exported as a Web Archive (WAR) file for deployment. Java servlets and other supporting Java classes are stored in the `src` folder inside the Java Resources directory. JSP files, HTML pages, style sheets, JavaScript files, and images are stored in the `WebContent` directory. Unlike its predecessor Java 2 Enterprise Edition (J2EE), in Java EE 5, deployment descriptors such as `web.xml`, `application.xml`, and `webservices.xml` are optional. Instead, the server uses annotations and application packaging to determine the deployment details and the module types. In Rational Application Developer, the Web deployment descriptor (`web.xml`) is created by default alongside with the Web project. You can find it in the `/WebContent/META-INF` directory.

Creating a Java Object—DrivingRecord

Create a Java object used by the Web service as a return type and name it `DrivingRecord`.

1. Create a Java class.

    a. In the Enterprise Explorer view, expand `DriversWebServiceProject`, right-click Java Resources, and click New, Class.

    b. Enter `com.drivers.webservice` as the package and `DrivingRecord` as the class. This is the Java object type that the Web service will return.

    c. Make sure the public static void main (`String[] args`) box is not checked.

    d. Click Finish. The Java editor opens.

2. Code the `DrivingRecord` class.

    a. Add the code in bold using the Java editor.

```
package com.drivers.webservice;

public class DrivingRecord {
    private String name;
    private int convictions;


}
```

    b. The getters and setters can be generated automatically by selecting the Generate Getters and Setters menu item. Right-click on the Java editor and click Source, Generate Getters and Setters.

    c. Click Select All to generate getters and setters for both added fields.

    d. Click OK. The final class file is displayed as follows:

```java
package com.drivers.webservice;


public class DrivingRecord {
    private String name;
    private int convictions;

    public String getName() {
        return name;
    }
    public void setName(String name) {
        this.name = name;
    }
    public int getConvictions() {
        return convictions;
    }
    public void setConvictions(int convictions) {
        this.convictions = convictions;
    }

}
```

3. Click the Save icon to save the changes.

Creating a Web Service Java Class—DrivingRecordWebService

In this section, you create a Java class that acts as the back end of the Web service. The Java class in this example returns a mock-up Java object of type `DrivingRecord` that you created in the previous section. A Web service back-end could potentially do anything, such as processing information through a business process, connecting to database, or even invoking another Web service.

1. Create a Web service Java class named `DrivingRecordWebService`.

    a. In the Enterprise Explorer view, expand `DriversWebServiceProject`. Right-click Java Resources and click New, Class.

    b. Browse `com.drivers.webservice` as the package and enter `DrivingRecordWeb Service` as the class.

    c. Make sure the public static void main (`String[] args`) box is not checked.

    d. Click Finish. The Java editor opens.

2. Add the code in bold as follows. This code creates a new `DrivingRecord`.

```
package com.drivers.webservice;


public class DrivingRecordWebService {
    public DrivingRecord getRecord (String name){
        DrivingRecord newRecord = new DrivingRecord ();
        newRecord.setName(name);
        int random_value =
Long.valueOf(Math.round(Math.random()*10)).intValue();
        newRecord.setConvictions(random_value);

        System.out.println ("Invoking DrivingRecordWebService...");
        System.out.println ("Name: "+ name +", Convictions:
"+random_value);

        return newRecord;
    }
}
```

3. Click Save.

Creating a Web Service

Creating a Web service is extremely simple in Rational Application Developer. The Web service uses the `DrivingRecordWebService` Java class as the implementation.

1. Create a Java Web service.

    a. Right-click `DrivingRecordWebService.java` and click Web Services, Create Web Service.

    b. By default, Bottom Up Java Bean Web Service should be selected as the Web service type (see Figure 3.10).

    c. Click Next twice until you reach the Server Startup page.

    d. Click Start Server, and then wait until the server is started. The Web Service Wizard starts the WebSphere Application Server and deploys the generated Web service to the server.

    e. Click Finish. Now the Web service is up and running.

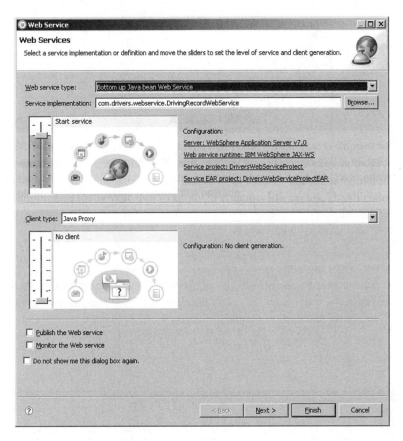

Figure 3.10   The Web Service Wizard

2.   When the wizard is complete, it means you have successfully created your first
     Web service. The wizard created some new artifacts in your project. They are
     `DrivingRecordWebServiceDelegate.java` and a Web service entry under the Ser-
     vices folder as shown in Figure 3.11.

Examining the WSDL Interface

You may wonder where the WSDL file is. Unlike Rational Application Developer v6.1, which
uses a default Web service runtime of JAX-RPC, Rational Application Developer v7.5 uses JAX-
WS as the default runtime; it does not require the presence of a physical WSDL file. Instead, the
WSDL file is dynamically generated. The Web services developed in Rational Application Developer v7.5 are backward compatible to WebSphere Application Server v6.1 if a feature pack is
installed on the server.

1.   View the WSDL file in the Web browser.

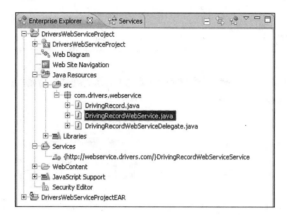

Figure 3.11   The generated Web service

    a. In a Web browser, enter `http://<host>:<port>/DriversWebServiceProject/` `DriversRecordWebServiceService?WSDL`. The host and port number might be different based on your computer's configurations. In a typical testing environment, the host is localhost, and the port number is 9080.

    b. Figure 3.12 shows the WSDL file. You will use this WSDL file in the next tutorial to invoke the Web service.

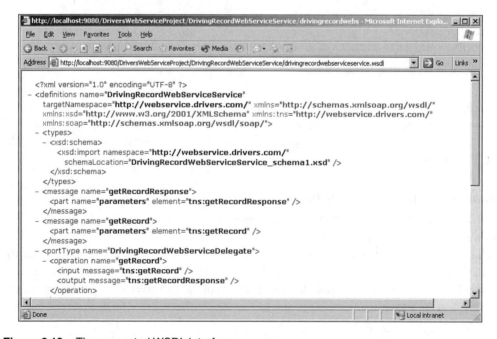

Figure 3.12   The generated WSDL interface

2. Alternatively, you can view the WSDL interface using the interface editor in the workbench.

   a. Expand Services in the Enterprise Explorer view in the workbench.

   b. Then right-click {http://webservice.drivers.com/}DrivingRecordWebService Service. Click Show, WSDL Interface to bring up the WSDL Interface editor as shown in Figure 3.13.

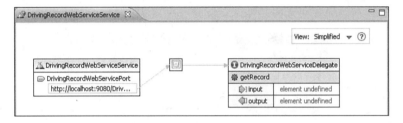

Figure 3.13 The generated WSDL interface in a WSDL Interface editor

Testing the Web Service

Rational Application Developer comes with a Web Service Explorer test client. It has three pages that can locate and test Web services from three sources: WSIL, Universal Description, Discovery and Integration (UDDI), and WSDL. In this example, the WSDL page will be used to invoke the driving record Web service you just created.

1. Launch the Web Services Explorer and load the WSDL interface for testing.

   a. In Rational Application Developer, click Launch the Web Services Explorer from the toolbar in the Java EE perspective, as shown in Figure 3.14.

Figure 3.14 Launching Web Services Explorer

   b. In the Web Services Explorer editor, click the WSDL Page icon, as shown in Figure 3.15.

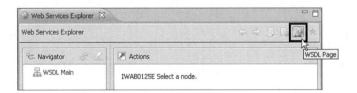

Figure 3.15 The WSDL Page in Web Services Explorer

  c. Click the WSDL Main URI.

  d. Click Browse to select the WSDL interface to call. The WSDL Browser window
      pops up.

  e. Select WebSphere Web Services WSDL documents from the Category drop-down
      box (see Figure 3.16). Notice that the WSDL URL is `http://localhost:9080/`
      `DriversWebServiceProject/DrivingRecordWebServiceService?WSDL`. The host
      and port number might be different depending on your computer's configurations.

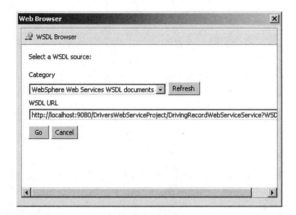

Figure 3.16   The WSDL page in Web Services Explorer

  f. Click Go to dismiss the WSDL Browser window.

  g. Click Go in the Web Services Explorer.

  2. Execute the WSDL operation to invoke the Web service.

  a. Click the `getRecord` operation.

  b. Click Add to add an argument. Then enter your name in the text field as shown in
      Figure 3.17.

  c. Click Go. The Web service is invoked, and Figure 3.18 displays the result in the bot-
      tom pane. The number of convictions will change with each call because this number
      is randomly generated in the `DrivingRecordWebService` implementation class.

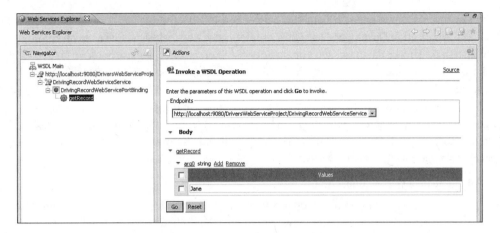

Figure 3.17 Invoking the getRecord operation of the DrivingRecordWebServiceService

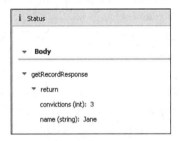

Figure 3.18 The results from the getRecord operation

Tutorial 3.2: Create a Database Table

In the previous tutorial, you created a Web service to provide the driving record for a particular driver. In this section, you create a database connection and database table using the database capability in Rational Application Developer. The Insurance Agent's Web Application that will be created in Tutorial 3.3 will store data in the database table created in this tutorial.

Create a Database Connection

Rational Application Developer has numerous relational database tools, or views, that can be accessed through the Data perspective. Some of the more important views in this perspective are the Data Project Explorer, Data Source Explorer, and SQL Results views. In the Data Source Explorer view, connections can be made to a list of supported relational databases. Some of the supported databases are IBM Cloudscape, IBM DB2 Universal Database, Derby, MySQL, Microsoft SQL Server, Sybase Enterprise Systems, and Oracle Database. Refer to the product help for a complete list of the supported databases.

In this step, you create a database connection to a Derby database that is shipped with Rational Application Developer. Derby is a simple-to-use Java-based database. It can employ any file system folder as a database, and you do not need to create the database before trying to establish a connection. You can select the Create database (if required) option to create the Derby database when the connection is established.

There is one key Derby limitation: It accepts only one database connection at a time. For example, if a WebSphere Application Server is already connected to the Derby database, an attempt to connect from the Database Explorer will fail. Keep this in mind if you choose to develop your applications with Derby.

1. Create a Derby connection.

    a. If the server is running, stop it now or you will not be able to establish a database connection. In the Servers view, right-click WebSphere Application Server v7.0 and click Stop.

    b. Switch to the Data perspective. Click Window, Open Perspective, Other. Then select the Show All check box and select Data. Click OK.

    c. Right-click Databases in the Data Source Explorer view in the bottom left of the perspective, and click New.

    d. Select Derby as the database manager, and scroll down in the JDBC driver drop-down box to select Derby 10.2—Embedded JDBC Driver Default. There are several Derby 10.2 selections; make sure you select the correct one.

    e. Enter any file system directory as the database location; for example, enter `C:\DerbyDatabases\InsuranceDB`. You do not have to physically create the folder in the file system; just type in a new folder name. Make sure the database name is `InsuranceDB`.

    f. Enter a username and password. The Derby database does not require a user ID or password. However, it is recommended that you enter the server user ID and password here, because the integrated WebSphere Application Server instance has security enabled by default. The Java Persistence API will use the username and password to connect to the database in the next tutorial.

    g. Make sure the Create database (if required) box is checked. If it is, the tool sets up the Derby database at that location.

    h. Select the Save password check box. See Figure 3.19.

    i. Click Test Connection to verify that a connection can be established. You should see a window that states that the connection is successful. Click Finish to create the connection.

The `InsuranceDB` connection is displayed in the Database Explorer view. Expand the connection to see `InsuranceDB`, as shown in Figure 3.20.

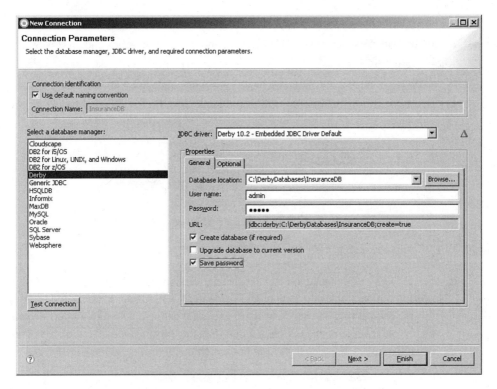

Figure 3.19 Create a new database connection

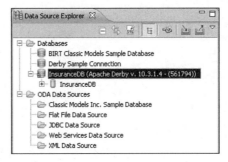

Figure 3.20 A new data source connection to the Derby database

Creating a Data Model

Right now, the database is empty. Use the Data Project Explorer view to create a data model that contains schemas and tables. A data model represents relational data objects that may or may not exist in the database. Later in this exercise, the data model will be deployed to an actual database.

1. Create a new physical data model.

    a. In the Data perspective's Data Project Explorer view, right-click and click New, Data Design Project.

    b. Type `InsuranceDataProject` as the project name and click Finish.

    c. Right-click `InsuranceDataProject` and click New, Physical Data Model as shown in Figure 3.21.

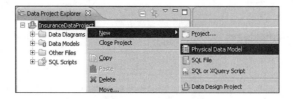

Figure 3.21   The menu item to create a physical data model

    d. Select Derby as the database and 10.2 as the version. The Create from reverse engineering option creates the data model from an existing database connection through reverse engineering. However, because you are creating a new data model, we select the Create from template option and use an empty physical model template to create a blank model. Click Finish as seen in Figure 3.22.

Figure 3.22   The New Physical Data Model Wizard

2. Create a schema named InsuranceSchema.

    a. Expand `InsuranceDataProject`, Data Models, `Database Model.dbm`, Database. Select Schema.

    b. Rename `Schema` to `InsuranceSchema` by single-clicking on the word `Schema` in the Data Project Explorer view.

3. Create a table named `AutoPolicyTable`.

    a. Right-click `InsuranceSchema` and click Add Data Object, Table. Type `AutoPolicyTable` as the table name and press Enter as shown in Figure 3.23.

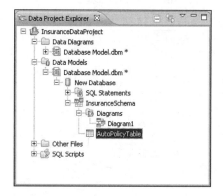

Figure 3.23   Create InsuranceSchema and AutoPolicyTable

4. Add new columns for the `AutoPolicyTable`.

    a. In the Properties view, switch to the Columns tab.

    b. Click New (the diamond-shaped button) to add a column. Then enter `id` as the column name. Select the Primary Key check box and select INTEGER as the data type.

    c. Click New. Enter `name` as the column name. Then select VARCHAR as the data type. Change the length to `100`.

    d. Click New. Enter `policy` as the column name. Then select INTEGER as the data type.

    e. Click New. Enter `convictions` as the column name, and select INTEGER as the data type (see Figure 3.24).

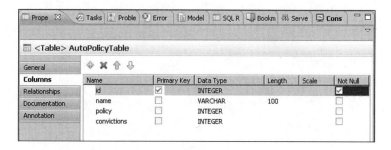

Figure 3.24   Columns in AutoPolicyTable

5. From the workbench, click File, Save All.

6. Generate a DDL file to be executed on the real database. The DDL file will contain the statements to create the schema and the table with the columns that we have specified.

a. In the Data Project Explorer, right-click the newly created `AutoPolicyTable` and click Generate DDL as shown in Figure 3.25.

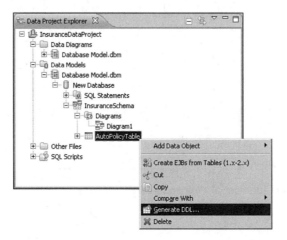

Figure 3.25   Generate DDL menu

b. In the Generate DDL Wizard, select the Fully qualified name check box. Make sure CREATE statements and Comments are selected. Then click Next as shown in Figure 3.26.

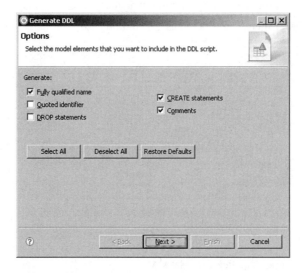

Figure 3.26   Generate DDL Wizard

c. Click Next two times, accepting all the default values. Then click Finish. This generates a DDL file named `script.sql` that can be executed to create the `AutoPolicyTable` in the database.

d. The generated DDL file is created under the `SQL Scripts` folder. Double-click `script.sql` to view the contents. The DDL should be as follows:

```
CREATE TABLE InsuranceSchema.AutoPolicyTable (
        id INTEGER NOT NULL,
        name VARCHAR(100),
        policy INTEGER,
        convictions INTEGER
    );


ALTER TABLE InsuranceSchema.AutoPolicyTable ADD CONSTRAINT
AutoPolicyTable_PK PRIMARY KEY (id);
```

7. Run the DDL file in the Derby database.

a. Right-click `script.sql` under the `SQL Scripts` folder and click Run SQL. This will create the `AddressTable` in the Derby database. Select `InsuranceDB` as the Connections as shown in Figure 3.27 and click Finish. You should see a message saying that the SQL script was run successfully in the SQL Results view.

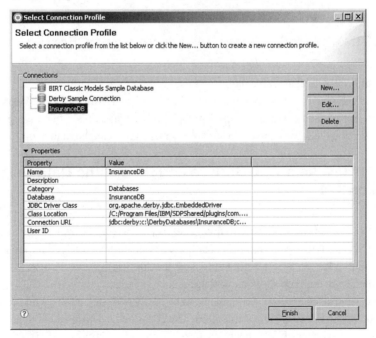

Figure 3.27   Run SQL Wizard

b. Expand your `InsuranceDB` connection in the Data Source Explorer until you see the `Tables` folder under the `InsuranceSchema`. You'll see the `AutoPolicyTable` you just created as shown in Figure 3.28. The schema and table names in Derby are not case sensitive.

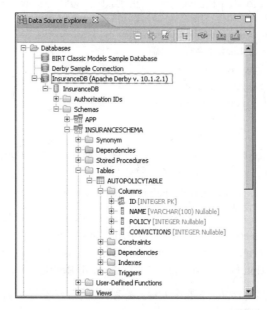

Figure 3.28   The AutoPolicyTable can be seen under the InsuranceDB connection.

In this tutorial, a database table named `AutoPolicyTable` in a Derby database is created. This table will be used by the Insurance Agent's Web Application in Tutorial 3.3. The Insurance Agent's Web Application performs two actions: invoking a Web service to obtain the driving record of the client, and persisting the information into the `AutoPolicyTable` created in this tutorial.

Tutorial 3.3: Invoke a Web Service and Persist the Data Using Java Persistence API

Invoking a Web service is rather straightforward in Rational Application Developer. Rational Application Developer provides a wizard that generates a proxy to the Web service from a WSDL file. The Web Service Client Wizard accepts either a physical file or a URI that points to a WSDL interface as input. After the Web service is invoked, the application uses the JPA to save the information obtained from the Web service to a database.

JPA is a standard that allows Java objects to be easily persisted into any relational database. It is part of the Java EE 5 EJB 3.0 specification. The JPA standard is designed to replace the container-managed persistence (CMP) beans in Java 2 Enterprise Edition (J2EE). Although JPA is part of the Java EE 5 standard, it can be used outside the Java EE container. It can also operate in a Java SE environment, which means that it can be run as a normal Java application not using WebSphere Application Server.

This tutorial covers two key elements of the JPA specification:

- Metadata annotations
- Persistence unit and `persistence.xml` file

The relationship mappings between a Java object and a database table are done through metadata annotations. Metadata annotations define how to map Java classes to relational tables. Listing 3.3 shows a snippet of a regular Java class with JPA metadata annotations. Such a class is normally referred to as an entity class. By annotating the Java class with JPA metadata annotations, you are essentially linking up Java classes with database tables. You can think of the annotations as the mappings between Java classes and database tables. JPA metadata annotations allow one Java class to be mapped to multiple database tables and vice versa.

Listing 3.3   Example of a JPA Entity Class File

```
import javax.persistence.Column;
import javax.persistence.Entity;
import javax.persistence.Id;

@Entity
public class AutoPolicyTable implements Serializable {
    private static final long serialVersionUID = 1L;

    @Id
    private int id;
    @Column (name = "name")
    private String another_name;
    private int policy;
    private int convictions;
...
}
```

The above entity class `AutoPolicyTable` is denoted with three JPA annotations: `@Entity`, `@Id`, and `@Column`. The `@Entity` metadata annotation marks the Java class to be a JPA entity. The `@Entity` annotation has an optional `name` element. If the `name` element is not specified, which is the case in this example, the JPA service assumes that the entity is mapped to a table with the same name as the entity. However, if the table name differs from the entity class name, `@Entity (name="AnotherTableName")` can be used to map the entity class to another table name.

The `@Id` annotation denotes the `id` field as the primary key field. The `@Column` annotation defines the mapping between a Java field and a table column. When the table column name is the same as the Java field, such as the policy and convictions variables, no annotation is required. However, when the column name differs from the Java field name, the `@Column` annotation can be used. In Listing 3.3, the Java field name `"another_name"` is mapped to a table column called `"name"`. Figure 3.29 summarizes how the `AutoPolicyTable` entity class is mapped to the `AutoPolicyTable` database table.

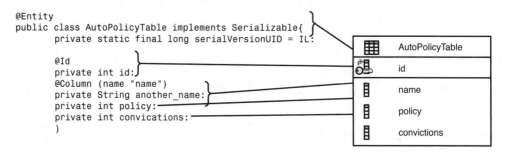

Figure 3.29   The AutoPolicyTable entity class mapped to the AutoPolicyTable in the database.

In the preceding example, the annotations are placed in front of the field declarations. We could have placed the annotations in front of the `getter` methods instead of the field itself, as shown in Listing 3.4. Both methods work the same way.

Listing 3.4   Example of an Annotation

```
private int id;
private String another_name;
private int policy;
private int convictions;

@Id
public int getId(){
    return id;
}
@Column (name = "name")
public String getAnother_name() {
    return another_name;
}
}
```

All the metadata information can be declared using annotations. Alternatively, the same information can be defined using an XML file. By default, the XML file is named `orm.xml`, which is placed in the META-INF directory under the classpath. Listing 3.5 shows an orm.xml file that maps the Java field "another_name" to the table column named "name".

Listing 3.5   Example of an orm.xml File

```
<?xml version="1.0" encoding="UTF-8"?>
<entity-mappings xmlns="http://java.sun.com/xml/ns/persistence/orm"
xmlns:xsi="http://www.w3.org/2001/XMLSchema-instance"
xsi:schemaLocation="http://java.sun.com/xml/ns/persistence/orm
http://java.sun.com/xml/ns/persistence/orm_1_0.xsd" version="1.0">
    <entity class="com.insurance.entity.AutoPolicyTable">
        <attributes>
            <basic name="another_name">
                <column name="name"/>
</basic>
</attributes>
    </entity>
</entity-mappings>
```

The orm.xml file is optional and is an alternative to using annotations. You may use one or the other or both to capture the metadata information. In this tutorial, only the annotations will be used. Annotations can be created in the Java editor or the annotation view, as shown in Figure 3.30.

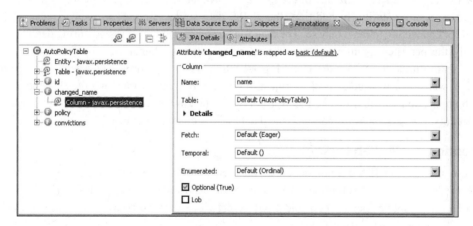

Figure 3.30   The annotation view

Rational Application Developer has tools and editors that assist in the creation of JPA projects, entity class, annotations, and orm.xml files. Although orm.xml is optional, persistence.xml is not. When a JPA project or JPA-enabled project is created, a persistence.xml is placed under the

META-INF directory. The persistence.xml file is where the persistence units are defined. A persistence unit lists the entity classes that are available for JPA persistence and defines the database connection information. Listing 3.6 is an example of a persistence.xml file.

Listing 3.6   Example of a persistence.xml File

```
<?xml version="1.0" encoding="UTF-8"?>
<persistence version="1.0" xmlns="http://java.sun.com/xml/ns/persistence"
xmlns:xsi="http://www.w3.org/2001/XMLSchema-instance"
xsi:schemaLocation="http://java.sun.com/xml/ns/persistence
http://java.sun.com/xml/ns/persistence/persistence_1_0.xsd">
    <persistence-unit name="InsuranceJPAProject">
        <jta-data-source>java:comp/env/InsuranceDB</jta-data-source>
        <class>
        com.insurance.entity.AutoPolicyTable</class>
        <properties>
            <property name="openjpa.jdbc.Schema" value="INSURANCESCHEMA"/>
        </properties>
    </persistence-unit>
</persistence>
```

In Listing 3.6, the persistence.xml file defines a persistence unit named "InsuranceJPAProject". It has one entity class available for JPA persistence, which is the AutoPolicyTable entity. In addition, the JDBC data source java:comp/env/InsuranceDB is used for connecting to the database. The data source is automatically created during deployment. Lastly, this persistence unit works with the INSURANCESCHEMA schema from the database.

In this tutorial, you use the Java EE perspective to create an Insurance Agent's Web Application, which is a JPA-enabled Web project to host the Web application and the JPA entity. The Web application will first invoke the Web service to obtain the driving record and then use the JPA entity to persist the information to the database you created in Tutorial 3.2.

Creating a JPA Web Project

To use a project for JPA development, you must enable JPA capability. You can either create a JPA project or create a Web project with JPA capability for developing a JPA application. The JPA Development perspective consolidates different views for your convenience. In this tutorial, you will use the Java EE perspective.

1. Create a Dynamic Web project named InsuranceJPAProject.

   a. Switch to the Java EE perspective. From the workbench, click File, New, Dynamic Web Project.

b. Type `InsuranceJPAProject` as the project name.

c. The default for configuration is Default Configuration for WebSphere Application Server v7.0.

2. Add the Java Persistence configuration to the project.

a. Click Modify, located to the right of the Configuration drop-down menu, to bring up the Project Facets window.

b. Select Java Persistence and click OK. The Configuration will become `<custom>`.

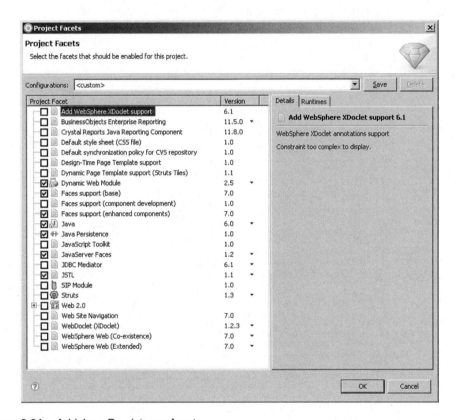

Figure 3.31   Add Java Persistence facet

3. Change the EAR project name to `InsuranceJPAProjectEAR`.

4. Click Next twice.

5. Configure the JPA settings.

a. Select `InsuranceDB` as the connection.

b. Select the Override default schema from connection check box.

   c. Select INSURANCESCHEMA from the Schema drop-down box.

   d. Select the Annotated classes must be listed in persistence.xml radio button as shown in Figure 3.32. This option requires the entity classes to be listed explicitly. Using this option allows your project to be more portable because not all of the runtime can discover the entity classes on the fly. The other option, Discover annotated classes automatically, automatically discovers the JPA entity through the @entity annotation in the runtime.

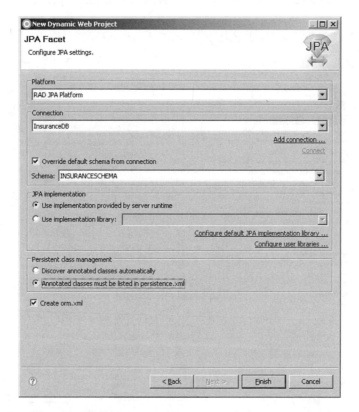

Figure 3.32 Configure the JPA Settings

   6. Click Finish. Click No if prompted to switch to the Web perspective. The structure of your newly created InsuranceJPAProject is shown in Figure 3.33.

Generating a Web Service Client

In this section, you generate a Web service client for the Web service created in Tutorial 3.1. The Web Service Client Wizard creates a set of classes that are considered to be packaged on the client side. It also generates a simple Java proxy class for invoking your Web service. Instead of

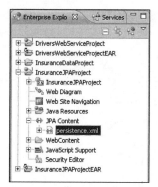

Figure 3.33   The structure of InsuranceJPAProject

using the Java proxy, we will be using the `@WebServiceRef` annotation in this tutorial. The client side files are required regardless of how you are calling the Web service. The Web Service Client Wizard requires the application server to be started.

1. Create a Web service client.

    a. Start the server from the Server view and wait until it is started.

    b. Right-click `InsuranceJPAProject` and click New, Other.

    c. In the New Wizard window, select the Show All Wizards check box to see all the available wizards, including those for the capabilities not currently activated.

    d. Expand the `Web Services` folder and select Web Service Client, as shown in Figure 3.34. Click Next.

2. Select the service definition for the Web service client.

    a. Enter `http://<host>:<port>/DriversWebServiceProject/DrivingRecordWeb ServiceService?WSDL` as the service definition, where the host and port typically are localhost and 9080, respectively. If the service definition is not found, check whether the server started successfully.

    b. Click Finish. The wizard creates a set of Web service client classes and a Java proxy.

3. The proxy named `DrivingRecordWebServicePortProxy` is generated in the `Java Resources` folder as shown in Figure 3.35. The other files are the Web service client stubs, which are needed on the client side. In the next section, you create the Insurance Agent's Web Application to call the Driving Record Web service.

Creating a Web Application to Invoke the Web Service

In this section, you create the Insurance Agent's Web Application that invokes the Driving Record Web service. The Web application is composed of a servlet handling the logic and a JSP file handling the presentation. The servlet uses an annotation to obtain a reference to the Web service created in the previous tutorial.

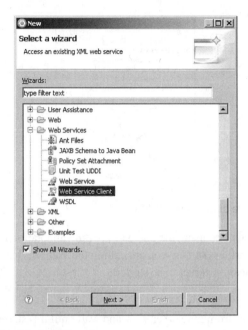

Figure 3.34   Create Web Service Client

Figure 3.35   The Web service proxy

1.   Create a servlet named `NewAutoPolicyServlet`.

    a.   In the Enterprise Explorer view, right-click `InsuranceJPAProject` and click New, Servlet.

    b.   Enter `com.insurance.servlet` as the Java package name.

    c.   Enter `NewAutoPolicyServlet` as the class name. Click Finish.

    d.   Add the bolded code and save the file. This code calls out to the Driving Record Web service. The annotation obtains a reference to the Web service through JNDI lookup. After the Web service is invoked, the result is set to the request attributes, which are forwarded to the presentation JSP.

```
package com.insurance.servlet;


import java.io.IOException;
import java.io.PrintWriter;


import javax.servlet.ServletException;
import javax.servlet.http.HttpServlet;
import javax.servlet.http.HttpServletRequest;
import javax.servlet.http.HttpServletResponse;
import javax.xml.ws.WebServiceRef;


import com.drivers.webservice.DrivingRecord;
import com.drivers.webservice.DrivingRecordWebServiceDelegate;
import com.drivers.webservice.DrivingRecordWebServiceService;


/**
 * Servlet implementation class NewAutoPolicyServlet
 */
public class NewAutoPolicyServlet extends HttpServlet {
    private static final long serialVersionUID = 1L;

    @WebServiceRef(name = "DrivingRecordWS_Servlet")
    static DrivingRecordWebServiceService service;

    public NewAutoPolicyServlet() {
        super();
    }
    protected void doGet(HttpServletRequest request,
            HttpServletResponse response) throws ServletException,
```

```
IOException {
        performTask(request, response);
    }
    protected void doPost(HttpServletRequest request,
            HttpServletResponse response) throws ServletException,
IOException {
        performTask(request, response);
    }

    protected void performTask(HttpServletRequest request,
            HttpServletResponse response) throws ServletException,
IOException {
        try {
            DrivingRecordWebServiceDelegate port =
service.getDrivingRecordWebServicePort();
            DrivingRecord record = port.getRecord("Jane Fung");
            request.setAttribute("name", record.getName());
            request.setAttribute("conviction",
record.getConvictions());

getServletConfig().getServletContext().getRequestDispatcher("NewAutoP
olicyClient.jsp").forward(request,response);
        } catch (Exception e) {
            System.out.println(e);
        }
    }


}
```

2. Create a JSP for presentation. This JSP displays the request attributes that were set in the servlet.

   a. In the Enterprise Explorer view, right-click `InsuranceJPAProject` and click New, Web Page.

   b. Enter `NewAutoPolicyClient` as the filename and make sure JSP is selected as the template. Click Finish.

   c. Switch to the Source view of the JSP editor and enter the code shown in bold as follows.

   ```
   <!DOCTYPE HTML PUBLIC "-//W3C//DTD HTML 4.01 Transitional//EN"><%@page
       language="java" contentType="text/html; charset=ISO-8859-1"
   ```

```
            pageEncoding="ISO-8859-1"%>
<html>
<head>
<title>NewAutoPolicyClient</title>
<meta http-equiv="Content-Type" content="text/html; charset=ISO-8859-
1">
</head>
<body>
<p><b>Invoking Web Service</b><br>
Name: <%=request.getAttribute("name") %><br>
Convictions: <%=request.getAttribute("conviction") %></p>

<p><br>

</body>
</html>
```

d. Save the file by pressing Ctrl+S.

Running the Web Application in a Browser

1. In the Enterprise Explorer view, expand `InsuranceJPAProject`, `Java Resources`, `src`, `com.insurance.servlet`. Right-click the `NewAutoPolicyServlet.java` and click Run As, Run on Server.

2. Select an existing server and click Finish to automatically add the project to the server and run the servlet file in the internal browser. The result of the servlet file is displayed in Figure 3.36. The URI is `http://localhost:9080/InsuranceJPAProject/NewAuto PolicyServlet`, where the host and port can be different. If server security is enabled, the URI will use the HTTPS protocol with a default port number of 9443.

The servlet obtains a Web service reference through the annotation that can be used to invoke the Web service's operation. In this exercise, the Web service and the client run on the same Web-Sphere Application Server. However, a client and a Web service would run on different servers in a typical scenario. Because the client only needs the WSDL file to invoke the Web service, it does not matter where it is hosted. The result of running the servlet is displayed in Figure 3.36. You can see the line `Invoking DrivingRecordWebService` in the console view log.

Creating a JPA Entity

This section creates a JPA entity, which facilitates in persisting into the `AutoPolicyTable` database table. It uses annotation to identify the mapping between the entity class and the database table. Later in the tutorial, the entire entity Java class can be persisted into the database without writing JDBC code.

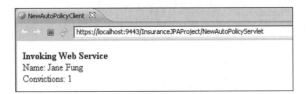

Figure 3.36   The result of NewAutoPolicyServlet

1. Create a JPA entity named `AutoPolicyTable`.

   a. Stop the server if it is running.

   b. In the Enterprise Explorer view, right-click `InsuranceJPAProject` and click New, Entity as shown in Figure 3.37. This creates a JPA entity that extends the `java.io.Serializable` interface. It also adds an `@entity` annotation to the class.

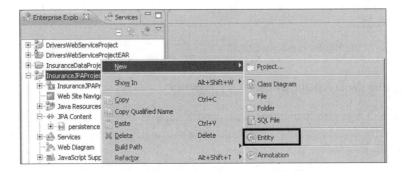

Figure 3.37   Create a JPA entity menu

   c. Enter `com.insurance.entity` as the package and `AutoPolicyTable` as the class. Click Next.

2. Add the property fields in the JPA entity.

   a. In the Entity Properties page, click Add to add the initial property fields for the class.

   b. Select `int` as the type and enter `id` as the name. Click OK as seen in Figure 3.38. This adds an equivalent line `private int id;` to the entity class.

Figure 3.38   Add a field in the JPA entity

    c.   Select the check box under the Key column.

    d.   Click Add. Select `java.lang.String` from the Type drop-down and enter `name` as the name. Then click OK.

    e.   Click Add. Select `int` from the Type drop-down and enter `policy` as the name. Click OK.

    f.   Click Add. Select `int` from the Type drop-down and enter `convictions` as the name. Click OK.

3.   Select Field-based as the access type. This adds the annotation in front of the field. The Property-based access type adds the annotation in front of the property `getter` method of the field. Click Next as shown in Figure 3.39.

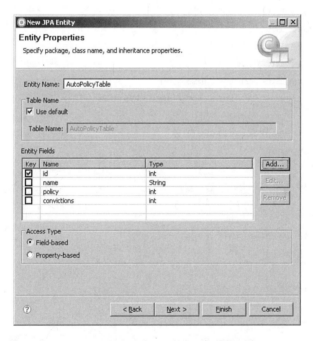

Figure 3.39   The Entity Properties dialog when creating a JPA entity

4.   Click Finish, and the Java editor opens. If you are prompted for Java Modeling capability or Web Service Modeling capability, click OK for both. The final source code for the file `AutoPolicyTable.java` is as follows. Click File, Save All to save all the files.

```
package com.insurance.entity;


import java.io.Serializable;
import java.lang.String;
```

```java
import javax.persistence.*;

/**
 * Entity implementation class for Entity: AutoPolicyTable
 *
 */
@Entity

public class AutoPolicyTable implements Serializable {


    @Id
    private int id;
    private String name;
    private int policy;
    private int convictions;
    private static final long serialVersionUID = 1L;

    public AutoPolicyTable() {
        super();
    }
    public int getId() {
            return this.id;
    }
    public void setId(int id) {
        this.id = id;
    }
    public String getName() {
        return this.name;
    }
    public void setName(String name) {
        this.name = name;
    }
    public int getPolicy() {
        return this.policy;
    }
    public void setPolicy(int policy) {
        this.policy = policy;
    }
    public int getConvictions() {
        return this.convictions;
```

```
    }
    public void setConvictions(int convictions) {
        this.convictions = convictions;
    }


}
```

5. Examine the `persistence.xml` file.

   a. In the Enterprise Explorer, expand `InsuranceJPAProject`, JPA Content. Double-click `persistence.xml` to open it in the editor, and switch to the Source view. The Entity Creation Wizard added the `AutoPolicyTable` class in the `persistence.xml` file. The menu item Synchronize Classes adds all the classes that are annotated with `@entity` into the `persistence.xml` file. You can find the menu item by right-clicking on the `persistence.xml` file.

```
<?xml version="1.0" encoding="UTF-8"?>
<persistence version="1.0"
xmlns="http://java.sun.com/xml/ns/persistence"
xmlns:xsi="http://www.w3.org/2001/XMLSchema-instance"
xsi:schemaLocation="http://java.sun.com/xml/ns/persistence
http://java.sun.com/xml/ns/persistence/persistence_1_0.xsd">
    <persistence-unit name="InsuranceJPAProject">

<class>com.insurance.entity.AutoPolicyTable</class>
    </persistence-unit>
</persistence>
```

Create a Utility Class

A utility class uses the JPA to use the entity. The code has three methods: `setup()`, `query()`, and `insert()`. The `setup()` method instantiates a JPA entity manager. The `query()` method queries all rows in the `AutoPolicyTable` table and returns the number of rows as the return type. The `insert()` method persists the `AutoPolicyTable` entity class into the database.

1. Create a utility class named `PolicyUtil`.

   a. In the Enterprise Explorer view, expand `InsuranceJPAProject`. Right-click Java Resources and click New, Class.

   b. Enter `com.insurance.util` as the package and `PolicyUtil` as the name.

   c. Make sure the public static void main (`String[] args`) box is not checked.

   d. Click Finish. The Java editor opens.

2. Add the code in bold as follows, and save the file.

```java
package com.insurance.util;


import java.util.List;
import javax.persistence.EntityManager;
import javax.persistence.EntityManagerFactory;
import javax.persistence.Persistence;
import com.insurance.entity.AutoPolicyTable;

public class PolicyUtil {
    private static EntityManagerFactory emf;
    private static EntityManager em;

    public static void setup() {
        emf =
Persistence.createEntityManagerFactory("InsuranceJPAProject");
        em = emf.createEntityManager();
    }

    public static int query() {
        int size=0;
        final List<AutoPolicyTable> list = em.createQuery(
                "select p from AutoPolicyTable p").getResultList();

        for (AutoPolicyTable current : list) {
            size ++;
            System.out.println("id = " + current.getId());
            System.out.println("name = " + current.getName());
System.out.println("policy = " + current.getPolicy());
            System.out.println("convictions = " +
current.getConvictions());
System.out.println ("===============================");
        }
return size;

    }

    public static void insert(AutoPolicyTable addr) {
        em.getTransaction().begin();
        em.persist(addr);
        em.getTransaction().commit();
    }
}
```

Set Up the JDBC Configurations in the Persistence XML File

This section sets up the JDBC configuration such that the Java Persistence API accesses the correct database and schema. A datasource is created automatically when the project is deployed to the server.

1. Configure the project for JDBC deployment to use the `InsuranceDB` connection.

   a. In the Enterprise Explorer, right-click `InsuranceJPAProject`. Click JPA Tools, Configure Project for JDBC Deployment.

   b. Make sure `InsuranceDB` is selected as the connection.

   c. In the Schema drop-down box, select `INSURANCESCHEMA` as seen in Figure 3.40.

   d. Click OK.

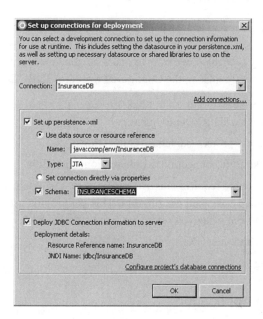

Figure 3.40   The Set Up Connections for Deployment Wizard

2. Examine the `persistence.xml` file again.

   a. This wizard sets up the JDBC deployment information in the `persistence.xml` file. Open that file. Expand `InsuranceJPAProject`, `JPA Content`. Double-click to open the `persistence.xml` file.

b. Change to the Source tab to review the datasource and schema information (See Figure 3.41) that the tool has specified automatically.

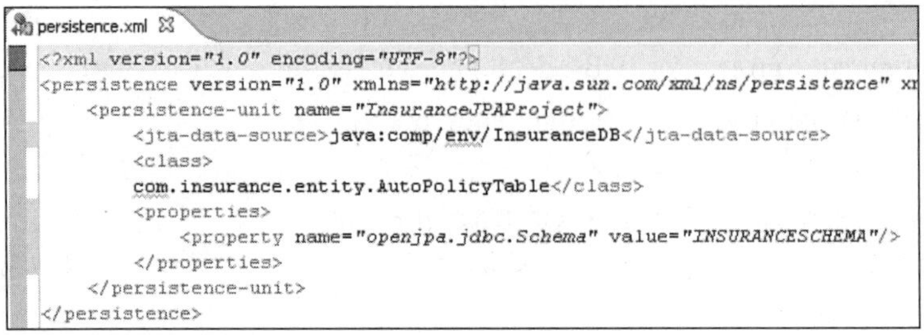

```
<?xml version="1.0" encoding="UTF-8"?>
<persistence version="1.0" xmlns="http://java.sun.com/xml/ns/persistence" xr
    <persistence-unit name="InsuranceJPAProject">
        <jta-data-source>java:comp/env/InsuranceDB</jta-data-source>
        <class>
        com.insurance.entity.AutoPolicyTable</class>
        <properties>
            <property name="openjpa.jdbc.Schema" value="INSURANCESCHEMA"/>
        </properties>
    </persistence-unit>
</persistence>
```

Figure 3.41 The persistence.xml file after the JDBC deployment information has been configured

3. If server security is enabled, we want to make sure that the user ID and password are supplied to the connection. Go to the Configure Project for JDBC Deployment dialog again.

a. In the Enterprise Explorer, right-click `InsuranceJPAProject`. Click JPA Tools, Configure Project for JDBC Deployment.

b. Click Configure project's database connections.

c. Under the Runtime connection details section, click Edit.

d. Select Data source requires a userid and password to obtain a connection. Make sure the user ID and password are filled in. This is the same user ID and password (See Figure 3.42) from when you set up the security in the WebSphere Application Server.

e. Click Finish and then OK.

f. Click OK again.

Modifying the Web Application

In the previous step, a utility class was created with three methods to access the entity class: `setup()`, `query()`, and `insert()`. These methods are used in the Insurance Agent's Web Application. Recall that you have already invoked the Driving Record Web Service in the servlet file. This step will further modify the servlet such that after the Web service is invoked, you will store the information in the database.

1. Modify the NewAutoPolicyClient.jsp file to create a new `AutoPolicyTable` entity class and insert it into the database. Then query the database to make sure it is inserted.

a. In the Enterprise Explorer view, expand `InsuranceJPAProject`, `Java Resources`, `src` folder, `com.insurance.servlet`. Double-click `NewAutoPolicyServlet.java` to open it.

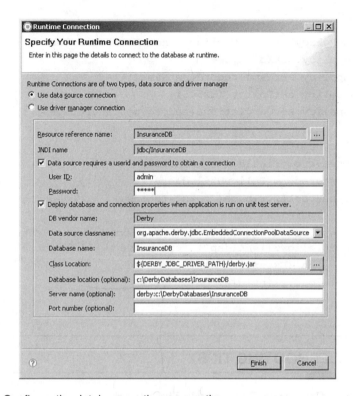

Figure 3.42   Configure the database runtime connection

b.   Insert the bolded code as follows into the `performTask ()` method. Then right-click on the editor and click Source, Organize Imports. Select `com.insurance.util.` `PolicyUtil` if there is more than one `PolicyUtil` class. Save the file.

```
protected void performTask(HttpServletRequest request,
HttpServletResponse response) throws ServletException, IOException {

  try {
DrivingRecordWebServiceDelegate port =
service.getDrivingRecordWebServicePort();
DrivingRecord record = port.getRecord("Jane Fung");
request.setAttribute("name", record.getName());
request.setAttribute("conviction", record.getConvictions());

PolicyUtil.setup();
System.out.println ("---- Before ----");
int size = PolicyUtil.query();
```

```
AutoPolicyTable newpolicy = new AutoPolicyTable();
newpolicy.setId (size+1);
newpolicy.setName(record.getName());
newpolicy.setPolicy (12345);
newpolicy.setConvictions(record.getConvictions());

PolicyUtil.insert(newpolicy);
System.out.println ("---- After ----");
int stored  = PolicyUtil.query();
request.setAttribute("rows", stored);

getServletConfig().getServletContext().getRequestDispatcher("N
ewAutoPolicyClient.jsp").forward(request,response);
   } catch (Exception e) {
System.out.println(e);
   }
}
```

TROUBLESHOOTING TIPS

DATABASE COLUMNS CANNOT BE RESOLVED

The JPA tooling in Rational Application Developer accesses the database to validate the entity class's annotated fields and the database table's columns. The errors can be the result of some other applications holding onto the database connection. Recall that Derby allows only one active connection at a time. If you still see errors stating that the database columns cannot be resolved, follow these steps to troubleshoot the errors.

a.   If the server is started, stop it. The server holds on to a Derby database connection. Switch to the Servers view. Right-click WebSphere Application Server v7.0 at localhost and click Stop.

b.   Check whether the database connection is still active in the Database Source Explorer. If it is, disconnect it. Switch to the Data perspective, expand Databases in the Database Source Explorer, and right-click InsuranceDB. Then click Disconnect.

c.   Perform a clean project to remove these errors. From the workbench, click Projects, Clean. Select Clean All Projects and then click OK. Now there should be no errors in the InsuranceJPAProject.

---

2.   Modify the `NewAutoPolicyClient.jsp` file to display the result of inserting a new row in the database.

a. In the Enterprise Explorer view, expand `InsuranceJPAProject` and the `WebContent` folder; then double-click `NewAutoPolicyClient.jsp` to open it.

b. Insert the bolded code as follows. This code adds two more import statements into the JSP file.

```
<!DOCTYPE HTML PUBLIC "-//W3C//DTD HTML 4.01 Transitional//EN"><%@page
    language="java" contentType="text/html; charset=ISO-8859-1"
    pageEncoding="ISO-8859-1"%>
<html>
<head>
<title>NewAutoPolicyClient</title>
<meta http-equiv="Content-Type" content="text/html; charset=ISO-8859-
1">
</head>
<body>
<p><b>Invoking Web Service</b><br>
Name: <%=request.getAttribute("name") %><br>
Convictions: <%=request.getAttribute("conviction") %></p>
<p><br>

<p><b>Storing into Database</b><Br>
Total of <%=request.getAttribute ("rows") %> rows are stored in the
database.

</body>
</html>
```

c. Save the file.

Running the Web Application

1. In the Project Explorer view, right-click the `NewAutoPolicyServlet.java` file and click Run As, Run on Server.

2. Select an existing server and click Finish to automatically add the project to the server and run the servlet file in the internal browser. This loads the following URI in the browser: `http://<host>:<port>/InsuranceJPAProject/NewAutoPolicyServlet`, where the host and port could be different based on your system configuration.

Results are displayed in the console and should be similar to the following. The servlet file invokes the Driving Record Web service to obtain the number of convictions for the customer and then stores that information in the Derby database. Then it forwards the request to the presentation JSP (See Figure 3.43).

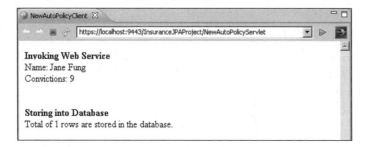

Figure 3.43   Running NewAutoPolicyServlet in the Web browser

```
00000022 SystemOut      O Invoking DrivingRecordWebService...
00000022 SystemOut      O Name: Jane Fung, Convictions: 9


00000021 SystemOut      O ---- Before ----
00000021 SystemOut      O ---- After ----
00000021 SystemOut      O id = 1
00000021 SystemOut      O name = Jane Fung
00000021 SystemOut      O policy = 12345
00000021 SystemOut      O convictions = 9
00000021 SystemOut      O ===============================
```

In addition, the browser displays something like the following figure.

TROUBLESHOOTING TIPS

DATASOURCE NAMENOTFOUND

If you encounter a datasource NameNotFound error when executing the servlet file, do the following:

a.   Switch to the Servers view. Right-click WebSphere Application Server v7.0 at localhost and click Add and Remove projects. Click Remove All to remove all projects.

b.   Add all projects to the server again. Right-click WebSphere Application Server v7.0 at localhost and click Add and Remove projects. Click Add All to add all projects.

Export the Project as an EAR File

After a developer has finished developing the projects, he normally packages them up as EAR files for the administrator to deploy to the server. Export both `DriversWebServiceProjectEAR` and `InsuranceJPAProjectEAR` as EAR files. These EAR files will be used in Tutorial 3.4 to deploy in the WebSphere Application Server.

1. Export `InsuranceJPAProjectEAR`.

    a. In the workbench of Rational Application Developer, right-click `InsuranceJPA ProjectEAR`. Click Export, EAR File. A Shared EAR file contains the source code where an EAR file gives you the choice of including the source.

    b. Click Browse to choose a destination to save the EAR file. Then click Finish.

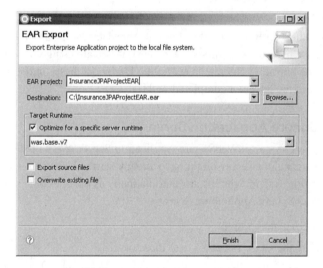

Figure 3.44   Export EAR dialog

2. Export `DriversWebServiceProjectEAR`.

    a. Right-click `DriversWebServiceProjectEAR` and click Export, EAR File. A Shared EAR file contains the source code where an EAR file gives you the choice of including the source.

    b. Click Browse to choose a destination to save the EAR file. Then click Finish.

Tutorial 3.4: Deploy an Application into a WebSphere Application Server

The application is completed and unit tested in Rational Application Developer. It's now time to deploy it to a production server. In this tutorial, the projects are deployed into a standalone WebSphere Application Server. Two EAR files have been exported from Rational Application Developer in Tutorial 3.3.

Set Up the Database

You may skip this step if you have completed Tutorial 3.2 on the same computer that is running WebSphere Application Server. Tutorial 3.2 created a Derby database at the `C:\DerbyData bases\InsuranceDB` location. This step sets up the database if you have not already done so.

1. From the CD-ROM, browse to `\chapter 3\tutorial 3.4\tutorial files\`.

2. Copy the entire `DerbyDatabases` directory to the `C:` drive. If you are using the tutorial files from the CD-ROM for this tutorial, the database is assumed to be located in `C:\DerbyDatabases\InsuranceDB`. However, if you are using your own EAR files from the previous tutorial, you have to set up the Derby databases at the drive that you have been using if you have not completed Tutorial 3.2.

Start the WebSphere Application Server

There are several ways to start a WebSphere Application Server. We will start it using the command prompt. The standalone server might have already started because it was by default registered with the operating system, which starts automatically as the operating system boots up.

1. Start the WebSphere Application Server.

   a. Open a command prompt.

   b. Change to the `<WAS_INSTALL>\bin` directory.

   Following is a directory example of a standalone server:

   `C:\Program Files\IBM\WebSphere\AppServer\bin`

   c. Enter `startserver server1`. When the server is started, you see the line `Server server1 open for e-business` as shown in Figure 3.45. If security is enabled, enter

   `startserver server1 -username <username> -password <password>`

Start the Integrated Solutions Console

1. In a Web browser, load the integrated solutions console. The URI is `http://<host>:<port>/admin`. For example: `http://localhost:9061/admin`.

2. Enter the user ID and password. Then click Log In as shown in Figure 3.46.

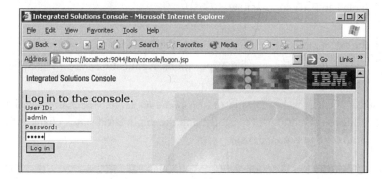

Figure 3.45   Start the server in the command prompt

Figure 3.46   Start the integrated solutions console

Install and Start the DriversWebServiceProjectEAR Enterprise Application

When installing the enterprise application, you have the option to install it as an individual enterprise application or as part of a business-level application. A business-level application (BLA) is a logical grouping of Java EE applications or non-Java applications that allow you to deploy and configure multiple applications. Having applications managed as a BLA, you can start and stop them as a logical group, which makes managing individual applications as a whole more convenient.

Because the Web service application and the Web application are two individual applications, for instance, we do not want to start and stop both of the applications together. The Web service application would likely be reused by other applications. Therefore, it is best to install them as an individual Enterprise application, which has a degree of separation and a simpler form of deployment.

1. Install a new enterprise application.

   a. In the administrative console, expand Applications, New Application.

   b. Click New Enterprise Application.

   c. Browse for the `DriversWebServiceProjectEAR.ear` file. Click Next.

d. Take the default value `Fast Path`. Click Next.

e. Click Next twice, and then click Finish. The EAR file will be installed.

f. Click Save to save it to the master configuration as seen Figure 3.47.

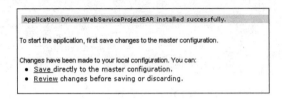

Figure 3.47   Install an EAR successfully

2. Start the `DriversWebServiceProjectEAR` application.

a. In the left navigation, expand Applications, Application Types, WebSphere enterprise applications.

b. Select the check box beside `DriversWebServiceProjectEAR` and click Start. The application is started successfully, and the application status changes from Stopped to Started (See Figure 3.48).

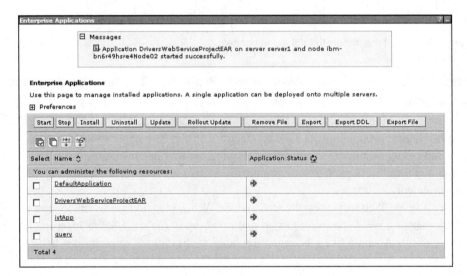

Figure 3.48   Start an EAR successfully

3. Make sure the application is running properly.

a. In another Web browser, load the URI `http://localhost:9081/DriversWebService Project/DrivingRecordWebServiceService`. This is the Web service endpoint. Figure

3.49 shows the running DrivingRecordWebServiceService. The host and port might be different depending on your system configurations.

Figure 3.49   Running the Web service endpoint

Install InsuranceJPAProjectEAR Enterprise Application

This `InsuranceJPAProjectEAR.ear` file contains the Web application that invokes the Driving Record Web Service.

1. Install the `InsuranceJPAProjectEAR` enterprise application.

    a. In the administrative console, expand Applications, New Application.

    b. Click New Enterprise Application.

    c. Browse for the `InsuranceJPAProjectEAR.ear` file. Click Next.

    d. Take the default value Fast Path. Click Next.

    e. Click Next twice, and then click Finish. The EAR file will be installed.

2. Click Save to save it to the master configuration.

Changing the Web Service Endpoint

During development, the Web application invokes the Web service that was running in the test server. In the previous step, we deployed the Driving Record Web Service into the production server, which has a different host name and port number. Therefore, configurations need to be changed for the `InsuranceJPAProjectEAR` Web application to communicate with the production version of the Driving Record Web Service.

1. Change the Web service binding of the `InsuranceJPAProjectEAR`.

    a. In the administrative console, expand Applications, Application Types, WebSphere enterprise applications.

    b. Click `InsuranceJPAProjectEAR`.

    c. Click Manage Modules under the Modules section as shown in Figure 3.50.

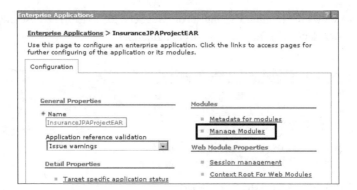

Figure 3.50   Manage modules

d. Click `InsuranceJPAProject`.

e. Click Web services client bindings under the Web Services Properties section as shown in Figure 3.51. We will be augmenting the Web service endpoint to point to the production version.

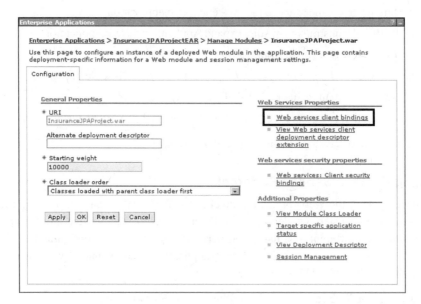

Figure 3.51   Web services client bindings

In this page, you will see two Web service clients. The `DrivingRecordWebService Service` is from the `DrivingRecordWebServiceService.java` file, which is the client stub. The other one named `DrivingRecordWS_Servlet` is introduced by the annotation in the servlet. This is the one we will be modifying to point to the production version of the Web service.

2. Edit the port information.

    a. Click Edit under the Port Information column of the `DrivingRecordWS_Servlet` Web service client (See Figure 3.52).

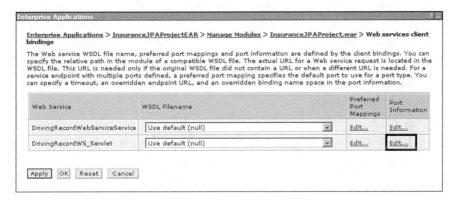

Figure 3.52 Editing port information of DrivingRecordWS_Servlet

    b. Enter `http://<prod_host>:<prod_port>/DriversWebServiceProject/Driving RecordWebServiceService` as the Overridden Endpoint URL as shown in 3.53. The host name and port number might be different depending on your server setup. Enter the host and port number of your production server.

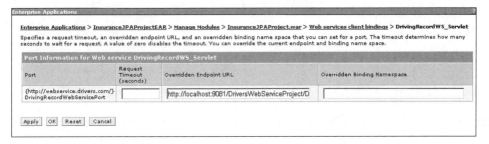

Figure 3.53 Editing port information of DrivingRecordWS_Servlet

    c. Click Apply.

3. Click Save. Pay attention that the endpoint only takes effect if the enterprise application is restarted.

4. Start the enterprise application.

    a. In the administrative console, expand Applications, Application Types, WebSphere Enterprise Applications.

b. Select the check box beside `InsuranceJPAProjectEAR` and click Start. The application is started successfully, and the application status changes from Stopped to Started.

Updating the JDBC Datasource

Most of the time, the database that is used during development is different from the database used in production. Therefore, the administrator needs to update the datasource in the enterprise application deployed on the server to point to the correct production database. WebSphere Application Server allows the administrator to change the datasource reference or the database name using the administrative console.

1. In the administrative console, expand Applications, Application Types, WebSphere enterprise applications.

2. Click `InsuranceJPAProjectEAR`.

3. Under the References section, click Resource references. You may change the JDBC datasource reference under the Target Resource JNDI Name column as shown in Figure 3.54.

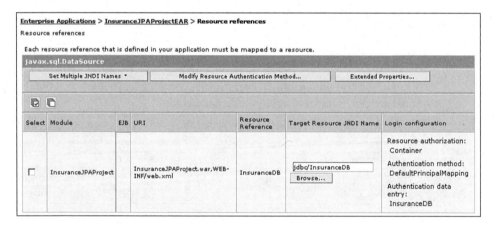

Figure 3.54   Changing the JDBC datasource in a deployed enterprise application

4. Because we are not really going to change the JDBC datasource, click Cancel. You may discard the changes if prompted.

Examine the Ports

Port numbers differ from server instance to instance, profile to profile. This step enables users to see the port number on the server they are running.

1. In the administrative console, expand Servers, Server Types, WebSphere application servers.

2. Click server1, which leads you to the Server Detail page.

3. Scroll down to the middle and click Ports under the Communications section. See Figure 3.55.

Figure 3.55 Ports

4. This page lists all the ports for this server as shown in Figure 3.56. If you have more than one instance of servers installed on the same machine or more than one profile, the ports for each server or profile are different, which is usually incremented by one. Here is where you can check for the port numbers.

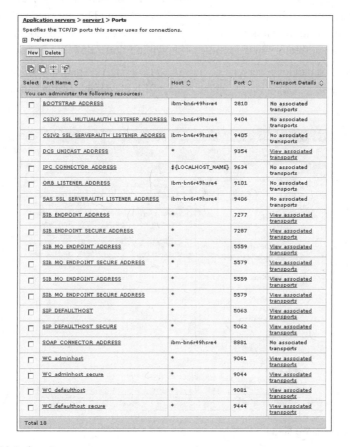

Figure 3.56 List of ports

5. Examine some of the ports used so far. The port WC_adminhost (for example, 9061) is for the administrative console. If security is enabled, WC_adminhost_secure (for example, 9044) would be used to load the admin console. WC_defaulthost (for example, 9081) and WC_defaulthost_secure (for example, 9444) are used for loading Web pages. The port numbers on your machine might be different depending on how many server instance and profiles you have on your computer.

6. Click Log Out.

Server Logs

WebSphere Application Server provides useful server logs. This step shows where all the logs files are.

1. Browse the server log location.

   a. In the file system, change to the WebSphere Application Server profiles directory. As mentioned before, the profiles directory could be installed in a completely different location that is outside the WAS_INSTALL directory. The log files are located in the logs directory in the profile as shown in Figure 3.57. For example,

   On a standalone server: C:\ProgramFiles\IBM\WebSphere\AppServer\profiles\ AppSrv01\logs\server1 where AppSrv01 is the default profile name.

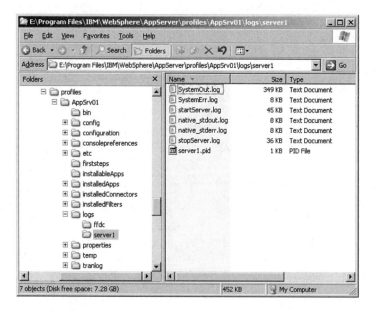

Figure 3.57   Server log files

2. When the server is running, `server1.pid` appears. If the server is stopped, this file is removed.

3. Run the Web application and look at the output in the log file.

    a. In another Web browser, load the URI `https://<prod_host>:<prod_port>/Insurance JPAProject/NewAutoPolicyServlet`. This is the Web service endpoint. The host and port might be different depending on your system configurations. Enter the host and port number of your production server.

    b. Open `SystemOut.log` in an editor. This file contains all the messages from the server and from System Out. At the bottom of the `SystemOut.log` file, you should see the System Out messages from the execution of the Web application as displayed in Figure 3.58.

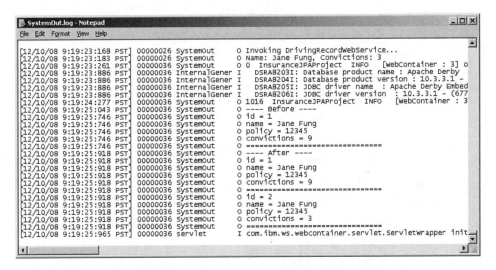

Figure 3.58   SystemOut.log file

The `SystemOut.log` file is not erased automatically when the server is restarted. The logs are appended to the end of the same log file. Therefore, it is recommended that you periodically clean up all the files in the `log` directory when the server is stopped. You cannot delete any of the files while the server is running. The `SystemOut.log` file has a size limit that you can modify from the admin console. When the file size limit is reached, the older logs are stored in another file with a year and time stamp (for example, `SystemOut_08.12.04_15.13.09.log`). The log files keep building up until you manually remove them.

Stop the WebSphere Application Server

1. Change to the `<WAS_INSTALL>\bin` directory of the command prompt.

2. Enter `stopserver server1`. This may pop up a dialog asking for the username and password. Alternatively, you can enter the following:

```
stopserver server1 -username <username> -password <password>
```

Summary

In this chapter, you glimpsed some of the features available in Rational Application Developer, which include Web tooling, Web service tooling, and Database tooling. There are many other features in Rational Application Developer that can help you create your SOA solution.

Tutorial Summary:

- Tutorial 3.1: Create, Deploy, and Test a Web Service
  - Create a Web project
  - Create a Web service
  - Test the Web service using the Web Service Explorer
  - Run in the embedded WebSphere Application Server
- Tutorial 3.2: Create a Database Table
  - Create a database connection
  - Create a data model with a schema and a table
  - Export the data model into an actual database
- Tutorial 3.3: Invoke a Web Service and Persist the Data Using Java Persistence API
  - Create a JPA Web project
  - Generate a Web service client
  - Create a Web application to invoke a Web service
  - Create a JPA entity and utility class to use it
  - Set up the JDBC configurations in the Persistence XML file
  - Run the Web application
  - Export the files into EAR for runtime deployment
- Tutorial 3.4: Deploy an Application into a WebSphere Application Server
  - Use the WebSphere Application Server admin console
  - Install the EAR files
  - Change the Web service endpoints
  - Look at the port number and the JDBC datasource
  - Examine the server log

CHAPTER 4

Service Governance with IBM WebSphere Service Registry and Repository

Product Overview

Service-Oriented Architecture (SOA) has become a hot topic in recent years. SOA enables companies to create new business processes or applications from existing services. It encourages reuse of services. Each service is a self-contained interoperable software unit, like a building block, that performs a particular task. SOA achieves loose coupling among the service consumers and service providers. A *service provider* provides reusable services. A *service consumer* discovers the services by some means and reuses them. A company can have many development teams creating services that are reusable.

How can services be shared across the organization? Maybe a simple spreadsheet or a database table could do the job. Developers creating reusable services could put an entry, including the description and service location, in the spreadsheet. People who want to reuse services can see the list and select what they want to use. It's a seemingly feasible solution.

The Scenario

Consider Tom's situation. As an experienced service developer, he has contributed to the spreadsheet for a long time. More than a dozen reusable services are under his name. As the year comes to an end, he finally has a bit of time to fix some bugs and add a few features for his services that are on the spreadsheet. Tom thinks: Can I just update the services? Will I break someone's code by doing so? Because he has no information on who is using his services, he just has to keep his fingers crossed and make the changes.

Tom's colleague Abby, an application developer, has developed several applications using the reusable services. The spreadsheet system has served her well and saved her lots of development time by allowing her to reuse existing services. One day her voice mail and Inbox are filled with complaints about her applications not functioning properly. After a dreadful day of investigation, she discovers some of the services that she had been using have changed. After a discussion with the service developer, Tom, about the issue, she politely points out that it mustn't happen again. Tom agrees to notify her by email when he updates the service to another version and promises to mark the old version as retired in the spreadsheet.

As time goes on, more application developers request that Tom notify them about different services they are using. Some developers want to know about services that are still under development, so that they can plan better. During a sleepless night, Tom wonders: Why do I have to do all these manually? There should be something that can help me. The next day Tom searches and comes across an article on IBM WebSphere Service Registry and Repository. He reads on with a sense of excitement. WebSphere Service Registry and Repository is exactly what he needs.

What Is WebSphere Service Registry and Repository?

WebSphere Service Registry and Repository (WSRR) is an industrial-strength tool that enables businesses to better manage and govern their services.

WSRR Capabilities

WSRR has five major capabilities: publish/find, manage, govern, and enrich.

Publish / Find   Services and their artifacts can be published to the Registry and Repository. The following artifacts can be published: Web Services Description Language (WSDL), XML Schema Definition (XSD), Extensible Markup Language (XML), WS-Policy, Service Component Architecture (SCA) Integration Module, MQ Services, and Binary Documents. The Registry and Repository also allows anything that does not have a concrete representation to be published as a *Concept*, which can be thought of as a generic object. Once services are published, they can be searched through the Web user interface, the Eclipse plug-ins, or the programming application programming interface (API). Besides manually publishing services, WSRR supports automatic discovery of services that are running in various runtime servers, which includes WebSphere Application Server, Microsoft .NET connection software, and Oracle Application Server.

Manage   *Service metadata* is the information about the service that can also be captured in the Registry and Repository. There are three types of service metadata:

- **Properties**—These are key/value pairs that can be predefined by the system or user defined.

- **Classifications**—These are like categories. You can classify service entities into different classifications. Classifications can be multidimensional, meaning a service entity can have multiple classifications.

- **Relationships**—These capture the associations between two entities. Some relationships are automatically derived when the service entities are published to the system. Some, known as *custom relationships*, can be built manually.

All the types can be applied to service entities within WebSphere Service Registry and Repository.

Govern A *service life cycle* is the process used to build and support the delivery of a service. As shown in Figure 4.1, WebSphere Service Registry and Repository comes with default life cycles that can be used for both service development and service discovery scenario. While the service is going through its natural development path, the services that are stored in the Registry and Repository can be advanced through the service development life cycle.

Figure 4.1 shows one of the life cycles from the *Basic Profile* that is shipped with the product. WebSphere Service Registry and Repository ships with two configuration profiles out-of-the-box – a *Basic Profile* and a *Governance Enablement Profile*. These configuration profiles are complete configuration for WSRR. For example, it contains life cycles, classifications, business model templates, access control roles and permissions, notifiers, validators, Web user interface (UI) configurations and etc. You can use one of the provided profiles as-is or you can extend on the profiles by adding your own configurations such as a lifecycle or a classification system. When a configuration profile is applied to a WSRR instance, configurations such as business models/concepts, access control, Web user interface (UI), life cycles, and classifications will be set up according to the profile.

WebSphere Service Registry and Repository by default has the *Governance Enablement Profile* activated. The *Governance Enablement Profile* was developed based on real life customer experience and the evolved best practices; therefore, it has more elaborate configurations. On the other hand, the *Basic Profile* contains the essential elements to get started with WSRR. It is recommended that a reasonable amount of forethought should be carried out before deciding on the profile.

The *Basic Profile* contains two life cycle paths as shown in Figure 4.1. The life cycle on the left path is used for service development and consists of six states: Created, Model, Assemble, Deploy, Manage, and Retired. The life cycle on the right path is used for service discovery. Existing services can be discovered from various runtime servers. When a service is discovered, it can be placed under governance automatically using the service discovery life cycle.

Any life cycles shipped with WebSphere Service Registry and Repository can be customized to fit your business's needs. All service entities within the Registry and Repository can be placed under the service life cycle. Beside the *Basic Profile's* life cycle, the *Governance Enablement Profile* provides a greater set of life cycles for users to choose from.

Enrich Once the service entities and metadata are published into the Registry and Repository, you can use them to do dynamic endpoint selection in an enterprise service bus (ESB). In the IBM ESB offerings, which include WebSphere ESB, WebSphere Message Broker, and WebSphere DataPower Appliance, there are nodes available to communicate with WSRR to obtain endpoints and metadata information to assist in the dynamic endpoint selections.

IBM WebSphere Service Registry and Repository fosters good behavior around the area of service management and governance. It is like a closet organizer that encourages you to manage your services properly. The rest of this section discusses a few of the capabilities in more detail.

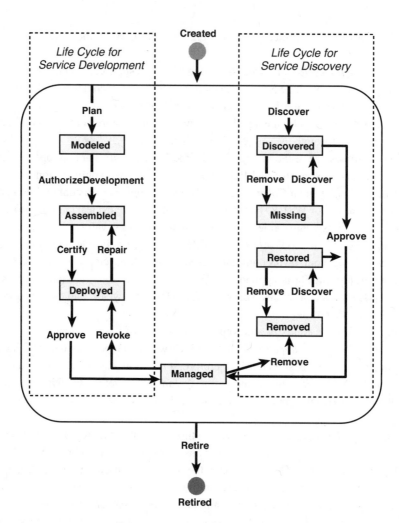

Figure 4.1   Default governance life cycle

The Publish/Find Capability

WebSphere Service Registry and Repository allows service entities to be published and located. One of the main ways to publish and find service entities is by using the Web user interface. The Web user interface has a URI of `http://<host>:<port>/ServiceRegistry`, as shown in Figure 4.2. Because WebSphere Service Registry and Repository is an application that is installed on top of WebSphere Application Server, the host and port used are no different from any other Web applications running on a WebSphere Application Server.

The Web user interface has different perspectives for different user roles. The perspective is selected based on the user role that is logged in. There are several perspectives out-of-the-box in the Governance Enablement Profile, which are Administrator, Business, Configuration, Development, General User, Operations, and SOA Governance as shown in Figure 4.3. Each perspective displays only the contents that the users in the role are allowed to see. The perspectives are configurable. In addition, new perspectives can be added for additional user roles. The user role and the perspectives only take effect if you have security turned on in the WebSphere Application Server.

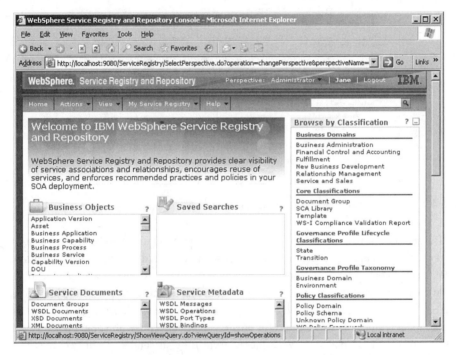

Figure 4.2   Web user interface welcome screen

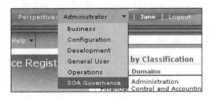

Figure 4.3   Web user interface perspectives

The service documents that can be published to the Registry and Repository are WSDL, XSD, XML, WS-Policy, SCA Integration Module, and Binary Documents. When you publish an artifact, you can provide the description and the version number. The artifact will be analyzed during the loading process, and if there are dependencies that are not in the repository, you will be asked to provide them in the publishing step, as seen in Figure 4.4. Once all the dependencies are resolved, you will have a choice to save the documents individually or as a document group. Saving the documents as a document group allows the users to see all the documents as a group. It is a user's preference as to which way to save the documents.

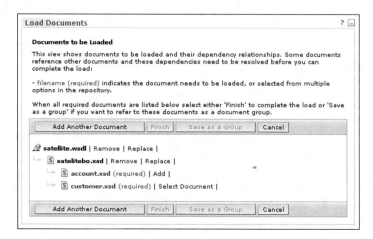

Figure 4.4   Web user interface loading documents

The service entities that do not have a concrete representation can be created as a concept. A *concept* can be thought of as a generic object that has a name, description, version number, and metadata such as properties, relationships, and classifications. At times, you may need to create multiple concepts with the same structures. For example, all the concepts would have a property named businessOwner. In that case, a business model template would make the job a lot easier. A business model template is like a mold for creating new concepts with some preset user-defined properties and relationship names. WebSphere Service Registry and Repository comes with some predefined business model templates. Some examples are Enterprise Application, Enterprise Module, Service Binding, and Service Interface. Besides these out-of-the-box business model templates, users may create their own business model templates.

Business model templates enable WebSphere Service Registry and Repository to perform validations on a concept instance. Validations include checking the type of property value, the type of target in a relationship, the number of targets allowed in a relationship, the contents allowed in a property, and the required fields. A business model template is based on the Web Ontology Language (OWL), which is the same language for creating the classification system. Figure 4.5 shows an example of a concept created based on a business model template. The template is named Service. It has a required field named businessOwner, which is identified by an asterisk. It has three relationships, where two are optional and one is mandatory. The targets that can be picked for a relationship are also validated. For example, the providedInterface relationship only allows a WSDL document to be selected. It is mandatory and allows multiple targets. Custom business model templates and lifecycles can be created in IBM WebSphere Service Registry and Repository Studio version 6.3.

Figure 4.5   Creating a new concept based on the Service template

Figure 4.6 shows a query wizard in the Web user interface that allows users to perform advanced searches for anything in the Registry and Repository. The wizard can search based on wild card names, namespace, version, property key, property value, and classifications.

The Query Wizard is one of the ways to locate artifacts within the Registry and Repository. The WebSphere Service Registry and Repository Studio provides another way to search for services to reuse. The studio is Eclipse based and it allows users to create profile configurations and connect to the WSRR. The studio can publish and find in the Registry and Repository. In Figure 4.7, the WSDL documents that are in the Registry and Repository are displayed in the Service Registry view in the studio workbench. You can directly import these documents into your Eclipse projects, and the documents' dependencies can be imported automatically. This feature provides a convenient way for application developers to obtain the service artifacts while they are searching for services to reuse.

WebSphere Service Registry and Repository also has a set of programming APIs that allow access to the Registry and Repository's data programmatically. There are several sets of programming APIs: Java API, Simple Object Access Protocol (SOAP) API, and REST interface reference. Both the Java and SOAP APIs can perform create, read, update, delete, and query functions. The Java APIs can further perform administrative functions such as updating the classification systems programmatically. The REST interface allows for lightweight clients to perform action on content and metadata by using HTTP requests.

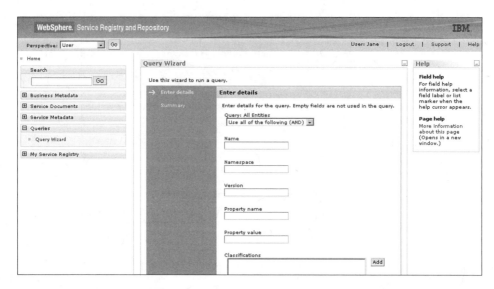

Figure 4.6   Web User Interface Query Wizard

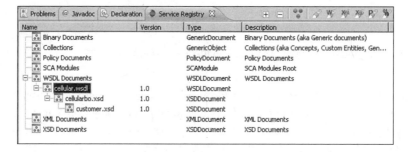

Figure 4.7   Eclipse plug-in Service Registry view

The Manage Capability

To properly manage service entities, you need service metadata. Properties, classifications, and relationships are metadata that can be applied to any service entities within the Registry and Repository. Properties are key/value pairs. When a service entity is published, it already comes with some default system-defined properties such as `creationTimeStamp` and `lastModifiedBy`. Optionally, users can create additional user-defined properties such as `MyProperty`, seen in Figure 4.8.

Classification is to assign a category to service entities. The classifications that you can put on the service entities are captured in the Configuration perspective under the Classification Systems section. Different governance profile include a different set of classification systems. For instance, there are three classification systems loaded out-of-the-box in the Basic Profile: Life Cycle Classifications, Policy Classifications, and Core Classifications. Users would likely

add their own classifications. In Figure 4.9, Organization Classifications is a user-defined classification system. The classification system is based on the Web Ontology Language (OWL),
which is essentially a text file. The classification system can be created and modified on the Web
user interface in the Configuration perspective or in the WebSphere Service Registry and Repository Studio version 6.3.

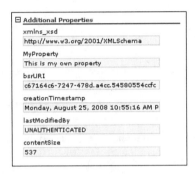

Figure 4.8   System-defined and user-defined properties

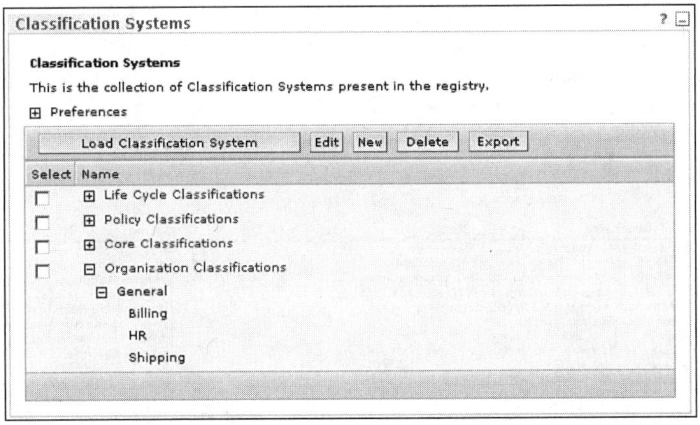

Figure 4.9   Classification systems

Relationship is another important topic, because it links the service entities, which enables
impact analysis. As the service artifacts are published to the Registry and Repository, some of the
relationships are automatically populated. Some relationship examples are the import relationship between an XSD and a WSDL or the relationship between an SCA module and an XSD.
Figure 4.10 shows some examples of the built-in relationships that are created automatically by
the Registry and Repository during publishing. On the other hand, user-defined relationships can
also be established between service entities.

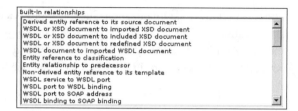

Figure 4.10   Built-in relationships

Once relationships are established, it is possible to perform impact analysis on a specific service entity. Remember in our scenario, our experienced service developer Tom was concerned whether his update of the service will affect others. Impact analysis is the perfect tool that can help him, as shown in Figure 4.11. He can find out using the impact analysis tool which entities depend on his code and what his code depends on. That way he can better understand the impact and the extent of the changes he plans to do.

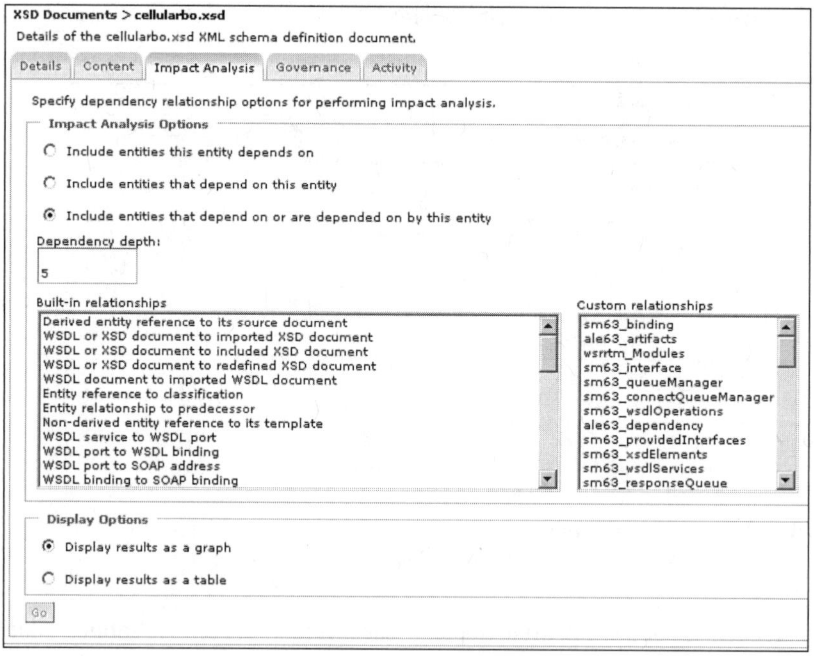

Figure 4.11   Impact analysis

Notification is another feature that the Registry and Repository provides. Users can create a subscription to be notified under some situations as shown in Figure 4.12. The application developer Abby in our example can set up a subscription to be notified when the service that she is using is updated or its life cycle state is changed to Retired. The target entities can be specified using a wild card name, namespace, version number, or the classifications, and users can listen to more than one operation.

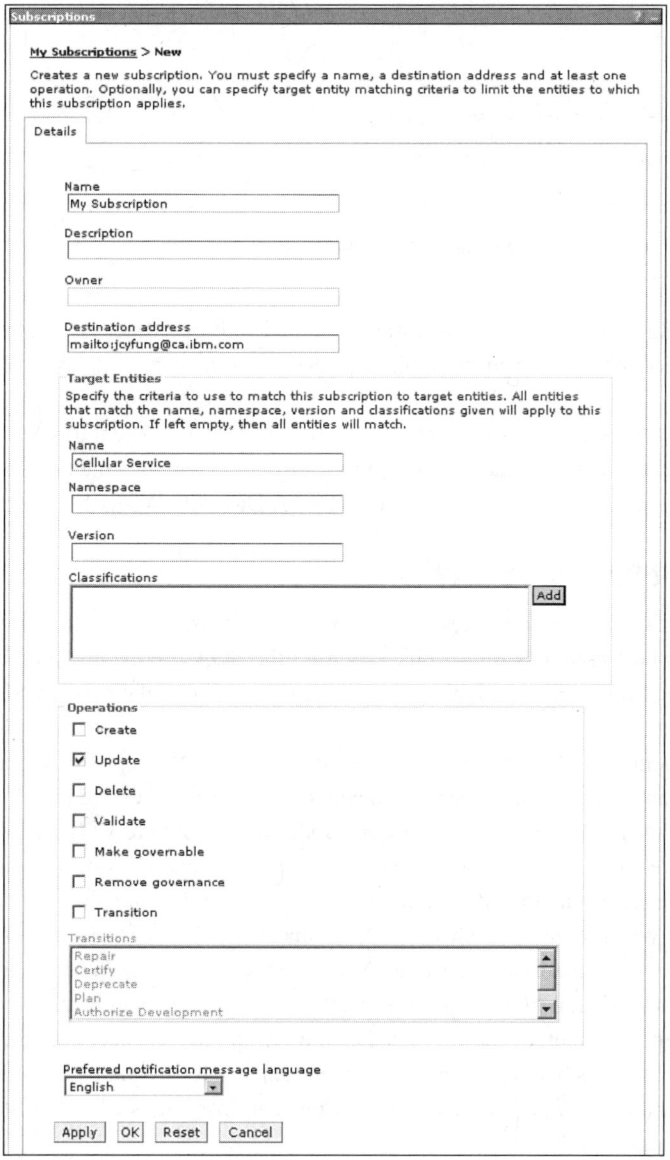

Figure 4.12 Subscriptions

The notification email is shown in Figure 4.13. This is a default email; however, the contents can be customized.

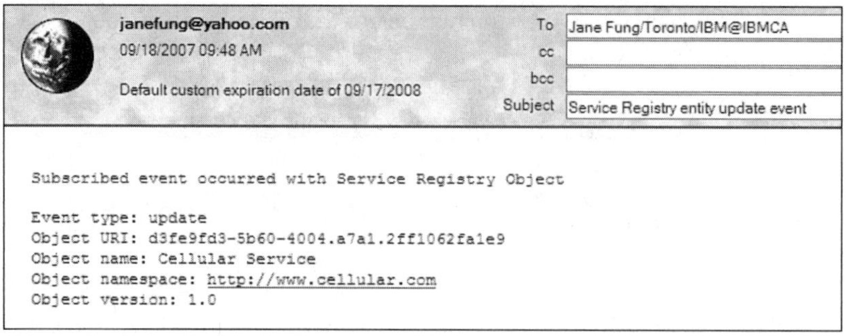

Figure 4.13   The notification e-mail

The Registry and Repository has a fine-grained role-based access control system. Once security is enabled in the WebSphere Application Server, users can set up user roles and their corresponding access rights.

WebSphere Service Registry and Repository has many other features that are not detailed in this chapter. For more information, you can visit the InfoCenter in the Reference section. The rest of the article will be a hands-on exercise on the "A Day with WSRR" scenario.

How Does It Support SOA?

WebSphere Service Registry and Repository can be used across the SOA life cycle. It features the governance and best practices for all phases within the SOA life cycle. WSRR allows users to manage their life cycle from development through deployment to their use by SOA runtimes and in service management.

Besides being a development time service repository, WebSphere Service Registry and Repository can act as a runtime registry from which the enterprise service bus can look up service metadata to make runtime endpoint selection. Both the WebSphere ESB and WebSphere Message Broker have an `EndpointLookup` node that can retrieve endpoint information from the service registry. The ESBs can then decide what endpoints to use to route the service to.

The IBM WebSphere DataPower SOA Appliance often acts as an enterprise service bus that mediates between a service consumer and a service producer. When a service consumer wants to access a service, it first reaches the DataPower appliance, which might perform transformation, policy enforcement, or routing. The DataPower appliance can communicate with the service registry such that its behavior can be altered in runtime. It can obtain a specific version or the most current version of WSDL Documents or Concepts from the service registry and route the service request accordingly.

WebSphere Service Registry and Repository acts as a repository for governing services in development time and as a runtime registry in runtime. It allows some nontechnical documents to be stored in repository, such as text files, document files, Portable Document Format (PDF) files, or pictures. However, it is not designed to store or govern documentations in mass. The Web-

Sphere Service Registry and Repository, Advanced Lifecycle Edition (ALE) provides such support. It can store and govern massive documentations and as well as services. This product bundles Rational Asset Manager and WebSphere Service Registry and Repository, which provide elaborate support for both documents and services governance for your entire organization.

Tutorial Overview

This chapter walks you through a hands-on exercise on the scenario "A Day with WSRR," where you will explore many of the capabilities in the Registry and Repository. This chapter assumes that you already have WebSphere Service Registry and Repository set up and the Eclipse plug-in installed in an Eclipse workbench.

A Day with WSRR Scenario

This scenario shows how to use WebSphere Service Registry and Repository in a typical development environment. The story has three users: a service developer, an application developer, and an administrator.

It has been a few months since Tom, the experienced service developer, found a solution to help his company manage and govern services. They are now using WebSphere Service Registry and Repository across the organization to manage reusable services. Tom is determined to be a top service developer and continues to crank out reusable services day in and day out. He still follows the same development process that uses a software configuration management (SCM) system for his team's source version control needs. When Tom is satisfied with the service and decides it's ready to be shared, he publishes it to WebSphere Service Registry and Repository as a concept with a version number, description, and related files.

The service concept is also placed under life cycle management. As the service comes to its natural end, Tom moves it to the Retired state, and the party of interest is notified.

Tom remembers the painful discussion with his application developer, Abby, regarding his poor judgment of changing services blindly. In addition to the automatic notifications, he can now also proactively assess the impact of his changes by doing an impact analysis. WebSphere Service Registry and Repository has saved him time in managing all the services that he creates and has off-loaded many administrative tasks from his shoulders.

Abby is having an equally good time. Using the Web interface, she can clearly see all the services that are available for reuse. She can see the version number, determine if there are other published versions, and identify their life cycle state. To reuse a service, she simply imports the documents directly into the Eclipse workbench where her usual development work resides. As Abby chooses the services for reuse, she registers her application in WebSphere Service Registry and Repository as a concept. She no longer has to worry about a service changing without her knowledge; notifications are sent to her automatically. Life is good; everyone is happy.

This scenario is just one way an organization can use WebSphere Service Registry and Repository; it is certainly not the only way. For example, using a concept to represent a service is a user's preference. You could choose not to use a concept at all, and the scenario would still work fine.

The exercises in the following sections explain the interactions between service developer Tom and application developer Abby. The exercises also show the responsibilities of an administrator.

Tutorial 4.1: Set Up the Registry and Repository as an Administrator

- The administrator set up the Registry and Repository with business model templates and a classification system.

Tutorial 4.2: Publish a New Service as a Service Developer

- The service developer Tom has finished the development of the service and decides it is ready for sharing. He publishes the artifacts into the Registry and Repository.

- Tom creates a concept to represent the service and moves it through the governance life cycle. Alternatively, Tom could have created a concept before he starts development and before the service is designed. However, in our scenario, Tom's company decides to have the concept created after the service is deemed sharable.

Tutorial 4.3: Reuse Services as an Application Developer

- Abby, the application developer, searches for services she can reuse.
- While she searches, she creates a concept to represent her application.
- She imports the artifacts into the Eclipse workbench.
- As she chooses the services for reuse, she creates a relationship between the services and the application concept.

Tutorial 4.4: Update Existing Services as a Service Developer

- Tom plans to update one of the services. Before he does anything, he performs an impact analysis to see what effect it will have.
- He creates a version 2.0 of the service as a separate concept and changes the life cycle of the version 1.0 service to Retired.

System Requirements

The following needs to be set up fully to run all the tutorials:

- WebSphere Service Registry and Repository version 6.3.
- WebSphere Service Registry and Repository Studio version 6.3.

What Is Included in the CD-ROM?

The attached CD-ROM contains all tutorial files that are required to perform the tutorials. They are located in the individual tutorial directory under the `tutorial files` folder. In addition, the

CD-ROM includes step-by-step videos that illustrate the tutorials, which are located in the individual `tutorial` directory under the `videos` folder.

Tutorial 4.1: Set Up the Registry and Repository as an Administrator

Start WebSphere Service Registry and Repository if it's not already started.

1. From the Windows Start menu, select All Programs, IBM WebSphere, Application Server Network Deployment, Profiles, AppSrv01, Start the Server.

2. Wait until the server is started and load the URL `http://<host>:<port>/Service Registry` in a Web browser. For example, `http://localhost:9080/ServiceRegistry/`.

3. Enter any user ID in the WebSphere Service Registry and Repository console page and click Login. If the WebSphere Application Server's security is enabled, you are required to enter the user ID and password. Once you are logged in, your session will be expired and become invalid if you are idle for too long.

The Registry and Repository has the Governance Enablement Profile activated by default. Change to the Basic Profile for the learning purposes.

1. From the browser where the Web user interface is loaded, select Configuration from the Perspective drop-down box.

2. Expand Manage Profiles and select Configuration Profiles as shown in Figure 4.14.

Figure 4.14   The Configuration Profiles drop-down

3. Select BasicProfile_v63 and click Make Active as shown in Figure 4.15. This process may take a few minutes as WSRR replaces all of the configurations within the system. When the activation is successful, the status for the BasicProfiel_v63 is changed to Active.

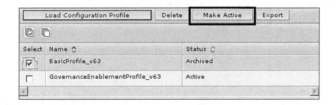

Figure 4.15   Activate the Basic Profile

Set Up the Business Model Templates

In this step, you as the administrator will load a business model system file that sets up two business model templates. A business model template is to facilitate the creations of concepts that have the same property and relationship names. One of the templates is called `Application` and has a property named `businessOwner` and a relationship named `referencedServices`. The template is created from an OWL file. Listing 4.1 is a snippet of the OWL file.

Listing 4.1   Code Snippet of the Application Template

```
<!-- Class Definitions for the Application Template -->
<owl:Class rdf:ID="Application">
    <rdfs:label>Application</rdfs:label>
    <rdfs:comment>Application template</rdfs:comment>
    <rdfs:subClassOf>
        <owl:Restriction>
        <owl:onProperty rdf:resource="#referencedServices" />
        <owl:minCardinality
rdf:datatype="http://www.w3.org/2001/XMLSchema#nonNegativeInteger">0</
owl:minCardinality>
        </owl:Restriction>
    </rdfs:subClassOf>
    <rdfs:subClassOf>
        <owl:Restriction>
        <owl:onProperty rdf:resource="#businessOwner" />
        <owl:cardinality
rdf:datatype="http://www.w3.org/2001/XMLSchema#nonNegativeInteger">1</
owl:cardinality>
        </owl:Restriction>
    </rdfs:subClassOf>
</owl:Class>

<!-- Property businessOwner -->
<owl:DatatypeProperty rdf:ID="businessOwner">
    <rdfs:label>businessOwner</rdfs:label>
    <rdfs:comment>businessOwner</rdfs:comment>
    <rdfs:domain>
        <owl:Class>
            <owl:unionOf rdf:parseType="Collection">
                <owl:Class rdf:about="#Application" />
                <owl:Class rdf:about="#Service" />
            </owl:unionOf>
        </owl:Class>
```

```
    </rdfs:domain>
<rdfs:range rdf:resource="http://www.w3.org/2001/XMLSchema#string" />
</owl:DatatypeProperty>

<!-- Relationship referencedServices -->
<owl:ObjectProperty rdf:ID="referencedServices">
    <rdfs:label>referencedServices</rdfs:label>
    <rdfs:comment>referencedServices</rdfs:comment>
    <rdfs:domain rdf:resource="#Application" />
    <rdfs:range rdf:resource="#Service" />
</owl:ObjectProperty>
```

You can create an OWL file manually by modifying the example file (ModellingSample.owl) supplied in the InfoCenter. Alternatively, you can create a business model OWL file using a Web-Sphere Studio Registry and Repository Studio. For your convenience, two sample OWL files for the tutorial illustration purposes are supplied in the attached CD.

If the Web user interface is not already loaded, load it in a browser using `http://<host>:<port>/ServiceRegistry`. Enter your username and password to log in, or enter any username if security is not enabled in the server.

1. Load the business model system.

   a. Make sure you are in the Configuration perspective. If not, select Configuration from the Perspective drop-down box.

   b. From the top navigation, expand Active Profile and click Business Model Systems.

   c. Click Load Business Model System as shown in Figure 4.16. The Registry and Repository has several business models already loaded out-of-the-box in the Basic Profile: Technical Model, WSRR Asset Business Model, and WSRR Service Model.

   d. Click Browse and select HelloWorld_BusinessModelSystem.owl, which can be found in the CD-ROM folder chapter 4\tutorial 4.1\tutorial files.

   e. Click OK. A message confirms that the upload was successful as shown in Figure 4.17.

2. Verify the business model template is loaded.

   a. Select User from the Perspective drop-down box to switch to the User perspective.

   b. In the top navigation, expand View and click Business Model Templates. You can sort the list of existing business model templates by clicking on the title in the table. For example, click on the table column title URI to sort by the URI. You will see both the Service and Application become business model templates and listed near the top of the table as shown in Figure 4.18. The other templates are from the out-of-the-box business model system.

Business Model Systems
?
Business Model Systems
This is the collection of business model systems in the registry.
Preferences
Load Business Model System
Delete
Export
Select
Name
Description
URI
Technical Model
http://www.ibm.com/xmlns/prod/serviceregistry/6/1/TechnicalModel
WSRR Asset Business Model
http://www.ibm.com/xmlns/prod/serviceregistry/v6r3/ALEModel
WSRR Service Model
http://www.ibm.com/xmlns/prod/serviceregistry/v6r3/ServiceModel
Total: 3

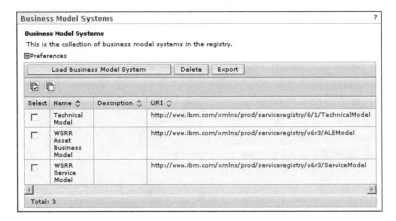

Figure 4.16 Load Business Model System menu

Business Model Systems
?
Messages
The upload was successful for configuration type: Business Model System.
Business Model Systems
This is the collection of business model systems in the registry.
Preferences
Load Business Model System
Delete
Export
Select
Name
Description
URI
HelloWorldBusinessModelSystem
HelloWorld Business Model System
http://www.ibm.com/helloworld
Technical Model
http://www.ibm.com/xmlns/prod/serviceregistry
WSRR Asset Business Model
http://www.ibm.com/xmlns/prod/serviceregistry
WSRR Service Model
http://www.ibm.com/xmlns/prod/serviceregistry

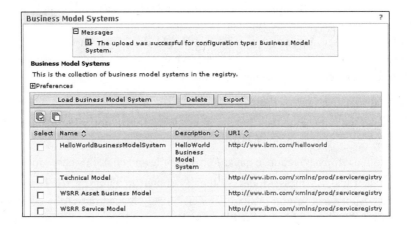

Figure 4.17 Business Model System was loaded successfully

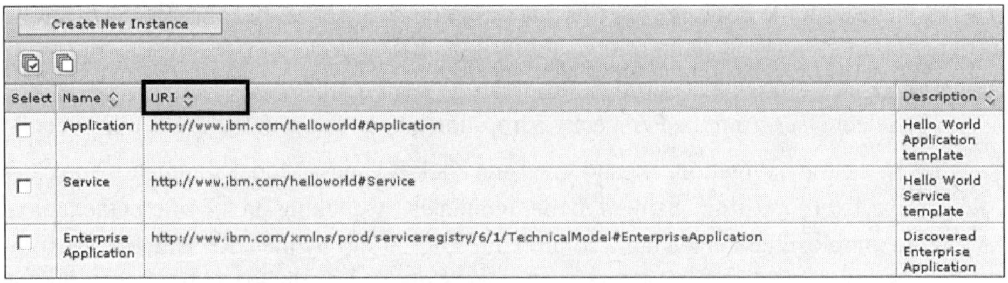

Create New Instance
Select
Name
URI
Description
Application
http://www.ibm.com/helloworld#Application
Hello World Application template
Service
http://www.ibm.com/helloworld#Service
Hello World Service template
Enterprise Application
http://www.ibm.com/xmlns/prod/serviceregistry/6/1/TechnicalModel#EnterpriseApplication
Discovered Enterprise Application

Figure 4.18 Service and Application business model templates

Load Classification System

A classification system is represented using a text-based OWL file. The following is a snippet from the OWL file. The classification system displayed in Listing 4.2 has a tree format, where the parent tree node is Environment and the children are Development, Test, and Production. The Registry and Repository Web user interface provides a classification editor in which classifications can be created visually.

Listing 4.2   Sample OWL File Code Snippet

```
<!---->
<!--WSRR   Sample root definitions  -->
<!---->
<owl:Class rdf:about="&wsrrgst;Environment">
    <rdfs:label >Environment</rdfs:label>
    <rdfs:comment>A base classification used to describe different
environments that services may be deployed to</rdfs:comment>
</owl:Class>

<!--   -->
<!--WSRR   Sample SOA Taxonomy definitions - Environments   -->
<!--   -->
<owl:Class rdf:about="&wsrrgst;Development">
    <rdfs:subClassOf rdf:resource="&wsrrgst;Environment"/>
    <rdfs:label>Development</rdfs:label>
    <rdfs:comment>The development environment</rdfs:comment>
</owl:Class>
<owl:Class rdf:about="&wsrrgst;Test">
    <rdfs:subClassOf rdf:resource="&wsrrgst;Environment"/>
    <rdfs:label>Test</rdfs:label>
    <rdfs:comment>The test environment</rdfs:comment>
</owl:Class>
<owl:Class rdf:about="&wsrrgst;Production">
    <rdfs:subClassOf rdf:resource="&wsrrgst;Environment"/>
    <rdfs:label>Production</rdfs:label>
    <rdfs:comment>The production environment</rdfs:comment>
</owl:Class>
```

1. Load the classification system.

    a. In the Perspective drop-down box, select Configuration.

b. From the top navigation, expand Active Profile and click Classification Systems.

c. Click Load Classification System.

d. Click Browse and select `SampleTaxonomy.owl` as shown in Figure 4.19, which can be found in the CD-ROM folder `chapter 4\tutorial 4.1\tutorial files`. Click Open to dismiss the File Selection dialog.

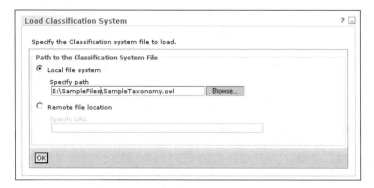

Figure 4.19   Load classification system

e. Click OK. The classification system WSRR Sample Taxonomy is loaded successfully, as seen in Figure 4.20.

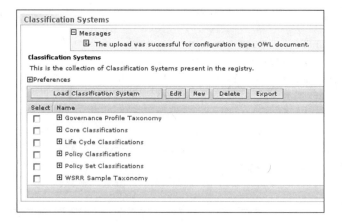

Figure 4.20   Load a user-defined classification system

You, as an administrator, have loaded a business model template and a classification system to the Registry and Repository.

Tutorial 4.2: Publish a New Service as a Service Developer

The service developer Tom has finished the development of the service and decides it is ready for sharing. He publishes the artifacts into the Registry and Repository. He then creates a concept for the service and moves it through the governance life cycle.

If the Web user interface is not already loaded, load it in a browser using `http://<host>:<port>/ServiceRegistry`. Enter your username and password to log in, or enter any username if security is not enabled in the server.

Import Service Documents

1. Import the WSDL document and its dependencies.

    a. From the browser where the Web user interface is loaded, select the User perspective.

    b. In the top navigation, expand Actions and click Load Documents.

    c. Click Browse and locate `chapter 4\tutorial 4.2\tutorial files\service_files\services\cellular\cellular.wsdl` from the CD-ROM.

    d. Make sure the document type is WSDL.

    e. Enter `1.0` as the document version.

    f. Click OK. Note that `cellularbo.xsd` is in red, which means it is required.

    g. Click Add, which is beside `cellularbo.xsd`.

    h. Click Browse and locate `chapter 4\tutorial 4.2\tutorial files\service_files\services\cellular\cellularbo.xsd` from the CD-ROM.

    i. Enter `1.0` as the document version. Click OK.

    j. Click Add, which is beside `customer.xsd`.

    k. Click Browse and locate `chapter 4\tutorial 4.2\tutorial files\service_files\lib\common\customer.xsd` from the CD-ROM.

    l. Enter `1.0` as the document version. Click OK. Figure 4.21 shows all the dependencies are resolved.

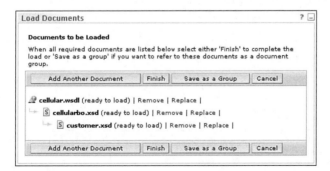

Figure 4.21   Load cellular service

m. Click Finish. The cellular service is loaded successfully, as shown in Figure 4.22. The service also has a text file that documents the details of the service. The text file can be imported as other documents.

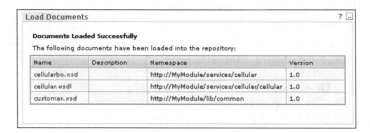

Figure 4.22   Successfully loaded the cellular service

2. Import the text file.

   a. In the top navigation, expand Actions and click Load Documents.

   b. Click Browse and locate `chapter 4\tutorial 4.2\tutorial files\service_files\` `services\cellular\cellular service details.txt` from the CD-ROM.

   c. Select Other as the document type.

   d. Enter `1.0` as the document version as shown in Figure 4.23.

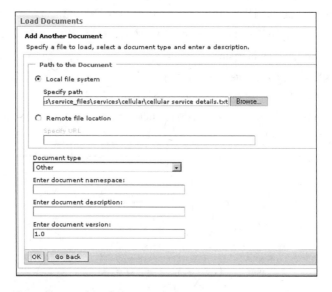

Figure 4.23   Load text file as other document

   e. Click OK and click Finish.

Create a Concept

In this step, a concept that is based on the Service template is created to represent the cellular service.

   1. Create a new instance of a business model template.

     a. Expand View in the top navigation and click Business Model Templates.

     b. Select the Service check box and click Create New Instance.

     c. Enter `Cellular Service v1.0` as the name.

     d. Enter `This service provides the accounting info for cellular customer` as the description.

     e. Enter `http://www.cellular.com` as the namespace.

     f. Enter `1.0` as the version.

     g. Enter your name as the businessOwner as shown in Figure 4.24.

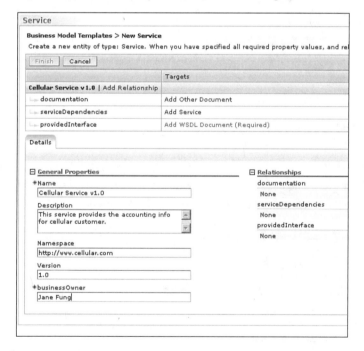

Figure 4.24   Create a cellular service concept

   2. Associate the text file with this concept.

     a. In the Add Relationship section on top, click Add Other Document to add the text file to this concept. The documentation relationship comes from the Service template of the business model OWL file.

     b. In the Add Target section, type * in the Name text field to search all the files that are other documents. This automatically displays the search result, as shown in Figure

4.25. Note that there is only one selection available in the Entity Type drop-down box. This is because the Service business model template has a restriction for the types that are allowed for this relationship. Only other documents are allowed to be "documentation" for a service.

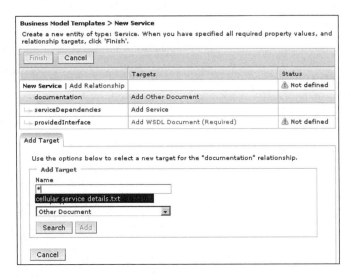

Figure 4.25   Add target for the other document

    c. Select `cellular service details.txt` from the drop-down.

    d. Click Add. The `cellular service details.txt` file is associated to the concept as a documentation relationship as shown in Figure 4.26.

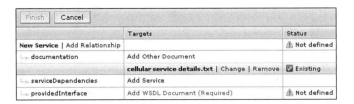

Figure 4.26   Add other documentation

  3. Associate a WSDL document to this concept.

    a. In the Add Relationship section on top, click Add WSDL Document (Required) to add a WSDL document as the provided interface to this concept.

    b. In the Add Target section, start typing `cell` in the Name text field. This searches all WSDL documents that start with the word `cell`. You will see `cellular.wsdl` in the drop-down as shown in Figure 4.27.

Figure 4.27 Add target for the WSDL document

   c. Select `cellular.wsdl` from the drop-down and click Add. All the relationships are added.

   d. Click Finish to create the concept.

Make the Concept Governable

All the entities within the Registry and Repository can be put under the governance life cycle. In this step, the company has decided to only create a concept when the service is already published. The first couple of stages in the *Basic Profile's* life cycle do not apply; therefore, in the tutorial we will quickly move through the first couple of stages. In reality, if the company's process is different from the out-of-the-box life cycle, the company should streamline and customize it.

   In this step, the cellular service concept is made governable following the service development life cycle and moved to the Managed state. Figure 4.28 shows where the Managed state is in the life cycle.

  1. Put the concept under governance.

    a. Expand View from the top navigation and select Concepts.

    b. Click Cellular Service v1.0.

    c. Click the Governance tab.

    d. Click Govern, and the life cycle governance state is moved to the Created state as shown in Figure 4.29. This step might take awhile if it's the first time running the Registry and Repository, because it needs to be initialized.

  2. Move the concept through the default life cycle.

    a. Select Plan from the Available State Transitions drop-down box. Click Transition, and the governance state is moved to Modeled.

    b. Take the default Authorize Development and click Transition again. The transition Authorize Development moves the governance state to Assembled.

    c. Take the default Certify and click Transition again. The transition Certify moves the governance state to Deployed.

    d. Take the default Approve and click Transition again. The transition Approve moves the governance state to Managed as shown in Figure 4.30.

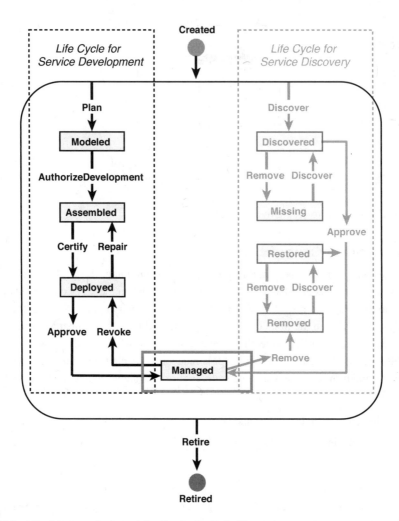

Figure 4.28   The Managed state of the Basic Profile's life cycle

In this tutorial, Tom successfully published the cellular service to the Registry and Repository. He created a concept to represent the service and moved the service concept to the Managed state in the life cycle.

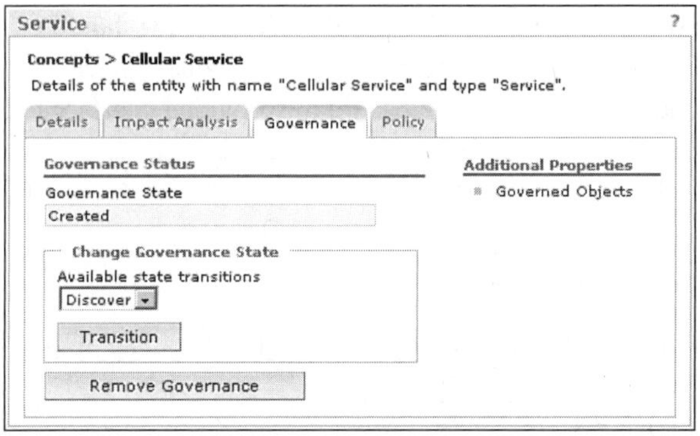

Figure 4.29 The life cycle is moved to the Created state

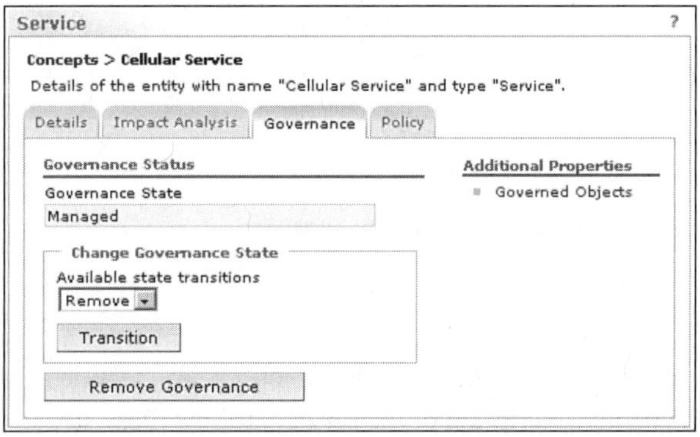

Figure 4.30 The governance state is at Managed

Tutorial 4.3: Reuse Services as an Application Developer

In this tutorial, we will see how Abby, the application developer, finds services and reuses them. If the Web user interface is not already loaded, load it in a browser using `http://<host>:<port>/ServiceRegistry`. Enter the username and password to log in. Select the User perspective.

Find Reusable Services

1. In the top navigation of the User perspective, expand Actions and select Query Wizard.

2. Search for existing services using the `*service*` search word.

    a. Select Concepts as the entity type in the drop-down box. Then click Next.

    b. Enter ***service*** in the Name section to search for any concepts that has with the word **service** anywhere in the name. In this example, a wild card name is used. Alternatively, you can use the Classification or any other fields for the query criteria. An example of Classification would be using a state from the default life cycle named `Managed`. The Managed classification can be found under the Life Cycle Classifications > State > Default Governance Life Cycle.

c.   Click Next and then Finish. The cellular service v1.0 should be returned as the result as displayed in Figure 4.31. Abby sees there is one service. She wants to know more details about it; therefore, she looks for the provided interface to get more information.

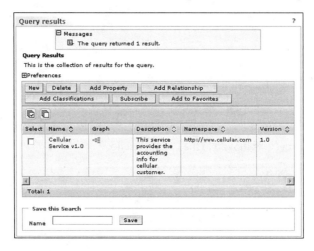

Figure 4.31   The query result from the query wizard

d.   Click Cellular Service v1.0.

3.   You should see the documentation in the Relationships section as shown in Figure 4.32. To look at the detail description of the service, follow these steps:

Figure 4.32   Explore the query result

a. Click `cellular service details.txt`.

b. Click the Content tab to see the content as shown in Figure 4.33.

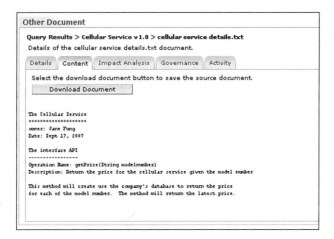

Figure 4.33 The content of the text file

4. As a developer, Abby has reviewed the service details. Click Logout to log out from the Web user interface.

Import Artifacts into Eclipse Workbench

After Abby reads the service details, she decides that it is the service she wants to use. From the `providedInterface` relationship, the file she needs to get is `cellular.wsdl`. In this step, she will use the WebSphere Service Registry and Repository Studio to obtain `cellular.wsdl` and its dependencies. The studio's plugins can be installed on any compliant Eclipse workbench which allows developers to use WSRR with the workbench of their choice.

1. Start the WebSphere Service Registry and Repository Studio workbench. You may take the default workspace or use a new workspace location.

2. Configure the WSRR location in the workbench's preference page to connect to the Service Registry and Repository.

a. From the workbench, click Window, Preferences.

b. Select WebSphere Service Registry and Repository (WSRR).

c. Click Add.

d. Enter `WSRR` as the alias name.

e. Enter the host name that WSRR is installed as host. For a default installation, the host is localhost.

f. Enter the HTTP port number as the port. For a default installation, the port is 9080. The completed preference page is shown in Figure 4.34.

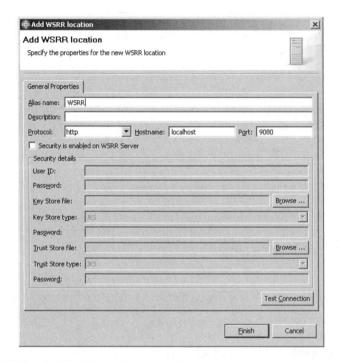

Figure 4.34   Add Service Registry preferences

g. Click Finish.

h. Click OK to close the Preferences window. Figure 4.35 shows the configured WSRR location.

3. Open the WSRR Content view and retrieve the existing WSDL documents from the Registry and Repository.

a. From the workbench, click Window, Open Perspective, Other. Select Java. Then click OK.

b. From the workbench, click Window, Show View, Other. Expand WSRR Content, WSRR Content. Then click OK.

c. In the WSRR Content view, right-click anywhere in the view and click Retrieve WSDL documents. The first time requires initializing the Service Registry plug-ins; hence, it may take a little bit of time.

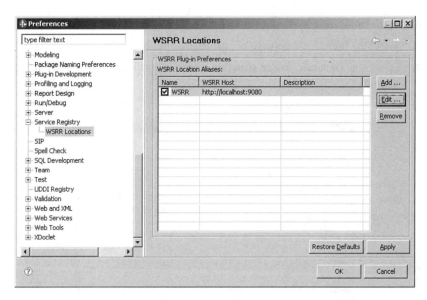

Figure 4.35   Set up the WSRR locations

d. The query result comes back with a list of WSDL documents that are stored in the Registry and Repository, including `cellular.wsdl` as shown in Figure 4.36. Click OK to dismiss the dialog.

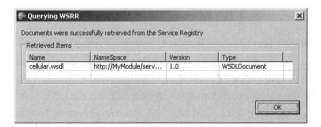

Figure 4.36   Retrieved items from the Service Registry and Repository

4. Create a new project to host the WSDL documents.

a. Create a new project. Click File, New, Other. Expand General, Project. Click Next.

b. Enter `MyProject` as the name. Click Finish.

5. Import the WSDL documents and all their dependent artifacts.

a. In the Service Registry view, expand WSDL Documents, right-click `cellular.wsdl`, and click Import Document. If you expand `cellular.wsdl`, you will see all its dependencies.

b. Select `MyProject` as the parent folder.

c. Select the Include all dependent artifacts/entities check box.

d. Select the Generate folder structure check box. Figure 4.37 shows the completed wizard.

Figure 4.37   Import WSDL document

e. Click Finish. The files are imported into the project as shown in Figure 4.38. The `cellular.wsdl` document is imported, as are all the dependent files. The folder structure is also properly recreated to avoid compilation errors. Abby can now continue the development of her application using the reusable services. If you are using other Eclipse-compliant workbenches, you might need to change to the Physical view to see the files as they might get filtered in other perspectives or views.

Figure 4.38   Import the WSDL document and its dependencies

Create an Application Concept

Abby has finished the development on the Eclipse workbench. In this step, she wants to create a concept to represent her application using the Web interface.

If the Web user interface is not already loaded, load it in a browser using `http://<host>:<port>/ServiceRegistry`. Enter your username and password to log in. Select the User perspective.

1. Create a concept for the application.

   a. In the top navigation, expand View and click Business Model Templates.

   b. Select the Application check box and click Create New Instance.

   c. Enter `Cell Phone Application v1.0` as the name.

   d. Enter `This is an application` as the description.

   e. Enter `http://www.cellphoneapp.com` as the namespace.

   f. Enter `1.0` as the version.

   g. Enter your name as the business owner as shown in Figure 4.39.

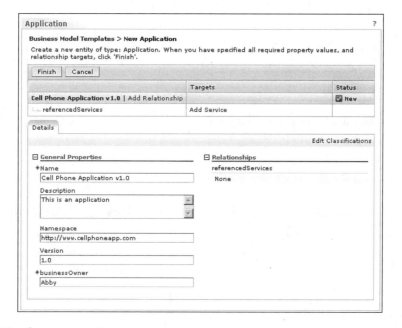

Figure 4.39   Create an application concept

2. Add the cellular service as the `referencedServices` relationship.

   a. In the Relationships section on top, click Add Service to add the cellular service as the referenced services. This means Abby's Cell Phone Application depends on the cellular service.

b. In the Add Target section, start typing `*Se` in the Name text field, and it will automatically become `*Service v1.0`.

c. Select Cellular Service v1.0 from the drop-down box as shown in Figure 4.40.

Figure 4.40   Searching for Cellular Service to be added as the relationship target

d. Click Add. The relationship is added, as shown in Figure 4.41.

Figure 4.41   The cellular service is added as the Cellular Application's relationship

3. Click Finish to complete the creation of the concept.

Tutorial 4.4: Update Existing Services as a Service Developer

In this tutorial, Tom will update the cellular service to version 2.0. He will perform an impact analysis and then deprecate the version 1.0 of the service. If notification is enabled and Abby has created a subscription, she will receive a notification on this change. Setting up the notifications is out of the scope of this article.

Impact Analysis

Tom wants to know the impact if he makes changes to `customer.xsd`. If the Web user interface is not already loaded, load it in a browser using `http://<host>:<port>/ServiceRegistry`. Enter the username and password to log in. Then select the User perspective.

1. Perform impact analysis on the `customer.xsd` file.

a. In the top navigation, expand View, Service Documents and click XSD Documents.

b. Click `customer.xsd`.

c. Click the Impact Analysis tab.

2. The impact analysis discovers what artifacts depend on `customer.xsd`.

   a. Select the Include entities that depend on this entity radio button.

   b. Change the dependency depth to 25.

   c. Hold the Shift key and highlight the following built-in relationships (2nd to 5th):

   - WSDL or XSD document to imported XSD document

   - WSDL or XSD document to included XSD document

   - WSDL or XSD document to redefined XSD document

   - WSDL document to imported WSDL document

   d. Highlight all custom relationships as shown in Figure 4.42.

Figure 4.42   Impact analysis on customer.xsd

3. Click Go. The result is as shown in Figure 4.43. You may change the orientation to Vertical to have the graph display vertically. If Tom changes `customer.xsd`, it affects

`cellularbo.xsd`, which affects `cellular.wsdl`. And that in turn affects both the Cellular Service and Cell Phone Application documents.

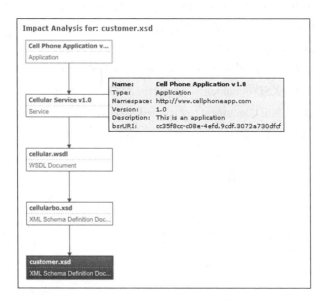

Figure 4.43   Impact analysis result

Load New Version of the Artifacts

Tom has decided nothing is out of the ordinary. Because he is going to keep the old service around, users to his service can slowly migrate to the new one. He has changed the artifacts files; he loads them into the Registry and Repository as version 2.0.

  1. Load a new version of the WSDL document and its dependencies.

    a. In the Web interface, expand Actions and click Load Documents.

    b. Click Browse and locate `chapter 4\tutorial 4.4\tutorial files\services_files\`
`services\cellular\cellular.wsdl` from the CD-ROM.

    c. Make sure the document type is WSDL.

    d. Enter `2.0` as the document version. Click OK.

    e. Click Replace to import the version 2.0 `cellularbo.xsd` instead of using the 1.0
`cellularbo.xsd` that is already in the repository.

    f. Click Browse and locate `chapter 4\tutorial 4.4\tutorial files\service_files\`
`services\cellular\cellularbo.xsd` from the CD-ROM.

    g. Enter `2.0` as the document version. Click OK.

h. Click Replace to import the version 2.0 `customer.xsd` instead of using the 1.0 `customer.xsd` that is already in the repository.

i. Click Browse and locate `chapter 4\tutorial 4.4\tutorial files\service_files\ lib\common\customer.xsd` from the CD-ROM.

j. Enter `2.0` as the document version. Click OK.

k. Click Finish. The documents should be loaded successfully, as illustrated in Figure 4.44.

Load Documents			? ▢
Documents Loaded Successfully			
The following documents have been loaded into the repository:			
Name	Description	Namespace	Version
cellularbo.xsd		http://MyModule/services/cellular	2.0
customer.xsd		http://MyModule/lib/common	2.0
cellular.wsdl		http://MyModule/services/cellular/cellular	2.0

Figure 4.44   Load cellular service version 2.0

Create a New Service Concept

Tom creates a new Service concept to represent version 2.0 of the service.

1. Create a new concept to represent version 2.0 of the cellular service.

a. Expand View in the top navigation and click Business Model Templates.

b. Select the Service check box and click Create New Instance.

c. Enter `Cellular Service v2.0` as the name.

d. Enter `Version 2.0 of Cellular Service` as the description.

e. Enter `http://www.cellular.com` as the namespace.

f. Enter `2.0` as the version.

g. Enter your name as the business owner.

2. Associate a WSDL document as the `providedInterface` relationship.

a. In the relationship section on top, click Add WSDL Document (Required) to add a WSDL document as the provided interface to this concept.

b. In the Add Target section, start typing `cell` in the Name text field. Two `cellular.wsdl` documents are found.

c. Select `cellular.wsdl` from the drop-down.

d. Click Search.

e. Select the `cellular.wsdl` check box, where the version is 2.0 as shown in Figure 4.45.

Figure 4.45   Select cellular.wsdl version 2.0 target

    f. Click Apply Selected Targets.

  3. Click Finish.

Optionally, you can move the service through the governance life cycle and associate it with a text description file.

Deprecate the Old Service Concept

  1. Locate the old service concept document.

    a. Expand View and click Concepts on the top navigation. All the concepts are listed as illustrated in Figure 4.46.

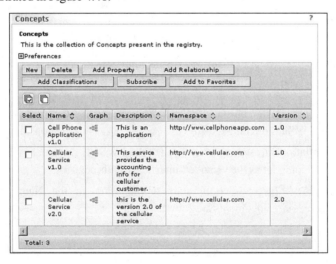

Figure 4.46   The Cellular Service version 1.0 concept

    b. Click Cellular Service v1.0.

  2. Move the Cellular Service v1.0 to the Retired state.

    a. Click the Governance tab. Currently Cellular Service v1.0 is at the Managed state.

    b. Select Retire from the Available State Transitions drop-down box.

    c. Click Transition to deprecate it, which will move it to the Retired state as shown in Figure 4.47.

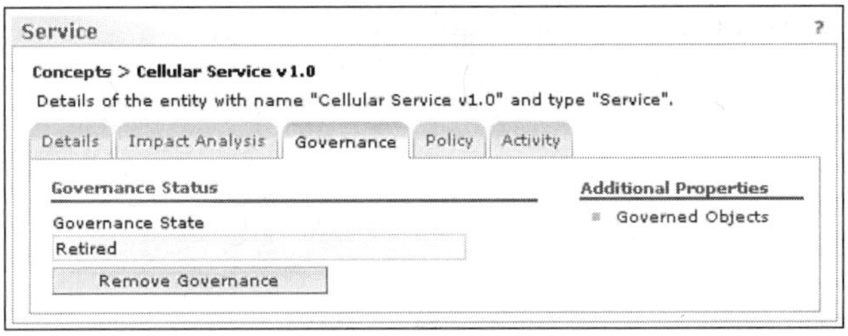

Figure 4.47   Deprecate the Cellular Service version 1.0

As Tom changes Cellular Service v1.0, if notification is set up, Abby receives notification from the system.

Summary

This chapter described how IBM WebSphere Service Registry and Repository governs services in development time. A key feature of the Registry and Repository that has not been extensively covered in this chapter is its capability to act as a runtime registry. In today's business world, many business models require a certain amount of dynamicity and fluidity. In some business situations, it might make sense to select services dynamically based on the information in the Registry and Repository such that the business model is more flexible. Furthermore, if the business is further along the SOA path in which documents in general require governance, the IBM WebSphere Service Registry and Repository, Advanced Lifecycle Edition would be a great choice.

    Tutorial Summary:

- Tutorial 4.1: Set Up the Registry and Repository as an Administrator
  - Set up the business model templates and a classification system
- Tutorial 4.2: Publish a New Service as a Service Developer
  - Publish artifacts into the Registry and Repository
  - Create a concept to represent the reusable service
  - Govern services with the governance life cycle
- Tutorial 4.3: Reuse Services as an Application Developer

- Search for reusable services
- Create a concept to represent the consumer application
- Import artifacts into the Eclipse workbench
- Create a relationship between the consumer application and the service entity
- Tutorial 4.4: Update Existing Services as a Service Developer
  - Perform impact analysis
  - Create a new service version
  - Deprecate the old version in the governance life cycle

Service Integration with IBM WebSphere Integration Developer and IBM WebSphere Process Server

Product Overview

WebSphere Integration Developer is an Eclipse-based development tool that builds on top of Rational Application Developer. WebSphere Integration Developer enables companies to build flexible Service-Oriented Architecture (SOA) solutions by assembling services. The concept for SOA is to make it easy for companies to create business processes by assembling existing or new services together. A *service* is a software function that has a componentized structure that can be used as a building block for creating composite business applications. In general, building a SOA solution encompasses both the creation and the assembly of services. WebSphere Integration Developer can do both. Some examples of services are business processes, business rules, human tasks, business state machines, and mediation flows in WebSphere Enterprise Service Bus (WESB). Business processes can be used to choreograph and assemble services to create new composite business applications.

WebSphere Integration Developer is designed to be used by integration specialists. The job of an integration specialist is to integrate existing services to create new IT solutions to meet the ever-changing business needs. This user does not have to be a Java, Web Services Description Language (WSDL), or XML Schema Definition (XSD) expert. This person focuses on integrating applications, automating systems, and providing new channels for customers. Figure 5.1 illustrates the relationship between the skill set of an integration specialist and other user roles.

An integration specialist takes over where a business analyst leaves off, developing the integration application, testing it, and debugging it. This person uses services to assemble solutions in WebSphere Integration Developer. Some examples of services include Web Services and Service Component Architecture (SCA) services. If you are already familiar with Web services, you know that Java classes, Enterprise JavaBeans (EJBs), and Microsoft .NET code can be made into Web services. SCA gives you a model to define interfaces, implementations, and references that are technology independent.

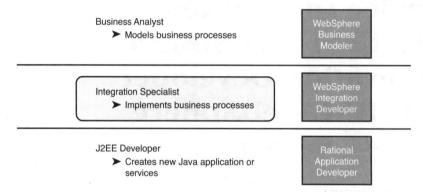

Figure 5.1   The relationship between the skill set of an integration specialist and other user roles

As mentioned previously, there are two aspects of usage in WebSphere Integration Developer. The first aspect is to create individual services that can be reused as building blocks. The second aspect is to create new business processes by assembling the service building blocks, which may or may not have originated from the WebSphere Integration Developer tooling.

Service implementation types are the implementations that you can create individual services with. There are many service implementation types that you can create services with. Some examples of service implementation types are business processes, business rules, business state machines, and human tasks. All service implementation types have a common characteristic; they are all described using an open standard WSDL interface.

An example of a WSDL interface file is shown in Figure 5.2. In this example, the operation is named `operation1` and is two-way. A two-way operation always has an input and an output message. Both the input and output message use a *business object* named `Employee` as their type.

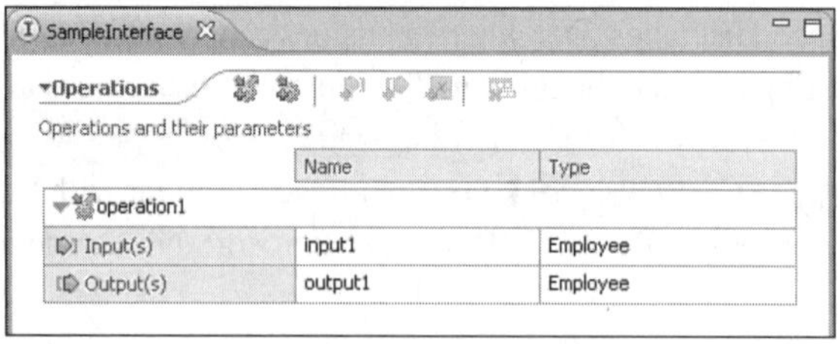

	Name	Type
▼ operation1		
▷ Input(s)	input1	Employee
▷ Output(s)	output1	Employee

Figure 5.2   Sample WSDL interface

PC world/Risk's orchestration service uses or has lot of BOs expressed/modeled in XSD's.

A *business object* is an object that captures business data. In WebSphere Integration Developer, business objects capture and exchange data between service implementation types. Figure 5.3 shows an example of a business object named Employee. It has four fields named empName, empRating, empBonus, and empStartDate. Each field has a type defined, which are string, int, double, and date respectively.

Figure 5.3 Sample business object

All artifacts created in the tooling are stored in modules. A *module* is basically a project where you store all your artifacts. You can also use a *library* to store some of your common artifacts that might be shared across several modules. A module that has a dependency on a library can access all the artifacts that are stored in the library.

A project might involve multiple library projects and modules. To organize them better, you can use an *integration solution* project to encapsulate them. This kind of project is mainly for organizing, which makes solution-related activities such as testing, working with a team environment, exporting, and importing much easier. In addition, every integration solution project comes with an automatically generated integration solution diagram. It shows the relationship between the different modules that are in the solution. Figure 5.4 displays a solution diagram, called ManufacturerSolution, that contains a ManufacturerSolution_Module calling out to a Web service.

When you are creating a module in the tooling, you are actually creating a Java 2, Enterprise Edition (J2EE) application. A module is packaged and deployed to the WebSphere Process Server as an Enterprise Archive (EAR) file. A library is simply copied to all dependent modules as a utility jar when deployed to a server. WebSphere Integration Developer comes with an embedded WebSphere Process Server (WPS) that allows you to unit-test right on the workbench.

Let's briefly go through the different service implementation types that you will build in this tutorial:

- **Business Processes** created in the tooling are based on an open-standard language named Business Process Execution Language (BPEL) for Web Services. BPEL is a language that automates business processes. IBM provides an IBM extension to the BPEL standard that provides more functionality, such as Java Snippet.

- **Human Task** component represents a task that a user needs to perform. A human task can be inserted into a long-running business process. The business process suspends execution until the human task is completed. The user uses the WebSphere Business Process

Choreographer Explorer to work on and complete the task, at which point, the business process continues its execution.

Figure 5.4   An example of an integration solution diagram

In the SCA, service implementation types expose their functions as services through interfaces. These service implementation types are known as *service components*. Service components can be wired to each other in an *assembly diagram*. Each *module* contains an assembly diagram that allows the interface of a *service component* to be exposed using open standards, such as Java or WSDL. In addition, it can be used to define the dependencies between different components by wiring the service components together in the assembly diagram.

Figure 5.5 shows a simple assembly diagram where two components are wired to each other. The ManufacturerProcess component has a dependency on the Supplier_Service_Import component.

Figure 5.5   Sample assembly diagram

In reality, a business integration solution will be much more complex than what you see in Figure 5.5. Not only can a component invoke another SCA component, it can invoke a regular Web service or even an EJB. Furthermore, it can expose itself as a Web service that can be used in other applications. In this tutorial, you will get a chance to create a business process by assembling from existing services.

After the business integration solution is developed in WebSphere Integration Developer, it can be deployed to a WebSphere Process Server. WebSphere Process Server, which is based on WebSphere Application Server, can execute standard-based and integration-based applications in a SOA environment. WebSphere Integration Developer contains an integrated WebSphere Process Server for testing. This tutorial explores some of the features of WebSphere Process Server.

Because WebSphere Process Server builds on top of WebSphere Application Server, all the basic server functions, such as installing and administrating an EAR, are identical to WebSphere Application Server. Similar to the WebSphere Application Server, WebSphere Process Server has a profile. A profile can be configured differently depending on the application deployed. By default, the profile directory on a standalone server is `<WAS_INSTALL>\ProcServer\profiles\ProcSrv01\`.

How Do They Support SOA?

Business Process Management (BPM) helps organizations streamline their business processes such that they are more capable of responding to rapid market change. It allows humans, application, and information to be integrated into business processes. BPM supports the notions to monitor, control, and continuously improve the business process operations. WebSphere Integration Developer allows organizations to quickly and easily bring people, applications, and information together to form streamlined business processes.

BPM with SOA is about enabling companies to create new business processes by assembling existing services together. Each of these services is like a building block that allows easy creation of composite business applications. WebSphere Integration Developer allows users to create the building blocks as well as assemble them. The building blocks can be regular Web services, business processes, business rules, business state machines, and so on. Assembling can be done using a business process and assembly diagram.

A major competency of WebSphere Integration Developer is assembling business services to create integration solutions that are SOA-based. In every business integration solution, there will be Business Process Choreographer, an enterprise service bus (ESB), or both. The major value proposition of WebSphere Process Server and WebSphere Integration Developer is that they provide business integration solutions with streamlined and efficient business processes and enhance communications between business partners and services with the ESB support.

WebSphere Integration Developer allows you to build SOA-based business integration solutions easily and quickly using the graphical interfaces. In addition, service implementation types can be exposed as SCA components that act as building blocks for other integration applications. The business integration solutions developed in WebSphere Integration Developer can be deployed to WebSphere Process Server. WebSphere Process Server supports the deployment of business processes and ESB mediation flows. A process that is deployed to the WebSphere Process Server can communicate with other parts of the SOA infrastructure. For instance, it can talk to the WebSphere Business Services Fabric to obtain the latest endpoint for dynamic endpoint selection. An ESB mediation flow can talk to WebSphere Service Registry and Repository for the latest metadata. In addition, business processes that are deployed can be made sharable and be put in the WebSphere Service Registry and Repository. This can help promote reusability across the organization.

Tutorial Overview

In this chapter you will use existing services to create a new business process by assembling them together.

The scenario features an ordering process of a car manufacturing company. When the car parts are low in supply, the ordering process for the part kicks in. It places an order to an external supplier, which returns the total price of the order. Next, the business process notifies the shipping personnel to pick up the items. The process has a response detailing the cost of the parts and the shipping status.

In this tutorial, you create a simple business process. BPEL business processes as well as other components in WebSphere Integration Developer are described by a WSDL interface.

Figure 5.6 shows a high-level picture of what we are going to build in this tutorial. The Manufacturer Ordering Process is a business process that is described by a Web Services Description Language (WSDL) interface, which has one input and one output element. Each of these elements is a business object. The business process is created by assembling services. In this sample, we will be using only one Web service. The business process calls the Web service using an invoke activity node through the WSDL interface file of the Web service. The Web service interface file also takes in a business object as input and returns the price in string as output. Although we are calling only one Web service in this example, the idea is similar for additional services. After the external service is invoked, the shipping personnel are notified using a human task component. A human task component represents a task that needs to be performed by a human. A human task component is also described by a WSDL interface. It can be invoked using the invoke node as an external component, similar to the way the Supplier's Web service is invoked, or it can be invoked using an inlined human task node in the BPEL palette. An inlined human task is embedded inside the BPEL business process. It can have access to the context information of the process, and it does not need to be wired in the assembly diagram. However, an inlined human task cannot be used if the human task component is not in the same module as the business process. In that case, an invoke node should be used. Using the invoke node to invoke a human task component provides more flexibility. It allows the human task component to be swapped in and out easily through the assembly diagram. In the tutorial, an inlined human task will be used.

The scenario is separated into three tutorials:

> Tutorial 5.1: Create a Business Process

> Tutorial 5.2: Assemble and Execute the Module

> Tutorial 5.3: Deploy to a WebSphere Process Server

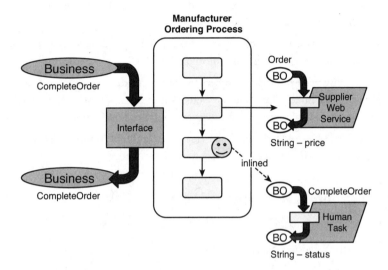

Figure 5.6   Sample ordering business process

System Requirements

The tutorial has been developed with the following products and environments.

- WebSphere Integration Developer v6.2 with Integrated WebSphere Process Server v6.2 is installed.
- WebSphere Process Server v6.2.

What Is Included in the CD-ROM?

The attached CD-ROM contains all tutorial solutions, which are Project Interchange files that can be imported into WebSphere Integration Developer and run. In addition, the CD-ROM includes videos that illustrate the tutorials step by step.

- **tutorial 5.1/tutorial files/SupplierService_WID62_V4.zip**—A project interchange file that contains initial setup files for the Supplier Web Service for Tutorial 5.1. To import it to WebSphere Integration Developer, select File, Import from the workbench menu bar. Expand Other and select Project Interchange. Click Next, and then follow the wizard's instructions.
- **tutorial 5.1/solution/ManufacturerSolution_V1.zip**—A project interchange file that contains a completed solution for Tutorial 5.1. To import it to WebSphere Integration Developer, select File, Import from the workbench menu bar. Expand Other and select Project Interchange. Click Next, and then follow the wizard's instructions.

- **tutorial 5.2/solution/ManufacturerSolution_ModuleApp.ear and SupplierService EAR.ear**—EAR files that are exported from the WebSphere Integration Developer after Tutorial 5.1 and 5.2 are completed.

- **tutorial 5.2/solution/ManufacturerSolution_V2.zip**—A project interchange file that contains a completed solution for Tutorial 5.1 and 5.2.

- **tutorial 5.3/tutorial files/ManufacturerSolution_ModuleApp.ear and SupplierService EAR.ear**—Essentially the same file as the Tutorial 5.2 solution. These EAR files can be installed on the WebSphere Process Server using the administrative console.

- **video**—The video folder contains the video files for all the tutorials discussed in this chapter. Open the HTML file in any browser to watch the video.

Tutorial 5.1: Create a Business Process

1. Start WebSphere Integration Developer if it's not already started.

   a. From the Windows Start menu, select All Programs, IBM WebSphere Integration Developer, IBM WebSphere Integration Developer V6.2, WebSphere Integration Developer V6.2.

   b. A dialog appears asking for the workspace directory. Just click OK to accept the default one.

   c. The first page is the Welcome page. Click Go to the Business Integration perspective, and you will be in the Business Integration perspective.

Import Existing Web Services to Workbench

This is a prerequisite step for the tutorial. Import the project interchange file to your workbench. The project interchange file contains the Supplier Web service.

1. Import an existing Web service to the workbench.

   a. From the workbench, select File, Import, Expand Other, Project Interchange, Next.

   b. Browse for the SupplierService_WID62_V4.zip from the attached CD (chapter 5/tutorial 5.1/tutorial files) and select all projects: SupplierServiceEAR and SupplierService.

   c. Click Finish. You will see the SupplierService and the SupplierServiceEAR projects imported into the workbench as shown in Figure 5.7.

Create an Integration Solution with a Library and a Module

Create an integration solution named ManufacturerSolution. In the Creation Wizard, you can also choose to create a library project and a module project that are referenced by the solution project.

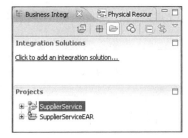

Figure 5.7 Business Integration view for the SupplierService projects

1. Create an integration solution with library and module projects.

   a. From the workbench, select File, New, Integration Solution.

   b. Enter `ManufacturerSolution` as the solution name. Click Next.

   c. Check both the Module Name and Library Name check boxes to create a new module and library with the default names as shown in Figure 5.8. This wizard page allows you to create a new module and library and select any existing projects to be part of the integration solution.

Figure 5.8 Creating a new integration solution project and its related module and library

d. Click Finish and you will see the solution project created as shown in Figure 5.9.

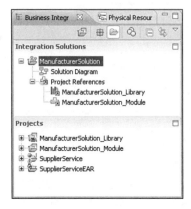

Figure 5.9   ManufacturerSolution project and its related module and library projects

Copy Interface Files from Existing Web Service

The business process that we are creating is being assembled from existing Web services. It will invoke an external Web service. To invoke an external Web service, the WSDL file for that Web service needs to be duplicated in the library or the module such that the business process can access it. In this case, we will copy the WSDL file into the library because the module also is visible to files that reside in the library.

1. Copy `Order.xsd` and `SupplierService.wsdl` into the `ManufacturerSolution_Library` project.

   a. Expand the project `SupplierService`, `WebContent`, `WEB-INF`, `wsdl`.

   b. Select both `Order.xsd` and `SupplierService.wsdl`.

   c. Click Edit, Copy.

   d. Select `ManufacturerSolution_Library`.

   e. Click Edit, Paste. See Figure 5.10.

   The external Web service has a WSDL file named `SupplierService.wsdl`. Its input uses a business object named `Order`, and its output is a string. The WSDL interface file for the business process will be using another business object named `CompleteOrder` that we will create in the next step. The `CompleteOrder` business object encapsulates the `Order` business object and a few more properties.

Create a Business Object

1. Create a new business object named `CompleteOrder`. The business object will be in the library project because it can be shared among multiple modules.

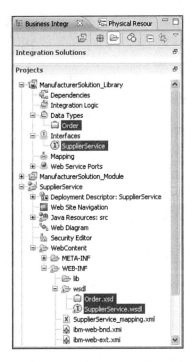

Figure 5.10   Copying XSD and WSDL files into a module project

a. In the Business Integration perspective under the Projects section, right-click `ManufacturerSolution_Library`. Click New, Business Object as shown in Figure 5.11.

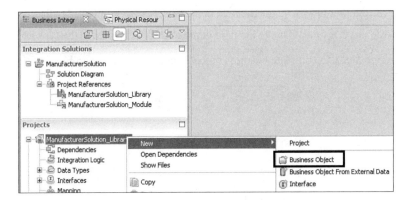

Figure 5.11   New Business Object menu item

b. Enter `CompleteOrder` as the name. Click Finish as shown in Figure 5.12.

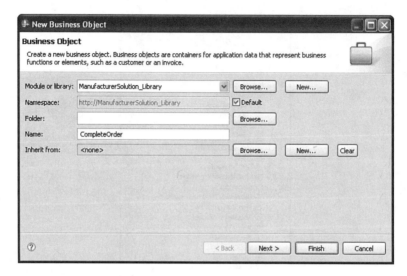

Figure 5.12 New Business Object Wizard

2. Add some fields to the business object.

   a. In the business object editor, right-click the business object and click Add Field.

   b. Enter Date as the field's name, and change the type to date.

   c. Add another field. Change the field name to EmployeeID and leave the type as string.

   d. Add another field. Change the field name to Order and change the type to Order, which can be found at the end of the drop-down list. This is the Order business object that comes from the external Web service.

   e. Add another field. Change the field name to TotalCost and change the type to double.

   f. Add another field. Change the field name to Status and leave the type as string.

3. Save the file. The complete business object should be as shown in Figure 5.13.

Figure 5.13 CompleteOrder business object

Create a WSDL Interface File for the Business Process

In this step, we will create a WSDL interface file for the business process. A business process and all other components in WebSphere Integration Developer are described by WSDL interface files. The interface for the business process will have one input and one output, which are of CompleteOrder type.

1. Create a new WSDL interface named ManufacturerProcessInterface for the business process.

   a. Right-click ManufacturerSolution_Library and click New, Interface.

   b. Enter ManufacturerProcessInterface as the name and click Finish as shown in Figure 5.14.

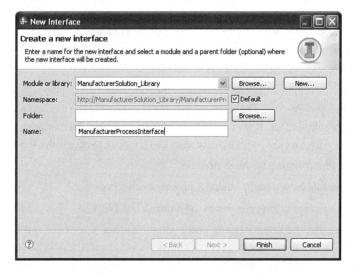

Figure 5.14   New Interface Wizard for ManufacturerProcessInterface

2. Create a new operation in the WSDL file.

   a. In the interface editor, click Add Request Response Operation.

   b. Change the operation name from operation1 to placeOrder.

   c. Change the input name from input1 to completeorder_input.

   d. Select CompleteOrder as the type for the input. The CompleteOrder business object is located at the end of the Type drop-down list.

   e. Change the output name from output1 to completeorder_output.

   f. Select CompleteOrder as the type for the output.

3. Save the file. Figure 5.15 displays the ManufacturerProcessInterface editor.

Figure 5.15   ManufacturerProcess interface editor

Create a Business Process

After we have created an interface file, we will create a business process named `ManufacturerProcess`. This business process will use the interface that was created in the previous step. It will have an invoke activity that calls out to an external Web service, followed by a human task activity that requires human interactions. There are also two other nodes in the business process that are for supporting purposes, such as copying and assigning variables.

1. In the Business Integration perspective, right-click `ManufacturerSolution_Module`. Click New, Business Process. The business process is created in the module project because it's not a sharable artifact. If you need to invoke this process from another module, you can expose it using an `Export` node and use an `Import` node to access the WSDL interface.

2. Create a long-running business process.

    a. Ensure that New default business process is checked.

    b. Enter `ManufacturerProcess` as the name. Click Next.

    c. Ensure that the Long-running process radio button is selected and the check box for Use WebSphere Process Server extensions is selected. Click Next. A long-running process and WebSphere Process Server extensions are needed to run a human task.

3. Use an existing WSDL file as the business process's interface.

    a. Select the Select an interface radio button.

    b. Click Browse to browse for the `ManufacturerProcessInterface` interface. Click OK.

4. Click Finish. Figure 5.16 displays the completed New Business Process wizard.

The new business process will look like Figure 5.17. Let's examine it a little bit. For each input and output messages in the WSDL interface, the business process contains a corresponding `Receive` and `Reply` node. The `Receive` node will receive the input message, and the `Reply` node will reply with an output message.

The variable `completeorder_input` is of type `CompleteOrder`, and it is used as an input message in the Receive node. The variable `completeorder_output` is also of type `CompleteOrder`, and it is used by the `Reply` node as the output message. If you click on the `Receive` or the `Reply` node and look at the Details tab in the Properties view, you can see the variable name and type.

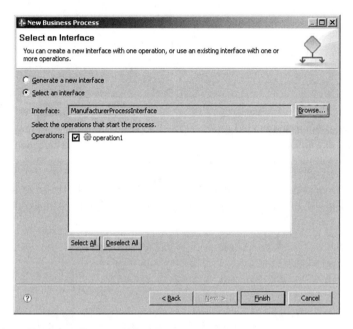

Figure 5.16   New Business Process Wizard

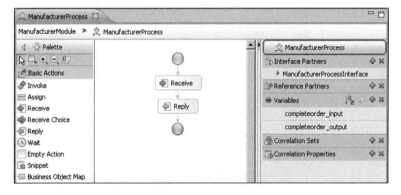

Figure 5.17   ManufacturerProcess business process

When someone invokes this business process, it needs to be provided with an input message of `CompleteOrder` type. This input will be received by the `Receive` node and is placed into the `completeorder_input` variable. When the business process completes its operation, the caller receives output of `CompleteOrder` type, where its value is provided by the `completeorder_output` variable.

Add a New Variable

Create a variable named `order` of `Order` type. This variable is used as the input to the external Web service.

1. In the business process editor, click Add a global variable to add a new variable. A dialog appears.

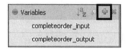

Figure 5.18   Add global variable button

2. Change the variable name to order.
3. Select Order as the matching data types as shown in Figure 5.19. To search for it, you can type o in the Filter by Type, Namespace, or File text field. Then click OK.

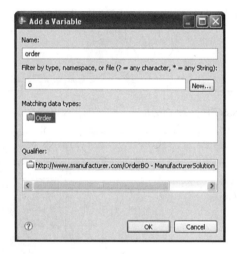

Figure 5.19   Create a New Variable Wizard

The order variable is created in the Variables section, as seen in Figure 5.20.

Figure 5.20   The order variable is created

Add an Assign Node

An Assign node is to assign the value from one variable to another. It is flexible enough to handle multiple variable assignments. The order variable created in the previous step will be used as input to the external Web service. However, before using the variable, we must assign some values to it. We can do that using an `Assign` node.

1. Add an `Assign` node to the business process.

   a. In the left palette of the business process editor, expand the Basic Actions section and select the `Assign` activity node as seen in Figure 5.21.

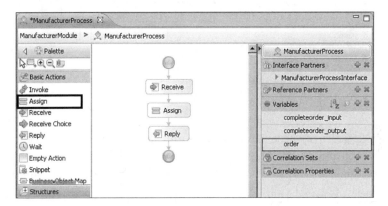

Figure 5.21 Assign node in palette

   b. Drop the node between the `Receive` and `Reply` activity nodes.

2. We want to assign from the `completeorder_input` Order variable to the `order` variable.

   a. In the properties view, switch to the Details tab.

   b. In the Assign From column, click Select From. Expand `completeorder_input` and select `Order : Order` as shown in Figure 5.22.

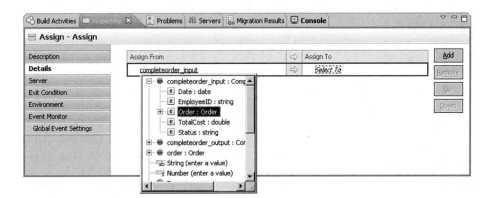

Figure 5.22 Select Assign From from the Assign Detail page

c. In the Assign To column, click Assign To. Select `order : Order`. This action assigns the `Order` element within the `completeorder_input` variable into the `order` variable as displayed in Figure 5.23.

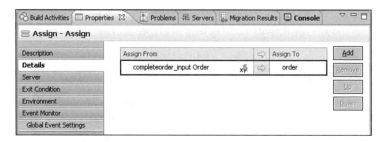

Figure 5.23   Assign activity's properties details

3. An `Assign` activity node allows multiple assignments of unrelated variables. Add a new assignment to copy the `completeorder_input` variable directly to the `completeorder_output` variable such that the original `CompleteOrder` information is preserved.

a. Click Add to add another assignment row.

b. In the Assign From column, click Select From. Select `completeorder_input`.

c. In the Assign To column, click Select To. Then select `completeorder_output`. The `Assign` activity node instantiates the `completeorder_output` variable and copies the contents of the `completeorder_input` variable. The complete detail page is shown in Figure 5.24.

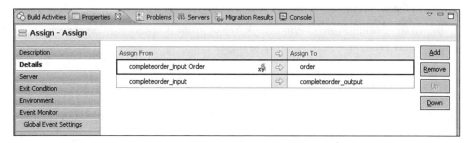

Figure 5.24   The completed Assign activity's properties details

4. Save the file.

Add an Invoke Node

An invoke node invokes external components such as external Web services, SCA components, Java Message Service (JMS) components, and so on. In this example, you will invoke an external Web service named `Supplier Web Service`. The Web service takes an input of type `Order` and returns a price in the type of `string`.

1. Add an `Invoke` activity node and name it `Place Order to Supplier`.

   a. In the left palette of the business process editor, expand the Basic Actions section and select the `Invoke` activity node.

   b. Drop the node between the `Assign` and `Reply` activity nodes.

   c. Change the activity name to `Place Order to Supplier` as shown in Figure 5.25.

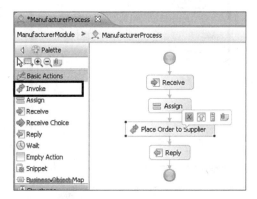

Figure 5.25   Adding an Invoke activity node

2. Create a reference partner named `Supplier` using the `SupplierService` interface.

   a. In the right toolbar, click the Add a Reference Partner icon to add a reference partner. A reference partner needs to be created when you send a message to a partner to invoke it.

   b. Change the name to `Supplier`.

   c. Select `SupplierService` as the matching interfaces. Then click OK as seen in Figure 5.26.

3. Set the invoke node to use the supplier as the partner.

   a. Select the `Place Order to Supplier` invoke node. In the Properties view, switch to the Details tab.

   b. Click Browse to browse the partner, and select Supplier.

4. Set the variables in the invoke node that are used to pass messages from the business process to the partner.

   a. Make sure the Use data type variables mapping check box is checked.

   b. Select `order : Order` as the Read from Variable of the Input(s) row.

   c. Select New as the Store into Variable of the Output(s) row.

   d. Enter `price_string` as the variable name as shown in Figure 5.27. Then click OK. This variable will be created with a `string` type by default and used as the output variable for the `Supplier` invoke node.

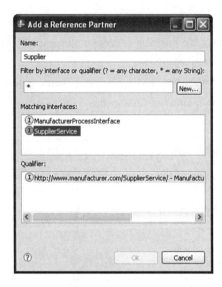

Figure 5.26   Creating a new reference partner

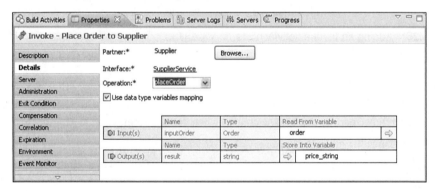

Figure 5.27   Adding an Invoke activity node

Add a Human Task Activity

In the previous step, we created an `Invoke` activity node to place an order to an external supplier. After the order is placed, the process notifies shipping personnel to pick up the order. This can be expressed as a human task. A human task is also described by a WSDL interface file. Therefore, we must first create an interface file. This interface will have `CompleteOrder` as the input type and `string` as the output type.

Create an interface named `ReceiveOrderHumanInterface`:

1. Create a new interface named `ReceiveOrderHumanInterface`.

    a. From the workbench, right-click the `ManufacturerSolution_Library`. Click New, Interface.

    b. Enter `ReceiveOrderHumanInterface` as the name and click Finish.

2. Add a request response operation with an input and output variable.

   a. In the interface editor, click Add Request Response Operation.

   b. Change the operation name from `operation1` to `receiveOrder`.

   c. Change the input name from `input1` to `completeorder` and select `CompleteOrder` as the type.

   d. Change the output name from `output1` to `status`, and select `string` as the type.

3. Save the file. The completed interface is as shown in Figure 5.28.

Figure 5.28   Human task interface file

4. Add the human task activity to the business process.

   a. Switch back to the `ManufacturerProcess` of the business process editor. In the left palette, expand `Human Workflow` section and select the human task activity node.

   b. Drop it between the `Place Order to Supplier` invoke node and the `Reply` node, and a dialog will appear.

   c. In the Add a Human Task dialog, change the name to `Receive Order`.

   d. Select `ReceiveOrderHumanInterface` as shown in Figure 5.29 and click OK.

5. The `ReceiveOrder` human task component is created automatically, and its editor will be loaded by default. This human task is inlined, meaning that it is embedded within the business process.

6. Set the input and output variables in the `Receive Order` human task node. These variables are used to communicate between the business process and the human task.

   a. Switch back to the `ManufacturerProcess` business process editor.

   b. Select the `Receive Order` human task node. In the properties view, switch to the Details tab.

   c. Select the Use Data Type Variables Mapping check box.

   d. Select the `completeorder_input : CompleteOrder` variable as the Read From Variable of the Input(s) row.

   e. Select New as the Store into Variable of the Output(s) row.

Figure 5.29 Add a Human Task dialog

f. Enter `receive_status_string` as the variable name as shown in Figure 5.30. Click OK. This variable will be created with a `string` type by default.

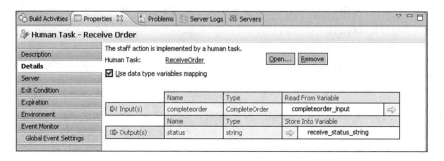

Figure 5.30 Adding a human task activity node

g. Save the file.

Add Visual Snippet Logic

A visual snippet is an activity node that allows you to do Java coding visually. It has built-in nodes that you can drag and drop and wire to perform specific Java functions. In this step, we will convert the `price_string` variable from a `string` to a `double` and assign it to the `completeorder_output` variable. The external Web service returns the price of the order in a `string` format. However, the `completeorder_output.TotalCost` variable is a `double` type;

therefore, a conversion is required. The visual snippet also assigns the `receive_status_string` to the status of the `completeorder_output` variable.

1. Add a snippet to the business process.

    a. In the left palette of the business process editor, expand the Basic Actions section. Scroll down by clicking on the down arrow, and select the `Snippet` activity node.

    b. Drop it between the `Receive Order` human task node and the `Reply` node.

    c. Change the name to `Setting Response Variable` as seen in Figure 5.31.

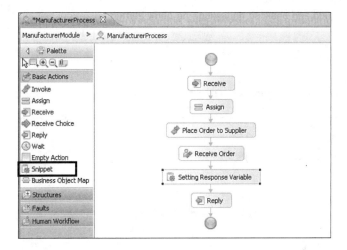

Figure 5.31 Adding Snippet activity node

2. Add an expression.

    a. In the properties view's Details tab, select `Expression` from the left palette.

    b. Drop it anywhere in the canvas.

    c. Click inside the `Expression` node and select `price_string` as shown in Figure 5.32.

3. Add another `Expression` node.

    a. Select `Expression` from the left palette and drop it on the canvas.

    b. Click inside the `Expression` node, expand `completeorder_output`, and select `TotalCost` as shown in Figure 5.33.

4. Add a `Standard` node. The `Standard` node provides many built-in functions such as printing to a log file or converting between different formats.

    a. Select `Standard` from the palette. A window labeled Add a Standard Visual Snippet appears.

    b. Expand the `converter` folder and select `convert string to double` as seen in Figure 5.34. Click OK.

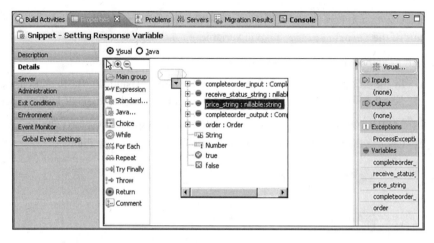

Figure 5.32 Select price_string as the expression

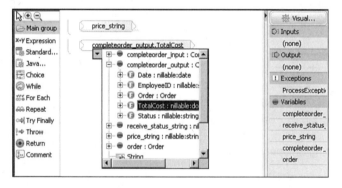

Figure 5.33 Select Price as the expression

   c. Drop the snippet anywhere onto the canvas as shown in Figure 5.35.

5. Connect the nodes.

   a. Connect the output of the `price_string` node to the input of the `convert string to double` node.

   b. Connect the output of the `convert string to double` node to the input of the `Completeorder_output.TotalCost` node as displayed Figure 5.36. This converts the `price_string` from a string to a double and puts the value in `completeorder_output.TotalCost`.

The next steps assign the `receive_status_string` to `completeorder_output.Status`. The visual snippet can perform multiple logical steps sequentially.

1. Add an expression for `receive_status_string`.

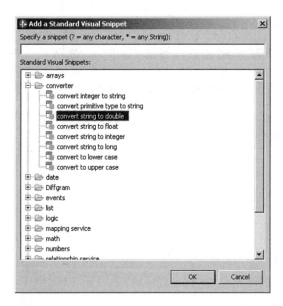

Figure 5.34   Select a standard visual snippet

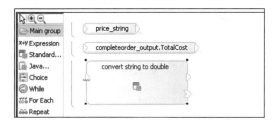

Figure 5.35   Adding a Convert String to Double visual snippet

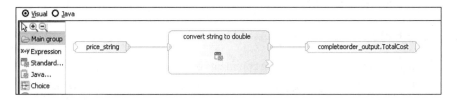

Figure 5.36   Connect the nodes in the visual snippet

 a. Select `Expression` from the left palette and drop it on the canvas.

 b. Click inside the `Expression` node and select `receive_status_string`.

2. Add another expression for `completeorder_output.Status`.

 a. Select `Expression` from the left palette and drop it on the canvas.

      b. Click inside the `Expression` node, expand `completeorder_output`, and select Status.

    3. Connect the output of `receive_status_string` to the input of `completeorder_output`. `Status`.

    4. Save the file. The complete business process is shown in Figure 5.37.

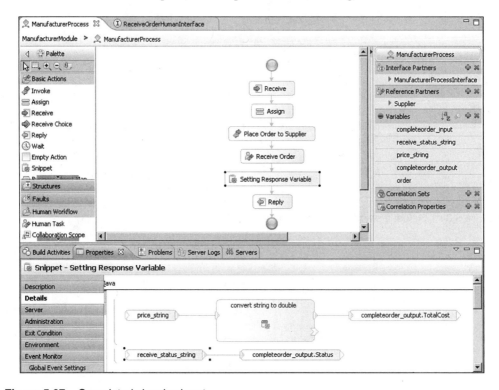

Figure 5.37   Completed visual snippet

Add Sticky Notes

    1. Sticky notes are handy for adding comments or to-dos.

      a. In the ManufacturerProcess editor, select Note on the left palette as shown in Figure 5.38. Drop it anywhere on the canvas.

Figure 5.38   The Note menu in the business process editor's palette

    b. Hover over the right edge of the note; there is an orange handle for association. Click the orange handle and connect it with the `Receive` node. We are making a note about the `Receive` node.

    c. Enter `TODO: write a description about the Receive node.` You might have to press Enter to break the sentence into two lines.

    d. Save all the changes.

  2. Switch to the Tasks view to see the to-do task. If the Tasks view is not opened, click Window from the workbench. Click Show View, Tasks as shown in Figure 5.39. Make sure all the changes have been saved to see the to-do task in the view.

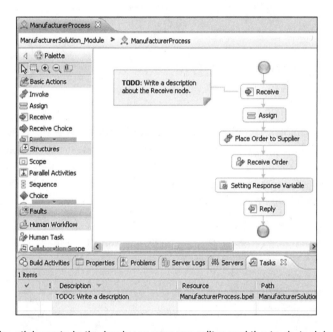

Figure 5.39   The sticky note in the business process editor and the to-do task in the task view

Tutorial 5.2: Assemble and Execute the Module

In Tutorial 5.1, we created a BPEL business process that invokes the Web service of an external supplier and notifies the shipping personnel to pick up the order through a human task. In this tutorial, we deploy the module and test it.

Assembling in the Assembly Diagram

The business process is now completed. Before you can execute the business process, you need to specify it and the external Web service in the Assembly diagram. In this step, the business process and the external Web service are assembled for deployment.

1. In the Business Integration view, expand the `ManufacturerSolution_Module` folder. Double-click Assembly Diagram. Right now the editor is completely empty; you need to add the `ManufacturerProcess` component into the editor.

2. Expand `ManufacturerSolution_Module`, `Integration   Logic`, `Processes`. Select `ManufacturerProcess` and drag it onto the assembly editor. Figure 5.40 shows that the ManufacturerProcess node is dragged into an assembly diagram.

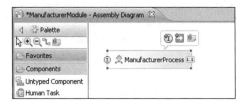

Figure 5.40   Adding the ManufacturerProcess component to the assembly diagram

3. Add an `Import` node.

   a. In the assembly diagram editor, expand the Components section and select Import on the left palette. Drop it on the canvas. The `Import` node brings the external service into the module for the `ManufacturerProcess` to use. On the other hand, an `Export` node exposes a component to the outside world for both WebSphere Process Server and non-WebSphere Process Server to use.

   b. Change the name to `Supplier_Service_Import`.

   c. Click Add Interface on the floating toolbar, as shown in Figure 5.41.

Figure 5.41   Adding an interface to the import

   d. Select `SupplierService` and click OK.

4. Connect the `ManufacturerProcess` component to the `Supplier_Service_Import` node. Hover the mouse over the right connection point of the `ManufacturerProcess` and connect it to `Supplier_Service_Import`.

5. Generate the Web Service Binding for the Import node.

   a. Right-click the Supplier_Service_Import node and click Generate Binding, Web Service Binding. A Web Service Import Details window should appear.

   b. Click Browse to use an existing Web service port, and select SupplierServiceSOAP as shown in Figure 5.42. Click OK.

Figure 5.42 Import Details Wizard

   c. Click OK to take the default SOAP 1.1/ HTTP using JAX-RPC transport.

   d. Click OK again.

6. Save the file. The completed assembly diagram is shown in Figure 5.43.

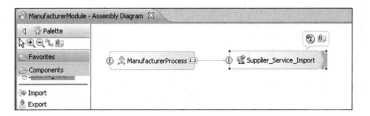

Figure 5.43 Completed assembly diagram

Exploring the Integrated Solution Diagram

An integrated solution diagram displays the relationships between the related projects within an integrated solution.

1. In the Business Integration view, expand ManufacturerSolution in the Integration Solutions view.

2. Open the Solution Diagram file by double-clicking it. The solution diagram is opened in the editor as shown in Figure 5.44.

Figure 5.44 The solution diagram in the Integration Solutions view

3. Double-click on the right connect point to see the external Web service as seen in Figure 5.45.

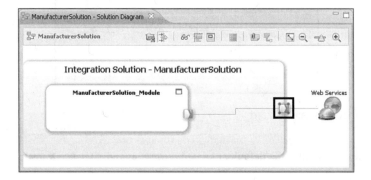

Figure 5.45 The solution diagram for ManufacturerSolution

4. You can see the content of the ManufacturerSolution_Module. Click the top-right icon Expand Module to Show Content (See Figure 5.46). In addition, you may hover over each entity to see the details. Also try out the buttons on the top toolbars to zoom in and zoom out.

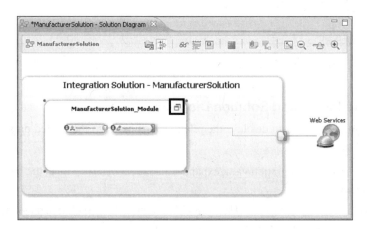

Figure 5.46 Expand module to show the content

5. Save the file and close the editor.

Deploy the Module Application to the Server

In this step, we will run the business process on the embedded WebSphere Process Server. By default, the WebSphere Process Server is already added to the Servers view. You need to add the project to the server.

1. Go to the Servers view. Right-click WebSphere Process Server v6.2 at localhost and click Start.

2. Wait until the server is started.

3. Right-click WebSphere Process Server v6.2 at localhost and click Add and Remove Projects as shown in Figure 5.47.

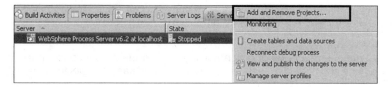

Figure 5.47 Add and remove projects

4. Click Add All to add all the available projects to the configured projects as shown in Figure 5.48. Then click Finish. You should see a progress bar on the bottom right publishing the project.

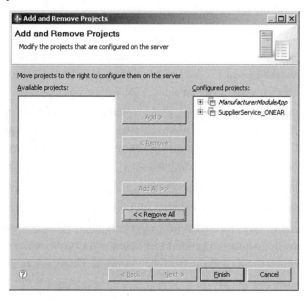

Figure 5.48 Add and Remove Projects Wizard

  5. Click OK to dismiss the dialog, and wait until the publishing is complete.

Run the Business Process

After adding the projects to the server, you can execute the BPEL business process using either the Business Process Choreographer Explorer or the Test Component framework. In this tutorial, we will run the BPEL process using the Test Component framework and the Business Process Choreographer Explorer to complete the human task activity. One of the major differences between the Business Process Choreographer Explorer and the Test Component is that the Business Process Choreographer Explorer can only run BPEL processes and work on the human tasks. In contrast, the Test Component framework can run all the SCA service components.

  1. Select Test Module in the assembly diagram to test the business process.

  a. In the assembly diagram, right-click the canvas and click Test Module. The test component editor should appear. Make sure that Component is set to `ManufacturerProcess`.

NOTE Do not select a node and right-click. Click on the empty space in the canvas. If you select a node and right-click, you will test only that node and not the entire module.

---

  b. Enter `0001` as the `ItemID` and `5` as the quantity. Click Continue on the left side of the editor and Finish in the Deployment Location window. Then enter the admin user ID and password. If you have not changed the user ID and password since the installation, accept the default and click OK if promoted for the admin password. The default ID is `admin`, as is the default password. Figure 5.49 shows that the process has been kicked off and is waiting for the human task to be completed.

  2. Open the Business Process Choreographer Explorer.

  a. To complete the human task, use the Business Process Choreographer Explorer. Right-click `WebSphere Process Server v6.2 at localhost` and click Launch, Business Process Choreographer Explorer (See Figure 5.50).

  b. The Business Process Choreographer Explorer is loaded on the internal browser. The default URL is `http://localhost:9080/bpc`. Optionally, you can open the Business Process Choreographer Explorer from an external browser using the URL. It can be used to start and administer both business processes and human tasks. Note that if you have more than one WebSphere Server installed, your port number might not be 9080.

  3. Complete the human task activity in the Business Process Choreographer Explorer.

  a. When the Business Process Choreographer Explorer is loaded, you are asked to log in because by default the embedded WebSphere Process Server has security turned on. Enter `admin` as the ID and `admin` as the password. Then click Login.

  b. Tasks are listed in the My To-Dos page as shown in Figure 5.51.

  c. Select the check box beside Receive Order and click Work on. You are brought to a detail screen.

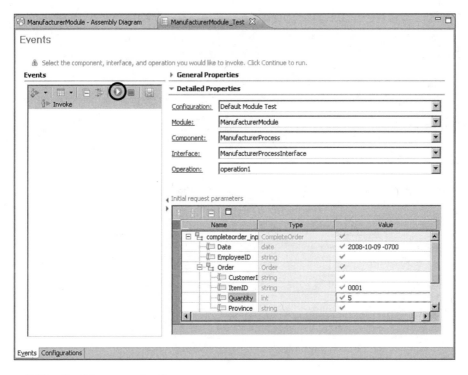

Figure 5.49 Test Component editor

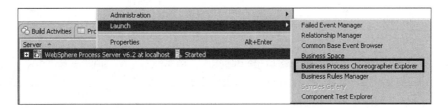

Figure 5.50 Launch the Business Process Choreographer Explorer

    d. Enter done in the status box as shown in Figure 5.52 and click Complete.

4. Switch back to the test component editor, and the process completes. The result is displayed in Figure 5.53. The completeorder_output variable contains the original order and the TotalCost and Status filled in by the business process.

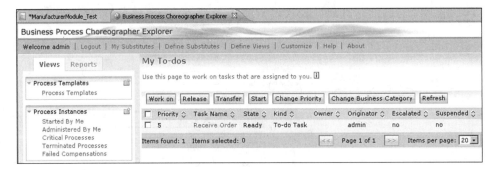

Figure 5.51   The My To-Dos page in the Business Process Choreographer

Figure 5.52   Complete a human task in the Business Process Choreographer Explorer

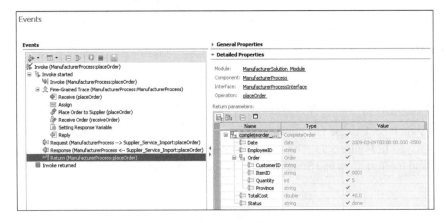

Figure 5.53   Test Component finish execution on the business process

Export the Projects as EAR Files

After developers finish developing the projects, they normally package the projects as EAR files for the administrator to deploy to the server. Export both `SupplierServiceEAR` and `ManufacturerSolution_ModuleApp` as EAR files. These EAR files will be used in Tutorial 5.3 to deploy in the WebSphere Process Server.

1. Export `SupplierServiceEAR` as an EAR file.

   a. In the workbench of WebSphere Integration Developer, right-click `Supplier ServiceEAR`. Click Export, EAR File. A shared EAR file contains the source code where an EAR file gives you the choice of including the source.

   b. Click Browse to choose a destination to save the EAR file. Then click Finish.

2. Export the `ManufacturerSolution` and its library and module as EAR files.

   a. Right-click `ManufacturerSolution` and click Export. Expand Java EE, EAR File. Then click Next. A shared EAR file contains the source code where an EAR file gives you the choice of including the source.

   b. Click Browse to choose a destination such as `ManufacturerSolution_ ModuleApp.ear` to save the EAR file. Then click Finish.

Tutorial 5.3: Deploy to a WebSphere Process Server

The enterprise application is completed and unit-tested in WebSphere Integration Developer. It's now time to deploy it to a production server. In this tutorial, the projects are deployed into a stand-alone WebSphere Process Server. Two EAR files were exported from WebSphere Integration Developer in Tutorial 5.2. The tutorial steps assume you are using a standalone server.

Start the WebSphere Process Server

There are several ways to start a WebSphere Process Server. We will start it using the command prompt. The standalone server might have already started because it was by default registered with the operating system and starts automatically as the operating system boots up.

1. Start the WebSphere Process Server.

   a. Open a command prompt.

   b. Change to the `<WPS_INSTALL>\bin` directory.

Directory example of a standalone server:

```
C:\Program Files\IBM\WebSphere\ProcServer\bin
```

   c. Enter `startserver server1` as shown in Figure 5.54. When the server is started, you see the line `Server server1 open for e-business`. If security is enabled, enter

```
startserver server1 -username <username> -password <password>
```

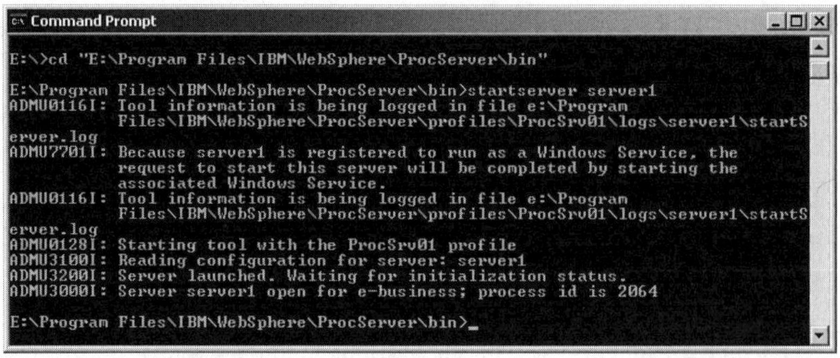

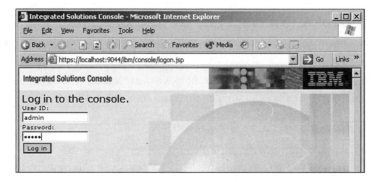

Figure 5.54   Start the server in the command prompt

Start the Integrated Solutions Console

1. In a Web browser, load the integrated solutions console. The URI is `http://<host>:`
   `<port>/admin`. For example: `http://localhost:9061/admin`.

2. Enter the user ID and password as shown in Figure 5.55. Then click Log In.

Figure 5.55   Start the integrated solutions console

Install and Start SupplierService Enterprise Application

Install the Web service as an individual Enterprise application to the WebSphere Process Server.
WebSphere Process Server builds on top of WebSphere Application Server; therefore, all the basic
server functions, such as installing and administrating an EAR, are identical to WebSphere Application Server.

1. Install the `SupplierServiceEAR`.

a. In the administrative console, expand Applications, Install New Application.

b. Browse for the `SupplierServiceEAR.ear` file. Click Next.

c. Click Next twice and click Finish. The EAR file will be installed as shown in Figure 5.56.

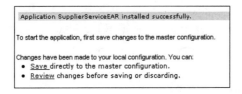

Figure 5.56 Install the SupplierServiceEAR successfully

d. Click Save to save the file to the master configuration.

2. Start the `SupplierServiceEAR` enterprise application.

a. In the left navigation, expand Applications, Enterprise Applications.

b. Select the check box beside the `SupplierServiceEAR` and click Start. The application is started successfully, and the application status changes from Stopped to Started as show in Figure 5.57.

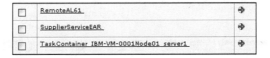

Figure 5.57 The SupplierServiceEAR is started successfully

3. In another Web browser, load the URI `http://<host>:<port>/SupplierService/ services/SupplierServiceSOAP` as shown in Figure 5.58. This is the Web service endpoint. The host and port might be different depending on your system configurations. For example, `http://localhost:9081/SupplierService/services/SupplierServicesSOAP`.

Figure 5.58 Running the Web service endpoint

Install ManufacturerSolution_ModuleApp Enterprise Application

This `ManufacturerSolution_ModuleApp.ear` file contains the Web application that invokes the Supplier's Web Service.

1. In the administrative console, expand Applications, Install New Application.
2. Browse for the `ManufacturerSolution_ModuleApp.ear` file. Click Next.
3. Click Next twice and then Finish. The EAR file will be installed.
4. Click Save to save the file to the master configuration.

Changing Web Service Endpoint

During development, the Manufacturer Ordering Process invokes the Supplier's Web Service that was running in the test server. In the previous step, we deployed the Supplier's Web Service into the production server, which has a different host name and port number. Therefore, configurations need to be changed for the business process application to communicate with the production version of the Web service.

1. Manage modules on the `ManufacturerSolution_ModuleApp`.

    a. In the administrative console, expand Applications, Enterprise Applications.
    b. Click `ManufacturerSolution_ModuleApp`.
    c. Click Manage Modules under the Modules section as shown in 5.59.

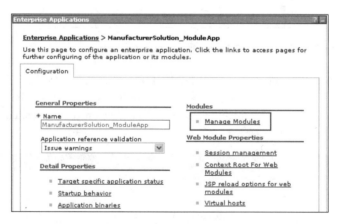

Figure 5.59   Manage modules

    d. Click `ManufacturerSolution_ModuleEJB`.

2. Change the Web service client bindings for the module.

a. Click Web Services Client Bindings under the Web Services Properties section as shown in Figure 5.60. We will be augmenting the Web service endpoint to point to the production version.

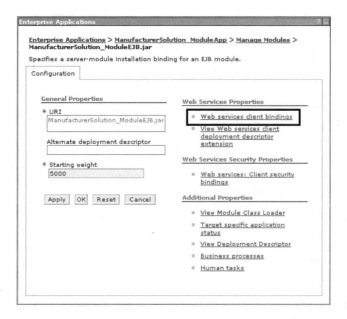

Figure 5.60 Web services client bindings

b. Click Edit under the Port Information column as shown in Figure 5.61.

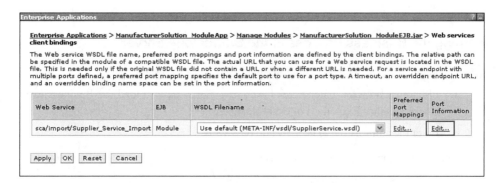

Figure 5.61 Editing port information of Supplier's Web Service

c. Change the host and port number in the Overridden Endpoint URL as shown in Figure 5.62. The host name and port number might be different depending on your server

setup. The URI is similar to `http://<host>:<port>/SupplierService/services/`
`SupplierServiceSOAP`.

Figure 5.62 Editing port information

    d. Click Apply.

    e. Click Save. Make sure the endpoint only takes effect if the enterprise application is restarted.

3. Start the `ManufacturerSolution_ModuleApp` enterprise application.

    a. In the administrative console, expand Applications, Enterprise Applications.

    b. Select the check box beside `ManufacturerSolution_ModuleApp` and click Start. The application is started successfully, and the application status changes from Stopped to Started.

Executing the Business Process in the Standalone Server

1. Load the Business Process Choreographer Explorer in a browser.

    a. In another browser, enter `http://<host>:<port>/bpc` to load the Business Process Choreographer Explorer. For example, enter `http://localhost:9081/bpc`.

    b. Enter the administrative user ID and password.

2. Start an instance of the business process.

    a. In the left navigation, click Process Templates.

    b. Select the check box for `ManufacturerProcess` as shown in Figure 5.63 and click Start Instance.

3. Add the input values.

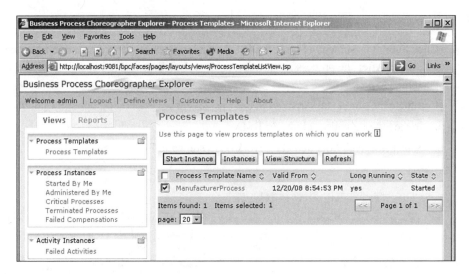

Figure 5.63   Start ManufacturerProcess instance

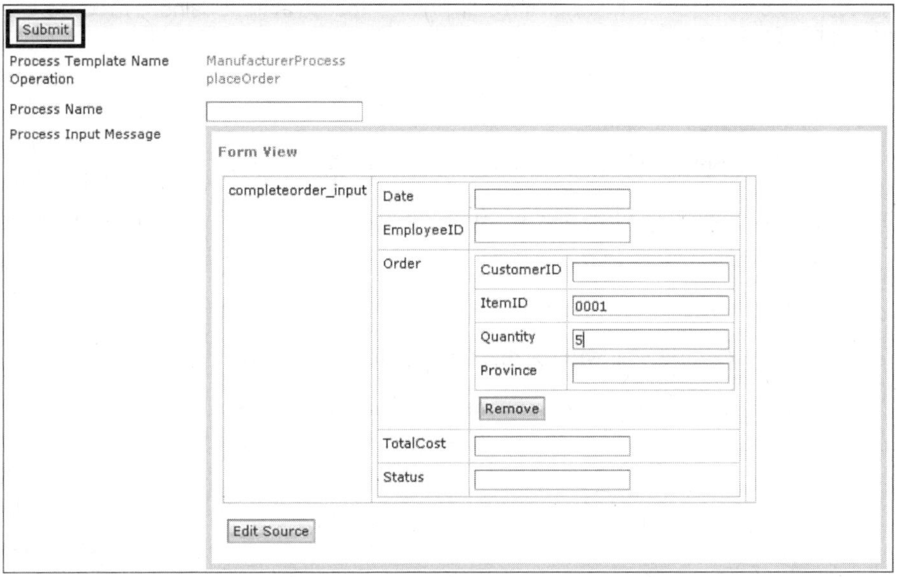

Figure 5.64   The input for the Manufacturer Business Process in the Business Process Choreographer Explorer

    a. Click Add to add an order object.

    b. Enter 0001 as the ItemID.

    c. Enter 5 as the quantity.

4. Click Submit as shown in Figure 5.64. This is a long-running process, and it has a human task node. After the process is started, a to-do task will be created awaiting the shipping personnel to pick up.

5. Complete the human task activity in the Business Process Choreographer Explorer.

    a. In the left navigation, click My To-Dos.

    b. Select Receive Order and click Work on as shown in Figure 5.65.

Figure 5.65 The input for the Manufacturer Business Process in the Business Process Choreographer Explorer

    c. Enter done as the status.

    d. Click Complete. The resulted plag is shown in Figure 5.66.

6. Open the system.log file. The log files are located in the logs directory in the profile. For example:

```
C:\Program Files\IBM\WebSphere\ProcServer\profiles\ProcSrv01\logs\server1
```

In the system.log file, you will see that the Supplier Web Service was invoked.

```
00000076 SystemOut     O ON - Ontario Supplier Service
00000076 SystemOut     O ===========================
```

Figure 5.66   Work on the task in Business Process Choreographer Explorer

Summary

This chapter described how to use the WebSphere Integration Developer and WebSphere Process Server to create and deploy a business process application. In the sample, a single Web service was used as the building block to create the application. However, in reality, you can create a choreographed process with many services as building blocks. Furthermore, the example we created is doing a point-to-point endpoint invocation. It is possible to have the endpoint selection logic delegated to an ESB. An ESB can decide which endpoint to invoke based on the information that is passed in. WebSphere Service Registry and Repository plays a vital role in SOA. It is a registry and repository that helps a company manage and govern services. It allows users to publish and find services that foster reuse, enable dynamic endpoint selection, and govern services through its service life cycle management capability. WebSphere Integration Developer, the IBM ESB offerings, and WebSphere Service Registry and Repository are integral parts of SOA that help enable the creation of dynamic and streamlined composite applications.

Tutorial Summary:

- Tutorial 5.1: Create a Business Process
  - Import existing Web services

- Create an integration solution
- Create business objects
- Create business processes
- Learn about Business process nodes: assign, JavaScript, invoke, human task
- Tutorial 5.2: Assemble and Execute the Module
  - Assemble in the assembly diagram
  - Use Import and Export in the assembly diagram
  - Explore the solution diagram
  - Test the business process using the `Test` component framework
- Tutorial 5.3: Deploy to a WebSphere Process Server
  - Install the EAR and modify the Web service endpoint
  - Run the business process using the Business Process Choreographer Explorer

CHAPTER 6

Service Connectivity with IBM WebSphere Message Broker

Product Overview

IBM SOA (Service-Oriented Architecture) Foundation offers three enterprise service bus (ESB) products: IBM WebSphere ESB, IBM WebSphere Message Broker, and IBM WebSphere DataPower Integration Appliance XI50. Users can implement one or all three of them in their SOA infrastructure depending on their requirements. WebSphere Message Broker is the solution for companies that need an ESB that delivers universal connectivity and transformation across heterogeneous information technology (IT) environments. WebSphere Message Broker is built on top of two key concepts: message transformation and business data routing between applications. By making full use of the transport and connectivity options from WebSphere MQ (message queue), WebSphere Message Broker offers additional routing and message transformation capabilities. It enables companies to integrate disparate applications without making changes to the existing applications. With its flexibility to handle protocols and data in different formats, business data can be transformed and routed to disparate applications across multiple platforms in exactly the format that is needed.

The Difference Between WebSphere MQ and WMB

WebSphere MQ is used hand in hand with WebSphere Message Broker. WebSphere MQ (formerly MQSeries) is a highly versatile software solution for application-to-application communication services regardless of where your applications or data reside. Whether on a single server, separate servers of the same type, or separate servers of different architecture types, WebSphere MQ facilitates communications between applications by sending and receiving message data via messaging queues. Applications then use the information in these messages to interact with Web browsers, business logic, and databases. WebSphere MQ is a class of middleware software known as message-oriented middleware (MOM). It is the industry standard in message queuing technologies. WebSphere MQ uses a set of small and standard application programming interfaces (APIs) that support a number of programming languages, including Visual Basic, NATURAL, COBOL, Java, and C across all platforms. With its open architecture, WebSphere MQ is flexible to work with other add-on products to facilitate many additional services such as message brokering (system integration, workflow), certificate security, monitoring, statistical reporting, analysis, wireless, and more. It is one of the most popular add-on products in the market.

WebSphere MQ provides a secure and reliable transport layer for moving data unchanged in the form of messages between applications. However, it is not aware of the content of the messages (that is, it does not understand the content of the data that it is delivering and will only move the data as it is supplied).

WebSphere Message Broker is built to extend WebSphere MQ, and it is capable of understanding the content of each message that it moves through the Broker. Customers can define the set of operations on each message depending on its content. The message processing nodes supplied with WebSphere Message Broker are capable of processing messages from various sources, such as Java Message Service (JMS) providers, HyperText Transfer Protocol (HTTP) calls, or data read from files. By connecting these nodes with each other, customers can define linked operations on a message as it flows from one application to its destination.

Let's go through some of the basic concepts of WebSphere Message Broker.

WebSphere Message Broker Basic Key Concepts

Table 6.1   Basic Key Concepts

Basic Key Concepts	Definition
Queue	A WebSphere MQ object that allows message queuing applications to put or get messages.
Queue manager	A WebSphere MQ object that provides queuing services to applications. A queue manager provides an API (the MQI) that enables programs to access messages on the queues that a queue manager owns.
Broker	A set of execution processes that hosts one or more message flows.
Broker domain	One or more brokers that share a common configuration, with a single configuration manager that controls them.
Configuration manager	An interface between the toolkit workbench and an executing set of brokers. It provides brokers with their initial configuration and updates them with any subsequent changes. It is the central runtime component that manages components and resources of a broker domain.

Table 6.1   Basic Key Concepts

Basic Key Concepts	Definition
Message flow	A sequence of processing steps that runs in a broker. It is composed of a number of message flow nodes that each represents a set of actions to be performed on the incoming message.
ESQL (Extended Structured Query Language)	A programming language that defines and manipulates data within a message flow.
Transformation node	A set of built-in nodes in WebSphere Message Broker to create new messages or augment the content of messages. There are two types of transformation nodes: ESQL transformation nodes (`Compute`, `Filter`, and `Database` nodes) use ESQL as the transformation language; Mapping transformation nodes (`Mapping`, `DataInsert`, `DataUpdate`, `DataDelete`, `Extract`, and `Warehouse` nodes) map the contents of a message to another message as well as store, retrieve, and update message contents from the database.
Message map	A complete transformation that has source objects that define the structure of inputs and target objects that define the structure of outputs. A message map is represented as a `.msgmap` file in the file system.
Message set	A container for a logical grouping of messages and associated message resources (elements, types, groups). It provides a business context for a set of messages.
Message definition	A container that holds one or more messages with the constructs that describe the logical and physical format of the message(s).

WebSphere Message Broker Toolkit

WebSphere Message Broker is composed of a runtime and a toolkit. The WebSphere Message Broker Toolkit is based on the Rational Software Development Platform, which is based on Eclipse. It enables customers to configure the system, develop message flows, and manage deployed environments. WebSphere Message Broker Toolkit offers the following four perspectives for users to develop, test, and administer message flows:

- Broker Application Development perspective
- Broker Administration perspective
- Debug perspective
- Plug-In Development perspective

Broker Application Development Perspective

This perspective is displayed by default when WebSphere Message Broker Toolkit is started. It allows users to develop and test message flows and message sets. It is divided into four views: Broker Development view (top left), Message Flow Editor view (top right), Outline view (bottom left), and Problems and Properties view (bottom right) for users to browse, navigate, and update application resources. Figure 6.1 shows the Broker Application Development perspective for the library book search service tutorial that will be exercised later in this chapter.

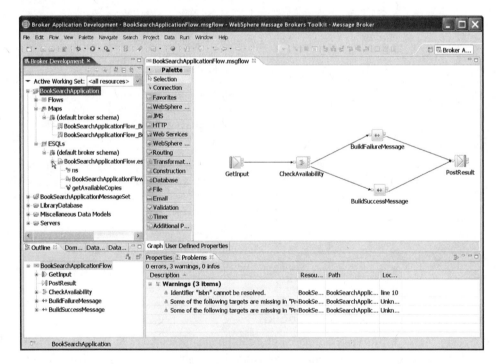

Figure 6.1   Broker Application Development perspective in WebSphere Message Broker

Broker Administration Perspective

In this perspective, users can define broker domain resources and manage configuration managers within broker domains. The Domain view allows users to update broker domain resources such as setting up broker domains, connecting or removing brokers, adding or removing execution groups, as well as creating and deploying broker archive (BAR) files.

Figure 6.2 shows the Domains view for the library book search service tutorial. The first item in the tree lists the configuration manager for the broker runtime and the queue manager details such as host location and listener port for WebSphere MQ queues. The next tree item, Broker Topology, stores the broker and collects information within a broker domain. Typically, it shows the available brokers, topics, and subscriptions on broker runtime along with the event log for problem determination. As illustrated in Figure 6.2, the library book search service tutorial has a configuration manager, WBRK61_DEFAULT_CONFIGURATION_MANAGER, which is defined within a queue manager WBRK61_DEFAULT_QUEUE_MANAGER residing on localhost with listener port 2414. A message flow for the library book search service, BookSearchApplicationFlow, is deployed in the default execution group of the broker, WBRK61_DEFAULT_BROKER.

Figure 6.2   Domain view in the Broker Administration perspective

Debug Perspective

This provides a graphical interface for users to test and debug message flows using the embedded flow debugger. Figure 6.3 shows a snapshot of the Debug Perspective. Users can carry out all debugging tasks, including adding/removing/disabling/enabling breakpoints and stepping into, stepping over, stepping out, and resuming message flows or source code in the Debug view. The message flow editor graphically displays the message flow being debugged. The Breakpoints and Variables view are fully enhanced to display details for the breakpoints and message content during execution.

Plug-In Development Perspective

This helps you develop user-defined nodes in the Message Broker Toolkit. A user-defined node is an Eclipse plug-in that adds a category of nodes to the message flow editor palette.

The tutorials of this chapter illustrate how to use the development perspective and the administration perspective to develop and deploy a message flow.

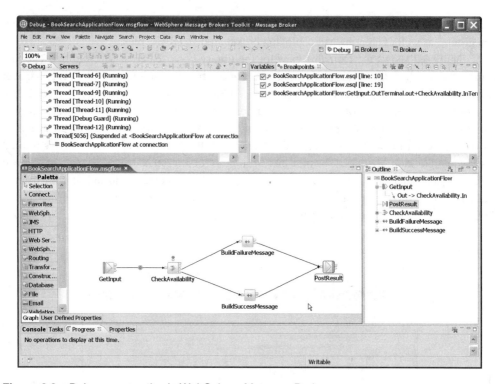

Figure 6.3   Debug perspective in WebSphere Message Broker

How Does It Support SOA?

WebSphere Message Broker provides a connectivity and integration solution for heterogeneous IT environments. As part of SOA Foundation, WebSphere Message Broker enables you to maximize flexibility as an enterprise service bus by doing the following:

- Leveraging existing resources much more widely
- Improving speed of implementation of changes to applications to respond to new opportunities, ensuring that application design and changes are focused on business logic rather than infrastructure details
- Accommodating and rapidly implementing IT changes as your business changes

WebSphere Message Broker gives you a flexible and dynamic infrastructure to simplify application integration. It allows you to assemble business services to create integration solutions for SOA. You can integrate many types of applications on a range of systems and enable them to exchange their data in real time.

In addition, WebSphere Message Broker adds services such as message routing, transformation enrichment, and support for various message distribution options and protocols to improve their flexibility and performance. It maximizes the value of your IT investment by broadening the range of environments that a connectivity layer can reach, such as hardware and operating system platforms and non-standards-based programming models, as well as Java 2 Platform, Enterprise Edition (J2EE) and .NET. With its robust design, scalable architecture, high performance, and ease of use, you can implement enterprise-wide SOA in stages.

Figure 6.4 shows an example of how WebSphere Message Broker can integrate existing applications running on legacy systems.

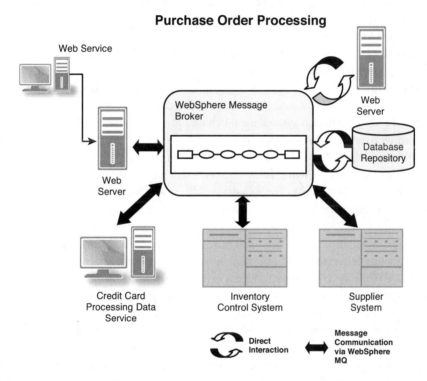

Figure 6.4   Integrating applications and connecting services using WebSphere Message Broker

Auto shop ABC Ltd. is a retail and wholesale auto parts business, serving both consumers and auto repair companies. Before integration, auto shop ABC Ltd. maintained its auto parts information, customers, and suppliers in DB2 Universal Database. An inventory control system for auto parts was in Customer Information Control System (CICS). Parts orders were received via phone or from its Web site. Then sales staff manually processed the orders by extracting customer information from DB2, checking whether the requested parts were in stock using 3270 terminals attached to a CICS subsystem, obtaining authorization for purchase amounts using a data service provided by the credit card processing center, and finally sending confirmation or rejection responses to customers via phone or mail. This purchase order process was labor intensive and not efficient enough to handle vast incoming orders.

Seeing this pitfall, auto shop ABC Ltd. decided to fully automate and integrate its purchase order processing system. There were two key points that the company was looking for in the new solution. First, the company wanted to leverage its existing assets as much as it could. It did not want to set up a new system or write a new application from scratch. Instead, it wanted to reuse its current inventory control system in CICS and keep the customer, supplier, and parts information databases in DB2. Second, the company was hoping the new solution would be able to let customers order auto parts over the Web and bypass as much human interactions as possible.

With the two key criteria in mind, auto shop ABC Ltd. searched for an ideal integration solution and decided to use WebSphere Message Broker to achieve its purchase order integration process. Auto shop ABC Ltd. realized that WebSphere Message Broker was the perfect fit for the company. It not only provided loose coupling for the company's existing infrastructure without making changes to its backend systems, but it provided connectivity and universal data transformation for its standard and non-standards-based applications and services across multiple platforms.

Under the new integration system, the purchase order request will be invoked directly from the enhanced Web services. Customers will use the Web service to send a purchase order request over the Web in Extensible Markup Language (XML) format—the structure and contents of which are defined by XML Schema. The Web Server will receive the request and send it to WebSphere MQ queue for processing. The request will be picked by the purchase order processing system running in the WebSphere Message Broker. The broker will interact directly with the DB2 database to extract customer information and the items' prices. After receiving the information from the database, the broker will build and send a message to the inventory control system in CICS by extracting requested parts information from the purchase order request. The message will be in CWF (Custom Wire Format), which is typically defined by the structure of a COBOL copy book or C Structure. As the CICS inventory control system processes the message, it will return a message in CWF format to the broker.

If the inventory system indicates that the requested items are in stock, the broker will invoke the data service of the credit card processing center to validate the credit card purchase. The broker will communicate with the credit card processing center using the Tagged Delimited Separated (TDS) message format. The TDS message format is predominantly used by banking and financial applications and by industry standard messages sets such as SWIFT and EDIFACT. Once a response is received from the credit card processing center, the broker will send an e-mail with confirmation/rejection response to the customers.

On the other hand, if the inventory system indicates that a part quantity in stock has gone below a threshold value or is insufficient to fulfill the order, it will create and send an XML format message to the supplier requesting more parts. The broker will then inform the customer via email about the shortage in inventory.

The preceding scenario fully demonstrates the versatility of WebSphere Message Broker in terms of dealing with various types of data formats (XML, CWF, and TDS) and performs data transformation and routing across different backend systems such as Web servers, email servers, DB2, and CICS. Further, it shows how to use WebSphere Message Broker to connect to existing services such as the purchase order Web service and the credit card processing data service in the scenario.

In this tutorial, you are going to implement a typical service: a library book search service that transforms and routes book search queries. The service receives a book search query in the form of an XML message in a WebSphere MQ input queue. Then a search is performed on the backend library database, and the search result is placed on a WebSphere MQ output queue for further processing. You will be able to build, deploy, and test your library book search service using WebSphere Message Broker Toolkit.

In general, WebSphere Message Broker is used to solve integration requirements ranging from simple two-application solutions to multi-application, multi-platform designs. Following are some of the benefits of doing this:

- Expanding your infrastructure without increasing the complexity
- Protecting your existing and ongoing investments in applications and data structures
- Seamlessly extending your connectivity capabilities

As companies expand and integration challenges multiply, WebSphere Message Broker can accommodate the changing needs with ease.

Tutorial Overview—Create a Library Book Search Service

This exercise lets you practice using WebSphere Message Broker Toolkit to implement a service to handle a library book search request. The search request comes in the form of an XML message in the input queue. Then, based on the availability of the book, a search response message is produced and placed on the output queue. You will be writing ESQL to implement a function to query the library database for the book. You will also be using the Mapping node that is supplied with the toolkit to create the search response message from the search request message. This service introduces you to the basic features and gives you hands-on experience to learn the fundamentals offered by WebSphere Message Broker.

Figure 6.5 shows the logistics of this library book search service.

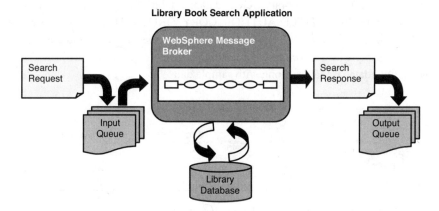

Figure 6.5   Library book search service

The following are the tutorials that are featured in this chapter:

- Tutorial 6.1: Configure Message Broker Toolkit with Predefined Databases and Runtime Artifacts
- Tutorial 6.2: Create the Message Flow and Message Set for the Library Book Search Service
- Tutorial 6.3: Deploy and Test the Library Book Search Service

System Requirements

The tutorial has been developed with the following products and environment:

- IBM WebSphere Message Broker version 6.1
  - IBM DB2 UDB Enterprise Server Edition, V9.1, is the chosen database for this tutorial.
  - IBM WebSphere MQ for Windows, V6.0, is the prerequisite for IBM WebSphere Message Broker version 6.1.
  - The Message Broker Runtime and the Message Broker Toolkit are installed.
  - For this tutorial, all of the above are installed on the same host.

Upon successful installation, follow the section "Tutorial Setup for Library Book Search Service" to prepare the environment needed for this tutorial:

- **IBM DB2 UDB Enterprise Server Edition**—Databases for WebSphere Message Broker and the library database used by the library book search service
- **IBM WebSphere Message Broker Runtime**—Configuration manager and Broker for message flow deployment and execution
- **IBM WebSphere MQ for Windows**—Queue manager and input/output queues for message flow

Figure 6.6 reveals the DB2 library BOOK database table after the setup. The database table contains five columns: ISBN, TITLE, AUTHOR, COPY_ORDERED, and COPY_AVAILABLE, where the ISBN is the primary key. The library book search message flow you are about to build will be using the sample data shown next for testing. In this tutorial, scripts are provided to create the following DB2 database tables along with sample data.

DB2ADMIN - DB2 - SAMPLEDB - SAMPLE.BOOK

ISBN	TITLE	AUTHOR	COPY_ORDERED	COPY_AVAILABLE
1234567	Introduction to He...	IBM Toronto Lab	10	10
156592262	Java In a Nutshell	David Flanagan	10	4
0470069821	Service Oriented ...	Robin Bloor, Judit...	5	2
0131510517	UNIX System Ad...	Evi Nemeth, Gart...	5	5

Figure 6.6   DB2 database for library book search service

Once you have the databases set up, you need to initialize the runtime environment to deploy and execute the library book search message flow. In this tutorial, you will use the Default Configuration Wizard provided within WebSphere Message Broker Toolkit to set up a basic configuration on your local machine.

Table 6.2 shows the runtime components created by the Default Configuration Wizard.

Table 6.2 Runtime Components Created by Default Configuration Wizard

Runtime Component	Name
Broker Domain	`Local_Domain`
Configuration Manager	`WBRK61_DEFAULT_CONFIGURATION_MANAGER`
Broker	`WBRK61_DEFAULT_BROKER`
Queue Manager	`WBRK61_DEFAULT_QUEUE_MANAGER`
Broker Database	`DEFBKD61`

With the basic domain configuration, you can deploy and execute the library book search message flow. Once the queue manager and runtime artifacts are created, you can see them in the Domains view within the Broker Administration perspective. Figure 6.7 shows the Domains view with WebSphere Broker runtime artifacts defined in this tutorial.

Figure 6.7 WebSphere Broker runtime artifacts for book search service

Last but not least, you will be creating three queues for use by the library book search service. You need an input queue to receive the incoming search request, an output queue to hold the search result, and a dead letter queue to store any invalid incoming messages (that is, search request messages that are not in the correct format). To ease the setup process, a script is provided to create these queues on your machine.

What Is Included in the CD-ROM?

In the CD included in this book, you will find a completed and configured library book search service for your reference. All the tutorials covered in this chapter have been recorded as videos on the CD-ROM.

1. **chapter 6/setup**—Contains the scripts to set up the environment needed for the Web-Sphere Message Broker tutorial.
   - /databaseSetup—DB2 script files and batch files for creating the library database and sample data.
   - /mqSetup—Script and definition file to create the queues within the WebSphere MQ manager.

2. **chapter 6/tutorial 6.1/solution/BookSearchDatabase&Server.zip**—A project inter-change archive that contains a configured data design project called LibraryDatabase and a configured server project called Servers.

3. **chapter 6/tutorial 6.2/tutorial files**—Contains the two XML schema definition files SearchRequest.xsd and SearchResponse.xsd needed to create the message definitions for the library book search service.

4. **chapter 6/tutorial 6.2/solution/BookSearchApplication.zip**—A project interchange archive that contains a configured message flow project called BookSearchApplication and a configured message set project called BookSearchApplicationMessageSet.

5. **chapter 6/tutorial 6.3/solution/BookSearchApplicationTestClient.zip**—A project interchange archive that contains a configured server project called Servers. This server project has the test client configuration file (.mbtest file) for testing the `BookSearchApplication message flow`.

6. **chapter 6/tutorial6.x/video**—The video folder contains the video files for all the tutorials discussed in this chapter. Open the Hypertext Markup Language (HTML) file in any browser to watch the video.

Tutorial Setup for the Library Book Search Service

Before you start the tutorial, you need to configure your environment for the library book search service. A set of scripts has been provided to set up the library database for you. Make sure that you have DB2ADMINS authority before running the scripts.

Databases Used by the Library Book Search Service

1. Review the provided script files found in the CD-ROM folder `chapter 6/setup/databaseSetup`.
   a. `createLibraryDB.bat`—This script creates the library database using the `mqsicreatedb` command provided by Message Broker runtime. This command creates

the database along with its Open Database Connectivity (ODBC) datasource name so that the broker can access it. If your system already has a database called SAMPLEDB, you can edit the script file to use a different name. Remember to replace SAMPLEDB with the new name wherever the library database is being referenced in the tutorial.

b. `createLibrarySampleData.cmd`—This script creates a BOOK table in the SAMPLE schema within the library database SAMPLEDB and populates it with sample data. If you have edited the script `createLibraryDB.bat` to use a different name for the library database, make sure you modify this script as well.

2. Create the library database and its ODBC datasource.

a. In the Windows taskbar, click Start, Programs, IBM WebSphere Message Brokers 6.1, Command Console.

b. Run the provided command file `createLibraryDB.bat` to create the library database SAMPLEDB and its ODBC datasource name. A successful command completion should be shown, similar to Figure 6.8.

c. Type `exit` to close the Command Console window.

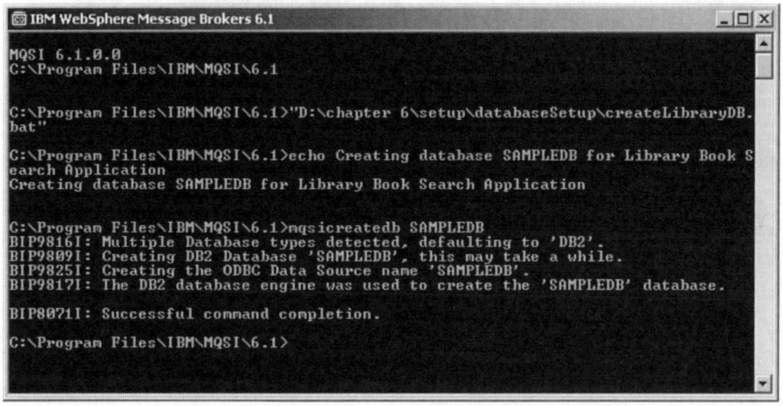

Figure 6.8 Running createLibraryDB.bat

3. Create the database table along with sample data.

a. Next, open the command window for DB2. In the Windows taskbar, click Start, Programs, IBM DB2, Command Line Tools, Command Window.

b. Run the provided command file `createLibrarySampleData.cmd` to create the BOOK database table along with sample data for the library book search service. The command should be executed successfully, similar to Figure 6.9.

c. Type `exit` to close the DB2 command window.

Figure 6.9   Running createLibrarySampleData.cmd

A DB2 library BOOK database table has been created with sample data for use with the tutorial.

WebSphere Message Broker Runtime Artifacts

WebSphere Message Broker Toolkit provides a Default Configuration Wizard for you to set up a basic broker domain configuration on your machine. If you already have a basic broker domain configuration on your machine, you can skip this step.

Before you run the Default Configuration Wizard, make sure your user account belongs to the Administrators group. Note that if your DB2 is not installed in the default location (that is, C:\Program Files\IBM\SQLLIB), you may encounter a database creation error about missing PATH variable for the DB2 ODBC driver or for the database installation location. Update your system PATH to include the bin directory of your DB2. For example, if your DB2 is installed onto

C:\SQLLIB, add the directory C:\SQLLIB\BIN to your PATH variable and restart the toolkit. This will resolve the problem.

1. Start WebSphere Message Broker Toolkit if it is not already started.

   a. In the Windows taskbar, click Start, Programs, IBM Software Development Platform, IBM WebSphere Message Broker Toolkit 6.1, WebSphere Message Broker Toolkit 6.1.

   b. A dialog appears asking for the workspace directory. Just click OK to accept the default one.

2. Create a basic broker domain configuration.

   a. The Default Configuration Wizard can be launched from the Message Broker Toolkit Welcome page, which is displayed the first time you launch the Message Broker Toolkit. If the Welcome page is not displayed, open it in the Message Broker Toolkit by clicking Help, Welcome.

   b. Click the Get Started icon in the Welcome page.

   c. Click the Create the Default Configuration icon.

   d. Click Start the Default Configuration Wizard. Follow the instructions to create a default configuration. If you already have a basic broker domain configuration on your machine, you will get a wizard disabled message. You can then skip this step and continue to the next section to create WebSphere MQ queues for the message flow.

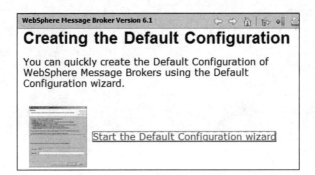

Figure 6.10 Starting the Default Configuration Wizard

You have created a default broker configuration for deploying and executing the library book search message flow.

WebSphere MQ Queues for Message Flow

If you are familiar with IBM WebSphere MQ, you can use its Explorer graphical interface to create the three queues INPUT, OUTPUT, and WMB.DEAD.LETTER in the default queue manager (that is,

WBRK61_DEFAULT_QUEUE_MANAGER) for use with this tutorial. Alternatively, you may also use the scripts provided to perform the same task.

1. Review the provided script file found in the CD-ROM folder `chapter 6/setup/mqSetup`.

   a. `webSphereMQSetup.bat`—This script file contains WebSphere MQ commands to create the queues within the default queue manager WBRK61_DEFAULT_QUEUE_MANAGER.

   b. `webSphereMQ.queues`—This file is fed to the `webSphereMQSetup.bat` script file to create the three queues used by the library book search service.

2. Create the MQ queues.

   a. Open an MS-DOS command prompt from the Windows taskbar.

   b. Change the directory to `chapter 6/setup/mqSetup`.

   c. Run the provided script file `webSphereMQSetup.bat`. The command should be run successfully, similar to Figure 6.11.

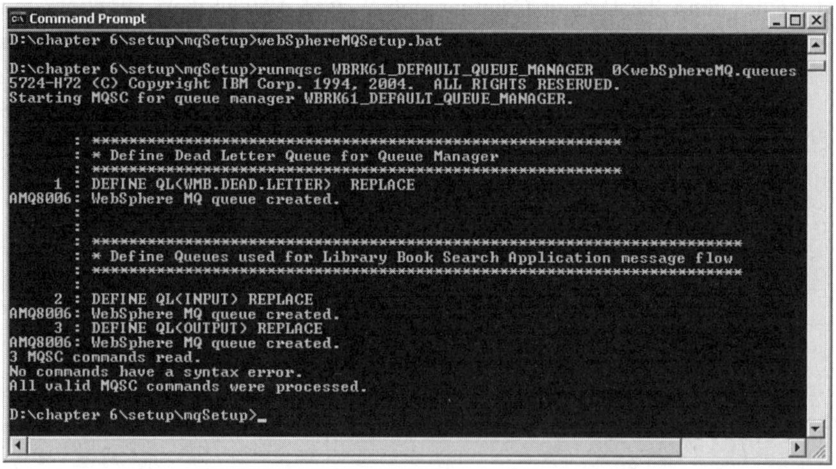

Figure 6.11   Running webSphereMQSetup.bat

3. You can examine the three queues created in WebSphere MQ Explorer.

   a. In the Windows taskbar, click Start, Programs, IBM WebSphere MQ, WebSphere MQ Explorer.

   b. Click IBM WebSphere MQ, Queue Managers, WBRK61_DEFAULT_QUEUE_MANAGER, Queues.

c. You should see the three queues INPUT, OUTPUT, and WMB.DEAD.LETTER in the Queues panel on the right.

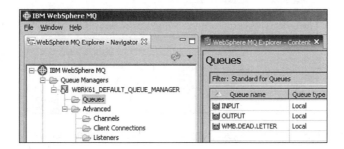

Figure 6.12   MQ Queues for the tutorial

You have created three MQ queues: an input queue to receive the incoming search request, an output queue to hold the search result, and a dead letter queue to store any invalid incoming messages for the library search application.

Tutorial 6.1: Configure Message Broker Toolkit with Predefined Databases and Runtime Artifacts

The WebSphere Message Broker toolkit is not aware of any database nor runtime artifacts that a user created on his system. To access any database from within a message flow in the toolkit, a user needs to establish a connection between the database on the system and the toolkit. This can be done by defining a database definition file in the toolkit. Similarly, a user needs to link up runtime artifacts with his workspace in order to manipulate these broker resources defined in runtime from the toolkit.

Configure the Library Database with the WebSphere Message Broker Toolkit

In this tutorial, the library book search message flow needs access to the library database (SAMPLEDB) to search for book availability. Therefore, you are going to create a new database design project LibraryDatabase using the New Database Definition File Wizard.

1. Create a new data design project LibraryDatabase.

    a. If you are not there already, click Windows, Open Perspective, Broker Application Development to go to the development perspective.

    b. From the workbench, click File, New, Database Definition.

    c. Click the New button beside the Data Design Project field to create a new data design project.

d. Type `LibraryDatabase` as the project name in the New Data Design Project page.

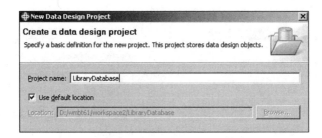

Figure 6.13   New Data Design Project page for the LibraryDatabase project

e. Click Finish.

2. Create the database definition file for `LibraryDatabase`.

    a. In the New Database Definition File page, verify that DB2 UDB is chosen in the Database field and the version is V9.1. (If your environment is using a different version of DB2, choose the right version as appropriate).

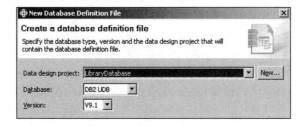

Figure 6.14   New Database Definition File Wizard for the library database

    b. Click Next to proceed to the Select Connection page.

3. Create a new database connection for the library database SAMPLEDB.

    a. Select the Create a New Connection radio button.

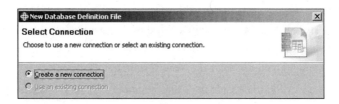

Figure 6.15   Connection page for the library database

b. Click Next.

c. In the Connection Parameters page, type SAMPLEDB as the database name in the Connection URL Details section. Verify that the rest of the fields such as the host and the port number in this section are correct.

d. In the User Information section (bottom-left corner), select your user ID from the pull-down menu and enter your password. If your user ID is not found from the pull-down menu, just type it in directly.

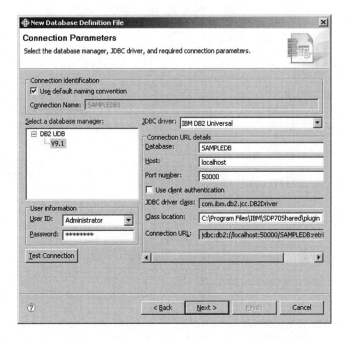

Figure 6.16   Connection Parameters for the library database SAMPLEDB

e. Click Test Connection to ensure that both database connections can be established. You should get the information dialog as shown in Figure 6.17 upon successful connection.

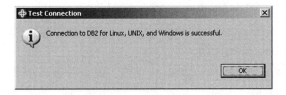

Figure 6.17   Informative dialog for successful database connection

    f. Click OK to close the dialog and click Next in the Connection Parameters page to move onto the Schema page.

4. Specify the schema for the library database SAMPLEDB.

    a. Select SAMPLE from the list of available schema in the Schema page, as shown in Figure 6.18. In the tutorial setup, you have already created the library database SAMPLEDB using the schema SAMPLE.

Figure 6.18   Schema selection page for SAMPLEDB

    b. Click Finish to complete the wizard. A project named LibraryDatabase is now created in your workbench.

5. Check the definition for the library database SAMPLEDB.

    a. Expand LibraryDatabase and double-click SAMPLEDB.dbm to open the file.

    b. An editor opens that shows the properties of the library database SAMPLEDB, similar to Figure 6.19.

6. Check the table definitions for the database table BOOK within SAMPLEDB.

    a. In the Broker Application Development perspective, click the Data Project Explorer tab in the bottom-left pane.

    b. Expand LibraryDatabase, Data Models, SAMPLEDB.dbm, SAMPLEDB, SAMPLE, BOOK.

    c. The table properties and columns definition for the BOOK database table are shown, similar to Figure 6.20.

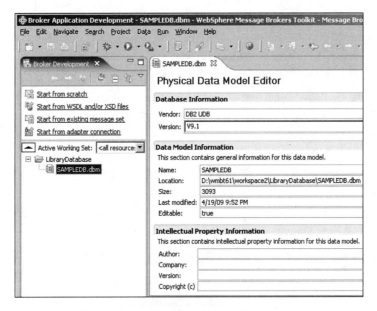

Figure 6.19   LibraryDatabase project in Broker Application Development perspective

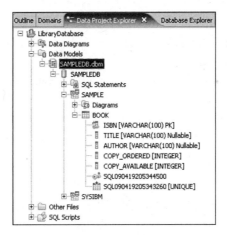

Figure 6.20   Data Project Explorer view for LibraryDatabase project

Set Up Association for WebSphere Message Broker Runtime Artifacts in Toolkit

WebSphere Message Broker Toolkit provides a Broker Administration perspective for users to manipulate broker resources defined in runtime. In particular, you can update broker domain resources such as setting up broker domains, connecting/removing brokers, adding/removing execution groups, and creating/deploying BAR files in the Domains view.

In the tutorial setup, you created a default broker domain configuration. If you are using a different workspace than the one you used to create the default configuration, you need to link up these runtime artifacts with your workspace such that any administrative tasks performed on these runtime artifacts can be forwarded to the corresponding runtime object.

1. Use the Domain Connection Wizard to create a new domain connection for the runtime artifacts you created earlier. Perform this step only if you are using a different workspace from the one you used to create the default configuration. Otherwise, you can jump to Tutorial 6.2 and skip this step.

    a. Switch to the Broker Administration perspective. In the workbench, click Window, Open Perspective, Broker Administration.

    b. Right-click on any white space in the Domains view at the bottom-left corner.

    c. Click New, Domain Connection.

Figure 6.21   Domains view with menu to open Domain Connection Wizard

    d. In the Create a Domain Connection page, type WBRK61_DEFAULT_QUEUE_MANAGER as the queue manager.

    e. Type 2414 as the port number. If you are using another queue manager, make sure that you have the right value for the name, host, and port fields for your queue manager. The window should look like Figure 6.22.

    f. Click Next to establish the connection between the toolkit and queue manager WBRK61_DEFAULT_QUEUE_MANAGER.

2. Create a new server project to store the connection configuration.

    a. Select Servers as the server project name.

    b. Type defaultConnection as the connection name, similar to Figure 6.23.

    c. Click Finish to close the wizard.

    d. Click Yes to confirm the creation of the new Servers project if it does not exist, as shown in Figure 6.24.

3. Once the connection has been established, you will see the status message The domain 'WBRK61_DEFAULT_QUEUE_MANAGER@localhost 2414' is connected at the bottom of the Domains view, as shown in Figure 6.25.

You have completed configuring WebSphere Message Broker Toolkit with its runtime artifacts. Now you are ready to create the message flow and message set for the library book search service.

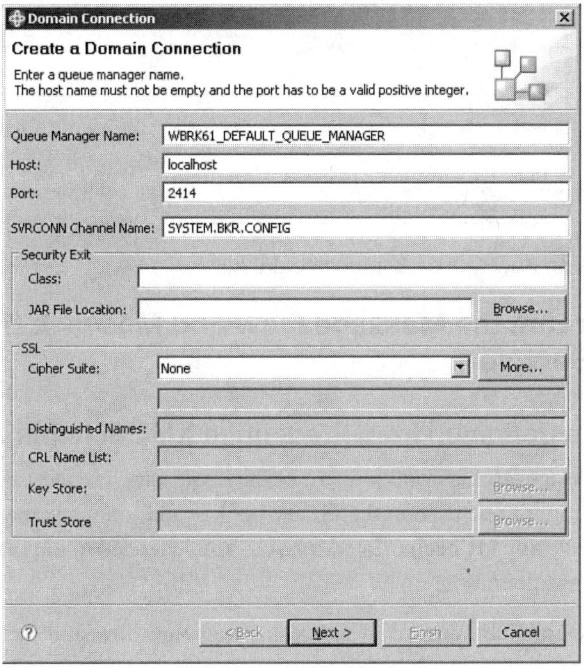

Figure 6.22   Domain Connection properties for queue manager
WBRK61_DEFAULT_QUEUE_MANAGER

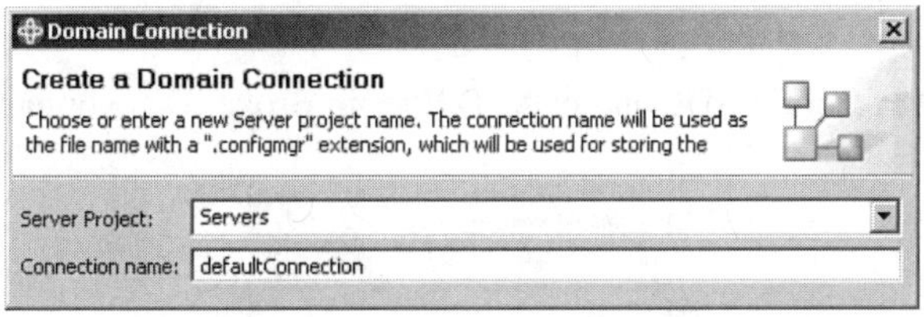

Figure 6.23   Naming page for server project and connection name

Figure 6.24   Confirmation dialog for server project creation

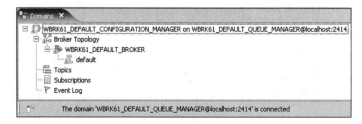

Figure 6.25   Domains view with broker runtime artifacts

Tutorial 6.2: Create the Message Flow and Message Set for Library Book Search Service

Create Message Definition from Predefined XML Schema

Use WebSphere Message Broker Toolkit to create the book search request and response message definitions that are going to be used in the library book search message flow. The XML schema for both messages have already been created for you. You just need to import them and create the corresponding message definition.

1. Open the QuickStart Wizard to create the message flow and message set project for book search service.

    a. Switch to the Broker Application Development perspective. In the workbench, click Window, Open Perspective, Broker Application Development.

    b. In the Broker Application Development perspective, click the arrow beside Active Working Set to expose the various QuickStart Wizard for Message Broker Toolkit.

    c. Click Start from WSDL and/or XSD Files in Broker Development view.

Figure 6.26   Shortcut for Quick Start Wizard

    d. In the Quick Start Wizard, type BookSearchApplication as the message flow project name.

    e. Uncheck Create a New Working Set for These Resources. Leave other fields as default. Click Next.

Figure 6.27   Quick Start Wizard for WSDL and XSD

2.   Create message definitions for book search request and respond.

   a.   Select the Use External Resources radio button in the Resource Selection dialog.

   b.   Click Browse beside the From Directory field and select the `chapter 6/tutorial 6.2/tutorial files` directory of the CD-ROM.

   c.   Select `SearchRequest.xsd` and `SearchResponse.xsd` and click Next.

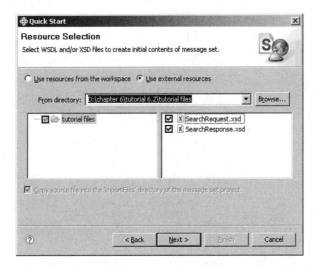

Figure 6.28   Selecting resource

d. In the Message Selection dialog, expand the hierarchy tree for `SearchRequest.xsd` and `SearchResponse.xsd`.

e. Select `SearchRequest` and `SearchResponse`, as shown in Figure 6.29.

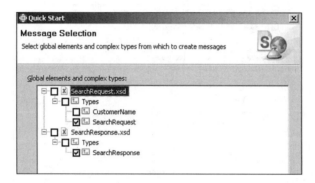

Figure 6.29   Create SearchRequest SearchResponse message definition from its complex type

f. Click Finish to close the New QuickStart Wizard.

3. The `BookSearchApplicationFlow` message flow should be opened automatically in the message flow editor. Upon completion, you should see the following four projects in the Broker Development view:

- `BookSearchApplication`
- `BookSearchApplicationMessageSet`
- `LibraryDatabase`
- `Servers`

Figure 6.30   Broker Development view for library book search service

4. Link the `BookSearchApplication` message flow project with the `LibraryDatabase` project.

    a. Right-click the `BookSearchApplication` project and click Properties.

    b. Click Project References.

    c. Check both the `BookSearchApplicationMessageSet` and `LibraryDatabase` projects.

    d. Click OK.

5. Examine the structure of the `SearchRequest` and `SearchResponse` messages in the `BookSearchApplicationMessageSet` project.

    a. Expand the tree structure under Message Definitions of the `BookSearchApplication MessageSet` project, and navigate to `SearchRequest.mxsd`.

    b. Double-click to open the message definition, as shown in Figure 6.31. You can see that the `SearchRequest` message definition has two element fields defined—`ISBN` and `CustomerName`—and both of them are of `string` type.

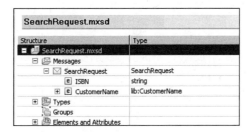

Figure 6.31   SearchRequest message structure

    c. Double-click `SearchResponse.mxsd` to examine the structure of the response message as well.

Now you have the message definitions for both the search request and the search response messages. You are ready to create the message flow for the library book search service.

Configure Message Flow with WebSphere MQ Queue

The `BookSearchApplication` message flow takes a book request in the form of a `SearchRequest` message from the WebSphere MQ queue `INPUT` and response with a `SearchResponse` message to the `OUTPUT` queue.

1. Add an `MQInput` node to the library book search message flow.

    a. Double-click the message flow `BookSearchApplicationFlow.msgflow` that can be found under the project `BookSearchApplication`, Flows, (default broker schema). This opens the message flow editor.

    b. Expand the WebSphere MQ tab within the message flow editor palette.

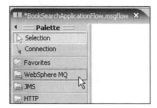

Figure 6.32   Palette in message flow editor

   c. Drag the MQInput node from the palette to the message flow editor canvas.

Figure 6.33   Dragging the MQInput node from the palette to the editor

   d. Right-click the MQInput node and rename it GetInput.

   e. Click GetInput to show its properties.

   f. Type INPUT as the queue name.

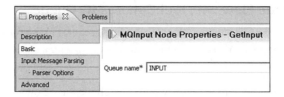

Figure 6.34   Properties view for GetInput node

  2. Add an MQOutput node to the library book search message flow.

    a. Drag the MQOutput node from the palette to the message flow editor canvas.

    b. Rename the node `PostResult`.

    c. Click the `PostResult` node to show its properties.

    d. Type `WBRK61_DEFAULT_QUEUE_MANAGER` in the Queue Manager Name field.

    e. Type `OUTPUT` in the Queue Name field.

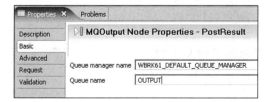

Figure 6.35   Properties view for PostResult node

Configure Parse Options for Input Message

The library book search service only takes messages in the format and structure defined in the `SearchRequest` message definition.

   1. Configure the `GetInput` node with parse options.

    a. Click the `GetInput` node to show its properties.

    b. Click the Input Message Parsing tab from the Properties view.

    c. Select `XMLNSC: For XML messages (namespace aware, validation, low memory use)` from the Message Domain list.

    d. Select `BookSearchApplicationMessageSet` from the Message Set list.

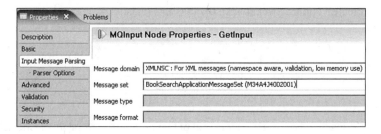

Figure 6.36   Parse option for input message

Creating ESQL for Library Book Search Query

Upon receiving the search request, the `BookSearchApplication` message flow searches the library database with the provided ISBN. Two different `SearchResponse` messages are generated according to the search result. In this case, a `Filter` node is used to perform the message routing.

    To conduct the database query, you need to write two ESQL routines to access the library database.

1. Add an ESQL node to the BookSearchApplication message flow.

   a. In the message flow editor canvas, expand the Routing tab within the message flow
      editor palette.

   b. Drag the Filter node to the canvas and drop it next to GetInput node.

   c. Right-click the Filter node and rename it CheckAvailability. The message flow
      should look similar to Figure 6.37.

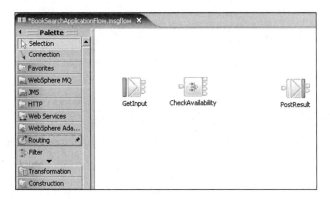

Figure 6.37   Message flow

2. Connect the CheckAvailability node with the GetInput node.

   a. Click Connection from the palette.

   b. Click the Out terminal of GetInput and click the In terminal of CheckAvailability
      to create a connection between the two terminals.

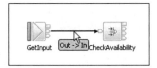

Figure 6.38   Connection between Out terminal of GetInput and In terminal of CheckAvailability

3. CheckAvailability needs to access the library database SAMPLEDB to check for book
   availability. Therefore, you need to configure the CheckAvailability Filter node
   with the datasource.

   a. Click Selection from the palette.

   b. Click CheckAvailability to show its properties.

   c. Type SAMPLEDB as the datasource.

4. Add ESQL code to `CheckAvailability` to perform a database query.

   a. Right-click `CheckAvailability` and click Open ESQL.

   b. A new ESQL file `BookSearchApplicationFlow.esql` is created with a module `BookSearchApplicationFlow_CheckAvailability`.

   c. Add the code in bold.

Listing 6.1   ESQL Filter Module BookSearchApplicationFlow_CheckAvailability

```
DECLARE ns NAMESPACE 'http://library';

CREATE FILTER MODULE BookSearchApplicationFlow_CheckAvailability
    CREATE FUNCTION Main() RETURNS BOOLEAN
    BEGIN
        DECLARE isbn REFERENCE TO Root.XMLNSC.ns:SearchRequest.ISBN;
        DECLARE availableCopy INTEGER;

        --if the ISBN cannot be found in the input message then we return false
        IF (isbn is NULL) THEN
            RETURN FALSE;
        END IF;


        -- search the library book database for the book ISBN and check for
availability
        SET availableCopy = THE (SELECT ITEM T.COPY_AVAILABLE FROM
Database.SAMPLE.BOOK AS T
        WHERE T.ISBN = isbn);

        -- if the book does not exist or none is available then return false
        IF (availableCopy >0) THEN
            RETURN TRUE;
        ELSE
            RETURN FALSE;
        END IF;
    END;
END MODULE;
```

5. In the same ESQL file, create another ESQL function, `getAvailableCopies()`, which will be used later in a `Mapping` node to retrieve the number of available copies. Add the following code for `getAvailableCopies()` after the END MODULE statement.

Listing 6.2   ESQL Function getAvailableCopies

```
CREATE FUNCTION getAvailableCopies(IN isbn CHARACTER ) RETURNS INTEGER
BEGIN
    DECLARE availableCopy INTEGER;

    -- get available copy
    SET availableCopy = THE (SELECT ITEM T.COPY_AVAILABLE FROM
Database.SAMPLE.BOOK AS T WHERE T.ISBN= isbn);

    RETURN availableCopy;

END;
```

Define the Logic of Message Flow

Two search response messages will be created depending on the result of the database query. If the book in search exists and is available in the library, you will create a SearchResponse message with the number of available copies. Otherwise, you will create a SearchResponse message with a comment to tell customers that the book is not available. You will use a Mapping node to create the SearchResponse message from the SearchRequest message.

1. Add two Mapping nodes—BuildFailureMessage and BuildSuccessMessage—to the library book search message flow.

   a. Switch back to the message flow editor canvas, and expand the Transformation tab.

   b. Drag the Mapping node to the canvas and drop it next to the CheckAvailability node.

   c. Right-click this Mapping node and rename it BuildFailureMessage.

   d. Create another Mapping node and name it BuildSuccessMessage. The message flow should look like Figure 6.39.

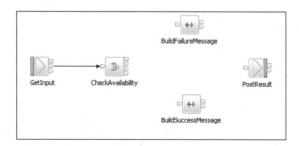

Figure 6.39   Message flow

2. If the book in search is available, a success search response message is created from the BuildSuccessMessage Mapping node. Connect the CheckAvailability Filter node with the BuildSuccessMessage Mapping node.

   a. Click Connection from the palette.

   b. Click the True terminal of CheckAvailability, and click the In terminal of BuildSuccessMessage to create a connection between the two terminals.

3. If the book in search is not available, a failure search response message is created from the BuildFailureMessage Mapping node. Connect the CheckAvailability Filter node with the BuildFailureMessage Mapping node.

   a. Click Connection from the palette.

   b. Click the False terminal of CheckAvailability and click the In terminal of BuildFailureMessage to create a connection between the two terminals. The message flow should look like Figure 6.40.

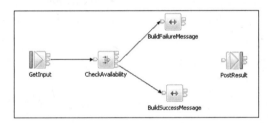

Figure 6.40   Message flow

4. The search response output messages from both Mapping nodes will be sent to the MQOutput node PostResult. Connect the Out terminals of both Mapping nodes to PostResult.

   a. Click Connection from the palette.

   b. Click the Out terminal of BuildSuccessMessage and click the In terminal of PostResult to create a connection between the two terminals.

   c. Repeat the same step for the BuildFailureMessage Mapping node.

   d. The completed BookSearchApplication message flow should look like Figure 6.41.

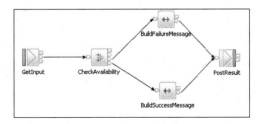

Figure 6.41   Overview of library book search service message flow

5. Configure the BuildSuccessMessage Mapping node with datasource SAMPLEDB. BuildSuccessMessage creates the search response message based on the database query on SAMPLEDB.

   a. Click the BuildSuccessMessage node to show its properties.

   b. Type SAMPLEDB as the datasource name.

6. Click File, Save All to save all the changes. Ignore the two errors about being unable to locate the map for the two mapping modes. You will create the mappings in the next section.

Create Mappings for SearchResponse Message

You will build the SearchResponse message from the SearchRequest message using mapping files. For successful database query, the message flow will create a SearchResponse message with ISBN, customer name, and number of available copies. ISBN and customer name are copied from the SearchRequest message, whereas the number of available copies will be retrieved from the library database using the ESQL function getAvailableCopies that you defined in the earlier steps.

1. Create the mapping for the BuildSuccessMessage Mapping node.

   a. Click Selection from the palette.

   b. Right-click the BuildSuccessMessage node and click Open Map. The New Message Map for Mapping Node dialog opens.

   c. In the Select Map Sources window, expand Messages and select SearchRequest as the map source.

   d. In the Select Map Targets window, expand Messages and select SearchResponse as the map target. The window should look like Figure 6.42.

   e. Click OK to close the dialog. The mapping editor opens automatically with the newly created map BookSearchApplicationFlow_BuildSuccessMessage.msgmap for the BuildSuccessMessage Mapping node.

2. ISBN and CustomerName are copied from the SearchRequest message to the SearchResponse message. Create the map for these two fields in the SearchResponse message.

   a. In the mapping editor, expand lib:SearchRequest and lib:SearchResponse.

   b. Drag ISBN from the lib:SearchRequest tree and drop it onto the ISBN of lib:SearchResponse. A mapping has been created for the ISBN field. A line between the source and the target ISBN in the mapping editor indicates that there is a map between these two fields.

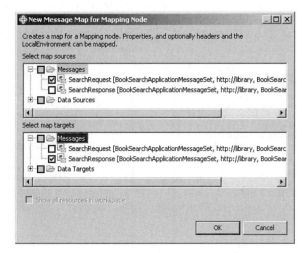

Figure 6.42   New Message Map Wizard for BuildSuccessMessage.msgmap

   c. The value for ISBN in the SearchResponse message is updated automatically to $source/lib:SearchRequest/ISBN in the Map Script pane and is shown in the expression editor.

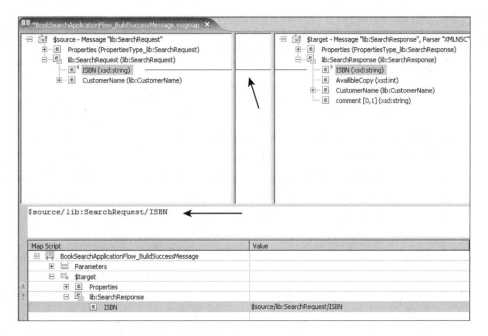

Figure 6.43   Mapping for ISBN in SearchResponse message.

d. Drag `CustomerName` from the `lib:SearchRequest` tree and drop it onto the `CustomerName` of `lib:SearchResponse`. The mapping looks like Figure 6.44.

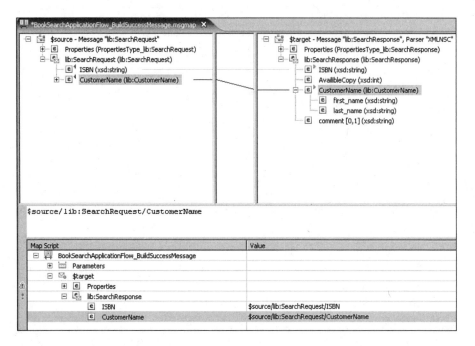

Figure 6.44   Mapping for CustomerName in SearchResponse message.

3. Next, you need to assign the value for `AvailableCopy` in the `SearchResponse` message. This value is retrieved using the ESQL function `getAvailableCopies`.

a. Right-click `AvailableCopy` on the `lib:SearchResponse` message tree and click Enter Expression.

b. In the expression editor, type `esql:` and then press Ctrl+Spacebar to invoke content assist for the available ESQL functions.

c. In the pop-up list, scroll down to User Defined ESQL Functions.

d. Click `esql:getAvailableCopies`, as illustrated in Figure 6.45.

e. Drag `ISBN` from the `SearchRequest` message on the source panel and drop it between the parentheses of `getAvailableCopies` in the expression editor. The `getAvailableCopies` ESQL function needs `ISBN` from the `SearchRequest` message as an input parameter.

f. You should have `esql:getAvailableCopies($source/lib:SearchRequest/ISBN)` as the value of `AvailableCopy` in the expression editor and in the Map Script pane, as shown in Figure 6.46.

Figure 6.45   ESQL content assist in the mapping editor

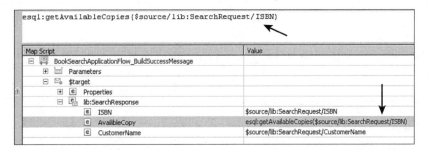

Figure 6.46   Mappings for BuildSuccessMessage

    g. You have completed creating the mapping for `BuildSuccessMessage`. Click File, Save to save the `BuildSuccessMessage` mapping file.

4. Create the mapping for the `BuildFailureMessage Mapping` node. The steps are similar to those earlier.

    a. Go back to the message flow editor.

    b. Right-click the `BuildFailureMessage` node and click Open Map. The New Message Map for Mapping Node dialog opens.

    c. In the Select Map Sources window, expand Messages and select `SearchRequest` as the map source.

    d. In the Select Map Targets window, expand Messages and select `SearchResponse` as the map target.

    e. Click OK to close the dialog, and a mapping editor opens.

5. `ISBN` and `CustomerName` are copied from the `SearchRequest` message to the `SearchResponse` message. Create the map for these two fields in the `SearchResponse` message.

    a. In the mapping editor, expand `lib:SearchRequest` and `lib:SearchResponse`.

    b. Drag `ISBN` from the `lib:SearchRequest` tree and drop it onto the `ISBN` of `lib:SearchResponse`.

    c. Drag `CustomerName` from the `lib:SearchRequest` tree and drop it onto the `CustomerName` of `lib:SearchResponse`.

6. Next, you need to assign the value for `AvailableCopy` in the `SearchResponse` message with a value of zero.

    a. Right-click `AvailableCopy` on the `lib:SearchResponse` message tree and click Enter Expression.

    b. In the expression editor, type `0`.

7. Add a comment for the failure search response message.

    a. Right-click comment on the `lib:SearchResponse` message tree and click Enter Expression.

    b. Type the comment including the quotation marks in the expression editor: `"The search item is not available in the library"`.

8. Your `BuildFailureMessage` mappings should look like Figure 6.47.

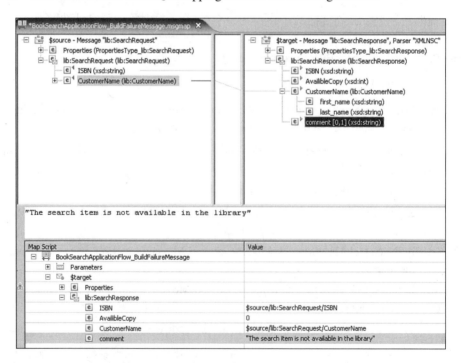

Figure 6.47   Mappings for BuildFailureMessage

9. Click File, Save All to save all the changes.

You have completed creating the message flow for the library book search service. You are now ready to test the library book search message flow.

Tutorial 6.3: Deploy and Test Library Book Search Service

Use the integration test client provided in WebSphere Message Broker Toolkit to test the `BookSearchApplication` message flow you just created.

Establish Connection with Broker Runtime

1. Before testing the `BookSearchApplication`, ensure that WebSphere Message Broker Toolkit and the predefined runtime artifacts are connected.

   a. Switch to the Broker Administration perspective.

   b. Right-click the predefined WebSphere Message Broker configuration manager (`WBRK61_DEFAULT_CONFIGURATION_MANAGER`) in the Domains view and click Connect.

Figure 6.48 Connect with the broker

2. Upon successful connection, the workbench status line is changed to `The domain 'WBRK61_DEFAULT_QUEUE_MANAGER@localhost 2414'` is connected. Figure 6.49 shows the Domains view after connecting to the broker `WBRK61_DEFAULT_BROKER`.

Figure 6.49 Domains view after connecting to WBRK61_DEFAULT_BROKER

Initialize the Test Client

1. Open the test client editor to test the library book search message flow.

a. Switch to Broker Application Development Perspective.

b. Right-click `BookSearchApplicationFlow.msgflow` in the Broker Development view and click Test Message Flow.

2. Next, you need to generate the structure for the `SearchRequest` input message.

   a. In the test client editor, right-click the table within the Message section and click Add Message Part.

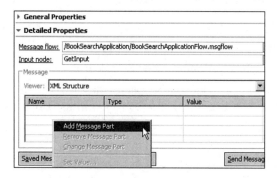

Figure 6.50　Adding a message part

   b. In the opened Type Selection dialog, select `SearchRequest` and click OK.

3. Enter test parameters for the search request message.

   a. As shown in Figure 6.51, type `1234567` as the ISBN.

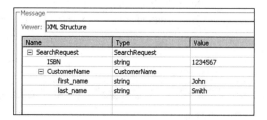

Figure 6.51　Input parameters for search request input message

   b. Type `John` as the first name.

   c. Type `Smith` as the last name.

Testing with Test Client

You have the test search request message ready. Now you can start testing the message flow.

1. Send the test input search request message to initiate the test client.

    a. In the test client editor, click the Send Message button to initiate the test client.

    b. In the Deployment Location dialog, select the default execution group for Web-Sphere Message Broker v6.1, as shown in Figure 6.52.

Figure 6.52 Deployment location for message flow

    c. Click Finish. The Test Client deploys the library book search service message flow to the broker WBRK61_DEFAULT_BROKER and sends the search request test message to the input queue of the library book search message flow. Note: If you get an error saying the configuration manager was unable to initiate the deploy, similar to Figure 6.53, try increasing the test client timeout value. Click Window, Preferences, Broker Development, Message Broker Test Client. Increase the seconds to wait for deployment completion and try again.

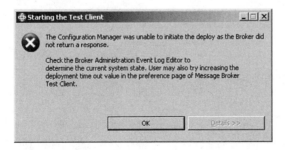

Figure 6.53 Deployment error

d. The message flow test events editor is updated with execution events. Wait until execution completes, as shown in Figure 6.54.

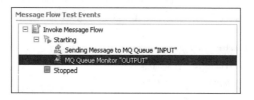

Figure 6.54   Message flow test events

2. Check the test result by examining the output message from the message flow `BookSearchApplicationFlow`.

   a. In the message flow test events editor, click `MQ Queue Monitor "OUTPUT"` to check the message that is placed on the `OUTPUT` queue.

   b. The `SearchResponse` output message is retrieved from the `OUTPUT` queue and showed in the `Message` section of the test client editor as shown in Figure 6.55. From the output `SearchRespone` message, you can see that the ISBN you have entered has 10 available copies in the library.

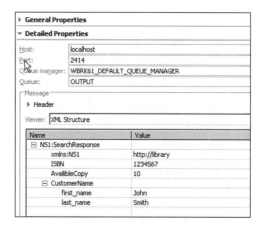

Figure 6.55   Sample output message for successful book search

3. Let's also test the message flow for a book search failure.

   a. Right-click Invoke Message Flow in the Message Flow Test Events pane and click Invoke.

b. This time, type `9876543` as the ISBN and `Bob Watson` as the customer name.

c. Click the Send Message button to start the test.

d. Wait until execution completes, and check the `SearchResponse` output message. Because the book with ISBN `9876543` does not exist in the database, you should see that the `AvailableCopy` field has a value of `0` and that it has the comment to inform you that the search item is not available in the library.

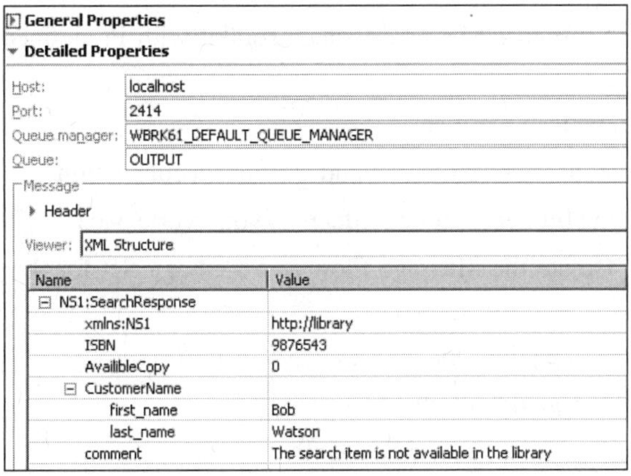

Figure 6.56   Sample output message for failure book search

4. You have completed testing the library book search message flow. Click File, Save to save the test client configuration file (`.mbtest` file) in the project `BookSearch Application` for future reference.

Summary

The library book search service in this tutorial has provided a high-level hands-on introduction to WebSphere Message Broker. You have followed step-by-step exercises to learn how to create a message flow service using ESQL and mappings, deploy the message flow service to Web-Sphere Message Broker runtime, and finally test it using the Unit Test Client.

Now that you have learned the basics of WebSphere Broker Toolkit and become more familiar with message flow, you can go one step farther by converting a message flow into a callable service. Using the set of Web Service SOAP nodes provided in WebSphere Message Broker Toolkit 6.1, you can turn the library book search service message flow from a standalone application to a callable Web service. In SOA, you can deliver message flows as services, or you can connect to services within a message flow. It is common to see a message flow that integrates with some existing business logic available as Web services in a consumer scenario. Furthermore, the Web service could be another message flow. This kind of design is known as the façade pattern. Façade pattern provides an easy to use interface to an otherwise complicated collection of interfaces or subsystems and is widely used in service integration scenarios.

In conclusion, WebSphere Message Broker gives you a flexible and dynamic infrastructure to simplify application integration. It allows you to assemble and connect business services to create integration solutions for SOA. You can connect and integrate many types of applications on a range of systems and enable them to exchange their data together in real time.

Tutorial summary:

- Tutorial 6.1: Configure Message Broker Toolkit with Predefined Databases and Runtime Artifacts
  - Create a data design project
  - Create a database definition file and establish a connection
  - Associate the broker runtime artifacts to your workspace
- Tutorial 6.2: Create the Message Flow and Message Set for the Library Book Search Service
  - Create a message flow and a message set project
  - Create a message definition
  - Add an `MQInput` node to a message flow
  - Add an `MQOutput` node to a message flow
  - Add an `ESQL` node to a message flow
  - Add mapping nodes to a message flow
  - Create mapping files
- Tutorial 6.3: Deploy and Test the Library Book Search Service
  - Initialize a test client
  - Test a message flow

CHAPTER 7

Collaboration with IBM WebSphere Portlet Factory and IBM WebSphere Portal

Product Overview

This chapter introduces you to two powerful software products that are suited for implementing a portal. The IBM WebSphere Portlet Factory provides a development environment for creating the applications for a portal. The IBM WebSphere Portal presents the tools for building and managing a portal and offers the hosting/runtime environment for a portal.

What Is a Portal?

A *portal* is a website that offers users a single point of access to a company's resources and services, requiring only one login to the website. It gives users personalized interaction with the resources and services, provides role-based access, and allows users to choose their experience and customize their own views of the website.

Users include employees, business partners, suppliers, and customers. "Company's resources and services" refer to applications, content, business processes, and people.

As an example, the following are some characteristics of a portal for a computer manufacturer.

- Using one login, employees can access applications from all departments, including human resources and technical support.

- An example of a personalized application is giving a different discount rate to customers based on their profiles. An example of personalized content is showing different news to business partners than suppliers.

- An example of role-based access is only allowing employees who are managers to see and to use the approved expense application.

- Users can add applications to their views, arrange applications, and customize the appearance of applications (for example, color).

Basic Portal Terminology

Concepts	Definitions
Portlet	To an end user, a portlet is a window on a portal website that displays information or provides a function. To a developer, it is an application.
Portlet application	A portlet application is a collection of related portlets that share the same resources. For example, these are images, properties, files, and classes.
Portal page	A portal page contains one or more portlets.
Portal website	A portal website is built with portal pages.

IBM WebSphere Portlet Factory

IBM WebSphere Portlet Factory provides a rapid development tool, WebSphere Portlet Factory Designer, to simplify and accelerate the creation of portlet applications. WebSphere Portlet Factory Designer, hereafter called Portlet Factory Designer, is a graphical tool that is a plug-in to Eclipse-based integrated development environments (IDEs).

With Portlet Factory Designer, you create projects, under which you develop models using builders and generate the resulting portlet applications from those models. Typically, no coding is required.

It is worth mentioning that IBM WebSphere Portlet Factory can be used as a development tool for creating Java 2 Platform, Enterprise Edition (J2EE) Web applications, although Web applications are not the focus of this chapter. The benefit is that you would create one model and use the same model to generate both a Web and a portlet application.

IBM WebSphere Portlet Factory Basic Concepts and Definitions

- Builder
  - A WebSphere Portlet Factory application is made up of builders. A *builder* is a software automation component that generates necessary application code. It has a simple wizard-like user interface for a developer to provide inputs. Based on the inputs, the builder generates code, including JavaServer Pages (JSPs), Java classes, and Extensible Markup Language (XML) documents. Each builder offers the function of an application design pattern, such as displaying a list of data from a backend data store. The IBM WebSphere Portlet Factory product ships with more than 160 ready-to-use builders at the time of writing this chapter and supports the creation of new builders. Builders are implemented using Java and XML.

- Model
  - Builders are assembled into models. A *model* is a made up of a number of builder calls. Web and portlet applications are generated from models. A well-designed application uses a model to provide data (a service provider model) and a different model to display the data (a service consumer/presentation model).

IBM WebSphere Portal

IBM WebSphere Portal has a complete set of portal capabilities to deliver business-to-business (B2B), business-to-consumer (B2C), and business-to-employee (B2E) portals. The capabilities include framework services, integration services, content services, and collaboration services.

Portals built using IBM WebSphere Portal are secure, personalized, and role-based with a unified user experience. These portals connect people, applications, business processes, and content (document and other types) so users can work productively and be more satisfied.

IBM WebSphere Portal software helps make it easy to create and maintain a portal. It is also faster. With a rich, responsive user interface based on Web 2.0 features, companies can provide self-service, collaboration, business intelligence dashboards, and more for their employees, partners, suppliers, and customers. As a result, they can respond quickly to business opportunities and drive business success.

IBM WebSphere Portal Basic Concepts and Definitions

- Portal server runtime
  - The portal server runtime is the execution environment for the portlets. It is also called the *portlet container*. It is a J2EE application that runs on the IBM WebSphere Application Server.
- Portlet versus servlet
  - Portlets can be administered while the Portal Server is running. For example, you can install/remove portlet applications and create/delete portlets and portlet settings. Portlets are more dynamic than servlets. Portlets may not send errors directly to browsers, forward requests, or write arbitrary markup to the output stream.
- Portal page layout
  - The *portal page layout* defines the number of content areas within the page and the portlets displayed within each content area.
- Themes
  - *Themes* represent the overall look and feel of the portal, including colors, images, and fonts.
- Skins
  - *Skin* refers to the appearance of the area surrounding an individual portlet. Each portlet can have its own skin.

IBM WebSphere Portal Key Capabilities

IBM WebSphere Portal has a broad set of capabilities. It provides you with a runtime server, services, tools, and many other functions. It is not the intention to list all the capabilities here, but let's look at a few key ones.

- Composite application and mashup framework
  - A *composite application* is a set of related and integrated services that support a business process. Users select components and logic from two or more applications to build a completely new application. You can derive that IBM WebSphere Portal itself is a security-rich composite application/view that assembles and delivers services in the form of portlets in the context of a business process.
- Web 2.0 support
  - Live Text presents "one-click" access to relevant supporting information that "pops up" on the page while executing a business process.
  - REST (Representational State Transfer) services further open the portal platform to composite mashup applications with services feeds from other Web applications.
  - Client Side Aggregation reduces server-side processing, which dramatically improves end-user performance.
- Single sign-on (SSO)
  - The basis for seamless, secure digital-identity-based access to multiple enterprise applications, systems, and networks.
- Role-based access
  - Offers advanced control over access to information, content, and applications based on users' roles and responsibilities in the organization.
- Personalization
  - Allows a portal or website to choose which content should appear for a particular user.
- Content management
  - Gives business users the ability to create and manage portal content without information technology (IT) intervention or support.
- Collaboration
  - Enables users to share information and collaborate within the context of an application in which they are working. Provides access to collaboration tools including instant messaging, Web conferencing, and team workspaces.
- Search
  - Functions include advanced search, search facets, search services, search scopes, search collections, adding custom links, summarizer, and search using different languages that the product supports. There are search services that come with IBM Web-

Sphere Portal, and you can add one or more. By adding custom links, users can do direct search using popular search engines.

How Do They Support SOA?

A *Service-Oriented Architecture* (SOA) is simply an IT architectural style that allows applications to be built to support today's business needs of flexibility and integration. *Flexibility* enables a business to change and adapt. *Integration* emphasizes the communication and interaction of business processes from end-to-end, both internally and externally with customers and suppliers.

IBM WebSphere Portlet Factory is part of the IBM SOA Foundation and supports the "assemble phase" of the SOA life cycle. Developing a SOA application basically involves creating a service provider model and a service consumer model. Additional SOA features include disconnected support via stub service models, automatic service testing, simple service documentation, dynamic service mapping, and service interface support.

IBM WebSphere Portal is part of the IBM SOA Foundation and supports the "deploy phase" of the SOA life cycle. The deploy phase includes a combination of creating the hosting environment for your applications and actually deploying those applications. IBM WebSphere Portal is a hosting environment for the user interaction logic of your SOA application. IBM WebSphere Portal gives you the user interface to SOA. Additional SOA features include accessing Web services from portlets, Web services for remote portlet (WSRP), integrating business processes, and composite applications.

By connecting/integrating a company's resources including people, applications, business processes, and content, IBM WebSphere Portlet Factory and IBM WebSphere Portal build portals that provide complete interaction and collaboration services.

Tutorial Overview

The tutorial in this chapter introduces you to IBM WebSphere Portlet Factory and IBM WebSphere Portal. It provides step-by-step instructions to give you a complete end-to-end experience from development to production. You will develop and test two portlets in a development environment using IBM WebSphere Portlet Factory, and then you will deploy/manage the portlets in a production environment using IBM WebSphere Portal.

End-to-End on Developing, Testing, and Deploying of a Portlet

The tutorial is based on a scenario about a company called PetCompleteServices building their portal Web site. PetCompleteServices is all about pets. It provides information and services for pets, including pet travel insurance, pet travel carrier, pet sitting, and lots more. Victoria is responsible for architecture and technology at PetCompleteServices. In her SOA plan for the company, the first step is to start with a portal. It is in PetCompleteServices' long-term plan to integrate with airline companies to provide travel services for pets. Claire is from the airline company HelloWorldAir and is always looking to work with new partners to provide first of a kind services for her customers to stay on top of the competition. Victoria and Claire have started working on the integration proposal.

The tutorial is divided into three parts (Tutorials 7.1, 7.2, and 7.3):

- In Tutorial 7.1, you will develop and test a simple portlet, called PetTravelInfo, which is expected to have the look and feel shown in Figure 7.1. This portlet displays static text.

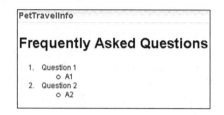

Figure 7.1   Look and feel of PetTravelInfo

The focus of this part of the tutorial is the basics of IBM WebSphere Portlet Factory. It covers projects, models, builders, portlets, testing of a model, and building the WAR file for deploying in production. If your intention is to have a hands-on end-to-end experience from development to production of a portlet, you can choose to follow only Tutorials 7.1 and 7.3.

- In Tutorial 7.2, you will develop and test a portlet, called ListPetTravelCompany, which is expected to have the look and feel shown in Figure 7.2. This portlet retrieves information from a database and displays the results in a simple table.

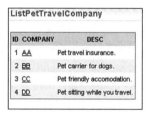

Figure 7.2   Look and feel of ListPetTravelCompany

The focus of this part of the tutorial is a well-designed SOA WebSphere Portlet Factory application. It covers service provider and service consumer models.

- In Tutorial 7.3, you will put PetTravelInfo and ListPetTravelCompany in a production environment. The result is shown in Figure 7.3. You will install the portlets in IBM WebSphere Portal and then add them to portal pages. Finally, you will grant permission to a new user to use the portlets.

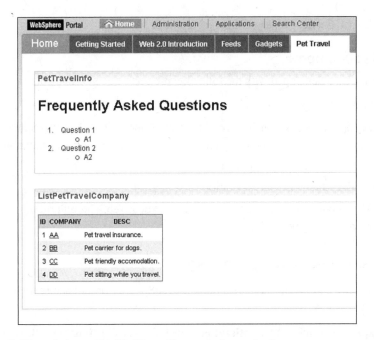

Figure 7.3   PetTravelInfo and ListPetTravelCompany in production

The focus of this part of the tutorial is on using tools to build a portal, including installing portlet application, creating portal pages, adding portlets to portal pages, and editing portal page layout; using tools to manage a portal, including giving access to users on new portlets; and single login to a portal website rather than to individual application.

Tutorial outline:

- Tutorial 7.1: Create and Test a Simple Portlet
  - Step 1: Create a project in IBM WebSphere Portlet Factory
  - Step 2: Create and test a simple portlet
- Tutorial 7.2: Create and Test a Portlet That Accesses a Database
  - Step 1: Create a service provider model
  - Step 2: Create a service consumer model
- Tutorial 7.3: Deploy a Portlet
  - Step 1: Install a portlet in IBM WebSphere Portal
  - Step 2: Add a portlet to a WebSphere portal page
  - Step 3: Access a portlet as a new user

- Step 4: Set access permissions for a portlet

System Requirements

The tutorial has been developed with the following products and environment.

- IBM WebSphere Portlet Factory version 6.1
  - An application server is needed for testing the model. The WebSphere Application Server instance WebSphere_Portal in the WebSphere Portal installation can be used.
- IBM WebSphere Portal version 6.1
- IBM DB2 Enterprise Server Edition version 9.1.4
  - This product is required for Tutorial 7.2. Your WebSphere Portal installation should be configured with DB2.

What Is Included in the CD-ROM?

In the CD included in this book, you will find the WebSphere Portlet Factory application and the tutorial recorded as videos.

1. **chapter 7/tutorial 7.2/solution/PetTravel.zip**—A WebSphere Portlet Factory archive file that contains the completed application for your reference. To import it to WebSphere Portlet Factory Designer, click File, Import from the menu bar. Then expand Other and click WebSphere Portlet Factory Archive. Click on Next and follow the wizard's instructions.

2. **chapter 7/tutorial 7.x/video**—Contains the video files for all the tutorials discussed in this chapter. Open the Hypertext Markup Language (HTML) file in any browser to watch the video.

Tutorial Setup

To prepare the environment for the tutorial, you will create a deployment configuration in WebSphere Portlet Factory, create a database and a table in DB2, and create a datasource in WebSphere Application Server.

WebSphere Portlet Factory—Create a Deployment Configuration

A *deployment configuration* is a set of properties that define your deployment information. An application server is needed for testing the models in the tutorial and you will create a deployment configuration for the application server instance. Your WebSphere Portal installation has two WebSphere Applications Server instances: server1 and WebSphere_Portal. In this section, you will create a deployment configuration for the WebSphere Application Server instance WebSphere_Portal.

1. Start WebSphere Portlet Factory Designer.

    a. Click Start, All Programs, IBM WebSphere, Portlet Factory, Designer.

    b. Click OK to accept the default workspace folder as shown in Figure 7.4.

Figure 7.4   Select a workspace

2. Create a deployment configuration.

    a. Click Window, Preferences as shown in Figure 7.5.

Figure 7.5   Set preferences

    b. Expand the WebSphere Portlet Factory Designer section and click Deployment as shown in Figure 7.6.

Figure 7.6   Select deployment preferences

    c. Click Add to create the deployment environment for deploying your projects as shown in Figure 7.7.

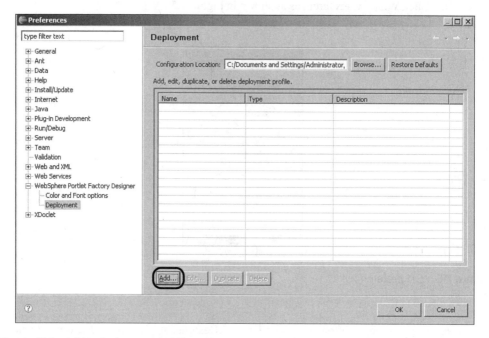

Figure 7.7   Add a deployment configuration

d. Table 7.1 shows you how to provide inputs for the New Deployment Configuration dialog. Click OK when you are finished with the dialog as shown in Figure 7.8. Make sure the WAS server `WebSphere_Portal` has been started.

Table 7.1 Input values for Deployment Configuration dialog

Parameters	Values
Configuration Name	Enter `WAS61` or provide a different name of your choice.
Description	Enter `WAS 6.1` deployment configuration or provide your own description.
Server Type	Select WebSphere Application Server 6.x from the drop-down.
Installed Applications Dir	Enter your WebSphere Portal installed directory. (Example: `C:\IBM\WebSphere\wp_profile\installedApps\ portalhost`).
Server Host	Enter your WebSphere Portal host name. (Example: `portalhost.ibm.com`).
Server Port	10040.
Specify Deployment Credentials	Select this check box.
WAS Server for deployment	Select `WebSphere_Portal` from the drop-down.
Admin User	Enter your WebSphere Portal Administrator user ID.
Admin Password	Enter your WebSphere Portal Administrator password.

e. A message indicating that the test to connect to the WAS server was successful is shown as in Figure 7.9. Click OK to close the window.

f. The new deployment configuration has been created successfully as shown in Figure 7.10. Click OK to close the Preferences window.

In this setup step, you have created a deployment configuration for deploying your projects.

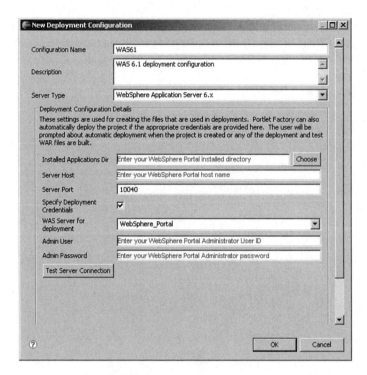

Figure 7.8   New Deployment Configuration dialog

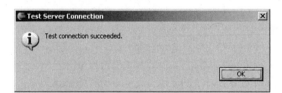

Figure 7.9   Test connection message

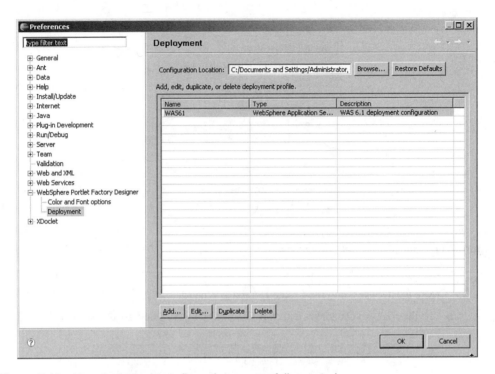

Figure 7.10   New deployment configuration successfully created

DB2—Create a Database and a Table

This is a setup step required by Tutorial 7.2.

1. Start the DB2 Control Center.

    a. Click Start, All Programs, IBM DB2, DB2COPY1 (Default), General Administration Tools, Control Center.

    b. Advanced view is the default for the Control Center View as shown in Figure 7.11. Simply click OK.

Figure 7.11   Specify Control Center view

2.   Create a database using the Create Database Wizard.

    a.   Right-click All Databases and click Create Database, Standard as shown in Figure 7.12.

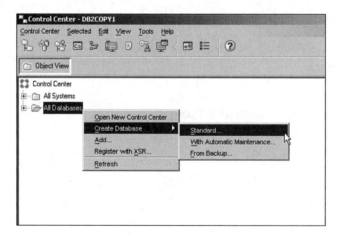

Figure 7.12   Invoke Create Database Wizard

    b.   Enter PetDB as the database name, and keep all other defaults as shown in Figure 7.13. Click Finish.

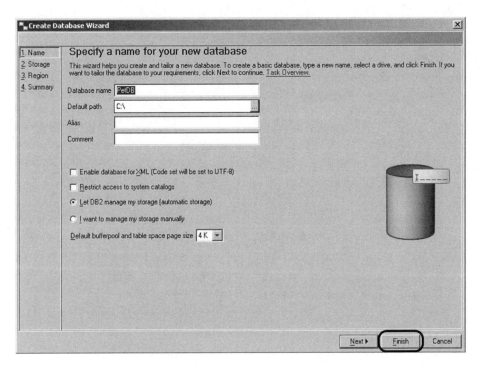

Figure 7.13 Specify database name

3. Create a database table using the Create Table Wizard.

    a. After database PetDB is created successfully, you are returned to the Object view. You should be able to see PetDB by expanding All Databases. To invoke the Create Table Wizard, expand PetDB. Then right-click Tables and click Create as shown in Figure 7.14.

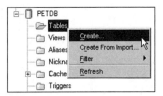

Figure 7.14 Invoke Create Table Wizard

    b. Enter PetTravelCompany as the table name as shown in Figure 7.15. Click Next.

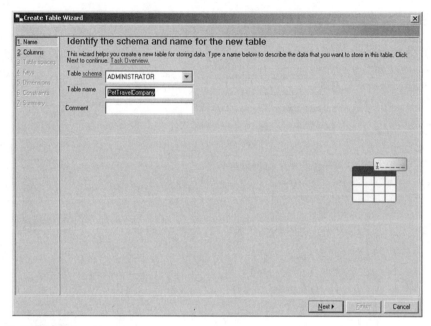

Figure 7.15   Specify table name

    c.   Click Add to add a column to the `PetTravelCompany` table as shown in Figure 7.16.

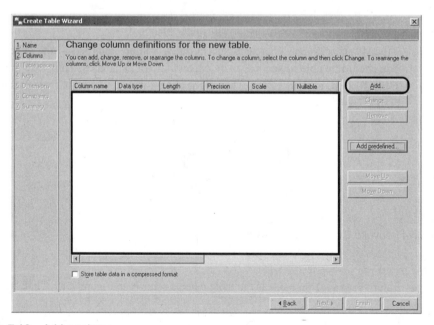

Figure 7.16   Add a column

d. Enter ID as the column name and select INTEGER from the drop-down for data type as shown in Figure 7.17. Click OK.

Figure 7.17 Add Column dialog

e. Use the Add button to add two more columns using the Table 7.2 as inputs.

Table 7.2 Inputs values for add column dialog

Column Name	Data Type	Length
Company	VARCHAR	50
Desc	VARCHAR	100

f. PetTravelCompany has three columns added as shown in Figure 7.18. Click Finish.

g. A message indicating that the table creation was successful is shown as in Figure 7.19. Click Close.

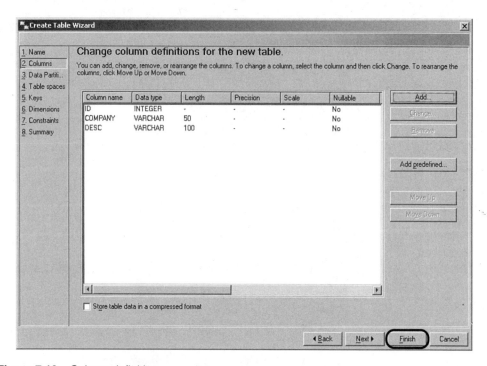

Figure 7.18   Column definition

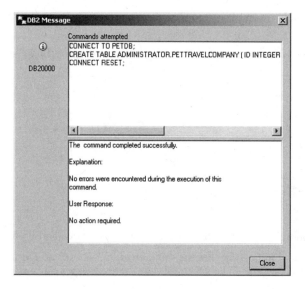

Figure 7.19   Table successfully created

h. To display the list of tables in the Contents pane, right-click Tables and click Refresh as shown in Figure 7.20. Do you see your newly created table PetTravelCompany in the Contents pane on the right side?

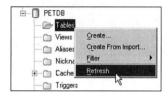

Figure 7.20 Refresh the list of tables

4. Add data to a database table.

a. To add data to the table PetTravelCompany, right-click PETTRAVELCOMPANY and click Open. as shown in Figure 7.21

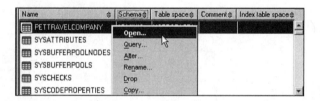

Figure 7.21 Open a table

b. Click Add Row to add a row to the table as shown in Figure 7.22. You will be doing this action four times to add four rows.

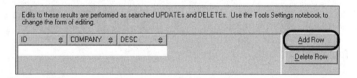

Figure 7.22 Add a row

c. Use table 7.3 as input when adding the four rows to the table.

Table 7.3	Input values for Add Rows

ID	COMPANY	DESC
1	AA	Pet travel insurance
2	BB	Pet carrier for dogs
3	CC	Pet friendly accommodation
4	DD	Pet sitting while you travel

> **d.** When all the rows have been added to the table, click Commit and then Close as shown in Figure 7.23.

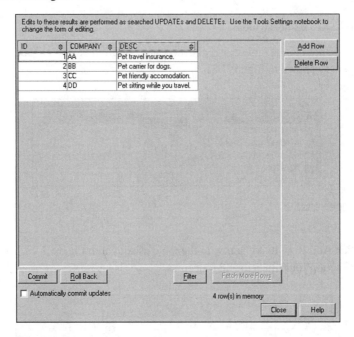

Figure 7.23	Table content

In this setup step, you have created a database and a table for creating a portlet that accesses a database.

WebSphere Application Server—Create a Datasource

This is a setup step required by Tutorial 7.2.

> **1.** Log in to WebSphere Application Server administration console.
>
> > **a.** Start the WebSphere Application Server administration console by opening a browser and entering the uniform resource locator (URL) `http://<hostname>:<port_number>/ibm/console`, where `<hostname>` is the fully qualified host name of

the machine that is running your WebSphere Portal and `<port_number>` is the administration console port number.

For example, enter `http://portalhost.ibm.com:10027/ibm/console`

    b. Log in using your administrator user ID and password.

2. Select the JDBC (Java Database Connectivity) provider.

    a. Expand Resources, JDBC and click JDBC Providers as shown in Figure 7.24.

    b. Click `wpdbJDBC_db2` as shown in Figure 7.25.

Figure 7.24   Go to the list of JDBC providers

Figure 7.25   Select the JDBC provider for the portal

3. Create a datasource.

    a. Under Additional Properties, click Data Sources as shown in Figure 7.26.

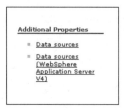

Figure 7.26   Go to the list of datasources

    b. To invoke the Create a Data Source Wizard, click New as shown in Figure 7.27. You will be creating a datasource for your database PetDB.

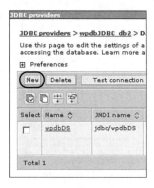

Figure 7.27   Invoke the Create a New Data Source Wizard

    c. In Step 1 of the Create a Data Source Wizard as shown in Figure 7.28, enter PetDB for the datasource name, jdbc/PetDB for the JNDI name, and select wpdbDSJAASAuth for the authentication alias. Click Next.

    d. In Step 2 of the Create a Data Source Wizard as shown in Figure 7.29, enter PetDB for the database name and your WebSphere Portal host name for the server name. An example of a host name is portalhost.ibm.com. Click Next.

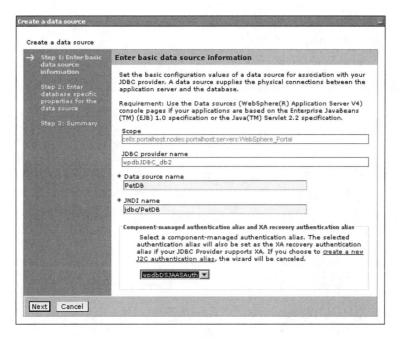

Figure 7.28   Step 1 of the Create a Data Source Wizard

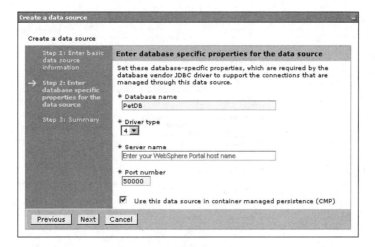

Figure 7.29   Step 2 of the Create a Data Source Wizard

   e. In Step 3 of the Create a Data Source Wizard as shown in Figure 7.30, simply review the information. Click Finish.

   f. Click the Save Directly to the Master Configuration link as shown in Figure 7.31.

In this setup step, you created a datasource for database `PetDB`.

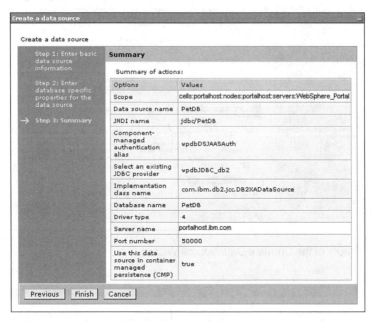

Figure 7.30   Step 3 of the Create a Data Source Wizard

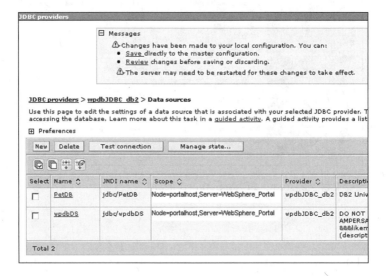

Figure 7.31   Save to master configuration

Tutorial 7.1: Create and Test a Simple Portlet

In this tutorial, you will create a project for all the models that will be built in Tutorials 7.1 and 7.2. You will then create a simple portlet.

Step 1: Create a Project in IBM WebSphere Portlet Factory

In this step, you will create a project in Portlet Factory Designer.

1. Launch the Create Portlet Factory Project Wizard to create a WebSphere Portlet Factory project.

   a. WebSphere Portlet Factory Designer should have been started in the "Tutorial Setup" section.

   b. Click File, New, WebSphere Portlet Factory Project to create a project as shown in Figure 7.32.

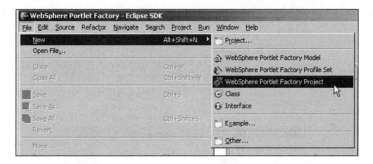

Figure 7.32 Create a WebSphere Portlet Factory project

   c. Enter `PetTravel` for the project name. Click Next as shown in Figure 7.33.

   d. There is no need to add feature sets to your project as shown in Figure 7.34. These feature sets provide additional builders that are not needed for this tutorial. Click Next.

   e. Select `WAS61` from the drop-down for application server deployment configuration as shown in Figure 7.35. Click Finish.

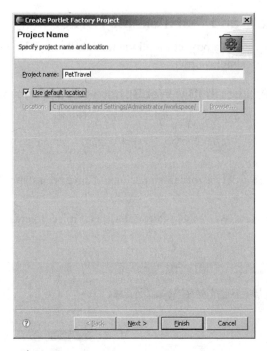

Figure 7.33   Enter the project name

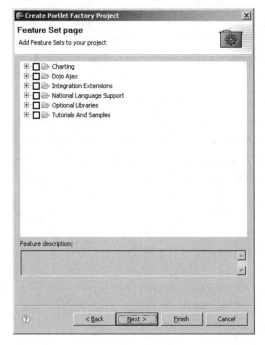

Figure 7.34   Select feature sets

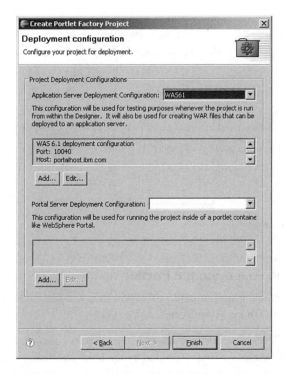

Figure 7.35 Specify application server deployment configuration

2. After the progress indicator, click No when asked whether you would like to deploy your project now as shown in Figure 7.36. You will be shown how to deploy your project in a development environment in a separate step.

Figure 7.36 Deployment Request dialog

3. Your project `PetTravel` has been created successfully and appears in the Project Explorer window as shown in Figure 7.37.

You have successfully created the project.

Figure 7.37   Project created

Step 2: Create and Test a Simple Portlet

In this step, you will create a simple model. You will then test the model using the deployment configuration you created in the setup section.

1. Launch the WebSphere Portlet Factory Model Wizard to create a Main and Page model. It is one of the sample models provided by the IBM WebSphere Portlet Factory product. A Main and Page model supplies a page and a main action that presents that page when the application is run.

   a. Right-click PetTravel and click New, WebSphere Portlet Factory Model as shown in Figure 7.38.

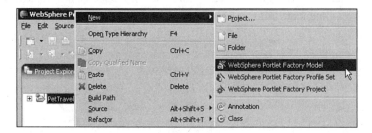

Figure 7.38   Create a new WebSphere Portlet Factory model

   b. Select PetTravel as the project as shown in Figure 7.39. Click Next.
   c. Under Factory Starter Models, select Main and Page as shown in Figure 7.40. Click Next.

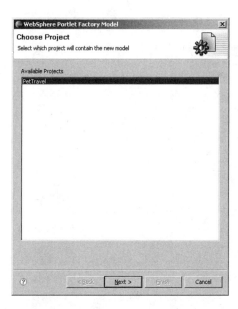

Figure 7.39   Select the project to contain the model

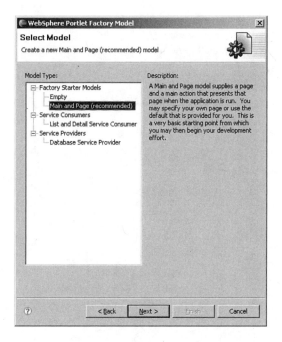

Figure 7.40   Select to create a Main and Page model

d. Keep all the defaults as shown in Figure 7.41. Click Next.

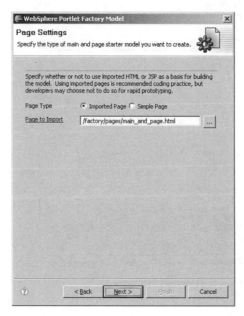

Figure 7.41   Specify page type

e. Enter `PetTravelFAQ` as the model name as shown in Figure 7.42. Click Finish.

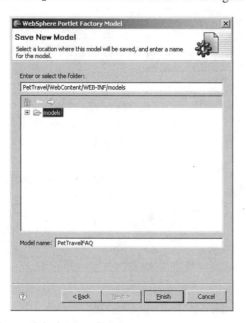

Figure 7.42   Specify the model name and save

2. Modify the content of the HTML page in the model.

   a. The `PetTravelFAQ` model has been created successfully as shown in Figure 7.43. The outline window at the bottom shows the list of builders in this model. Double-click the imported page builder `page1`.

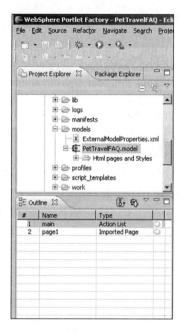

Figure 7.43 Main and Page model created

   b. Click Edit Page to modify the page content in HTML as shown in Figure 7.44.

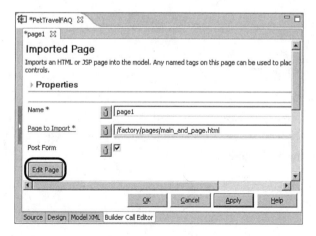

Figure 7.44 Edit page

    c. To modify the page content, follow the example as shown in Figure 7.45 or provide your own HTML content. Click Save Page, then Apply and OK to save changes for the builder.

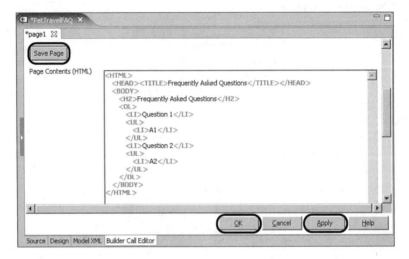

Figure 7.45 Modify page content and save builder changes

    d. Click File, Save to save changes for the model as shown in Figure 7.46.

Figure 7.46 Save model changes

3. Deploy the project for development testing.

    a. Right-click `PetTravel` and click Application Server WAR, Build WAR for Dev Testing as shown in Figure 7.47.

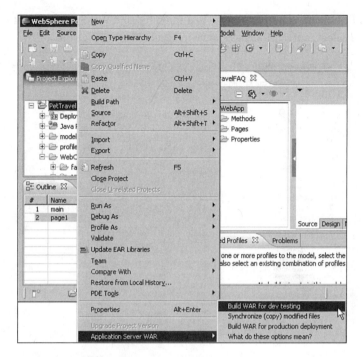

Figure 7.47 Deploy project for development testing

4. Test the model.

    a. Click the Run Active Model icon as shown in Figure 7.48.

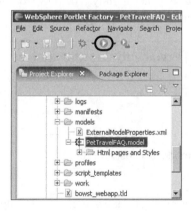

Figure 7.48 Run selected model

b. A little setup is needed for the first time. Expand WebSphere Portlet Factory Model and select Active Model as shown in Figure 7.49. Click Run.

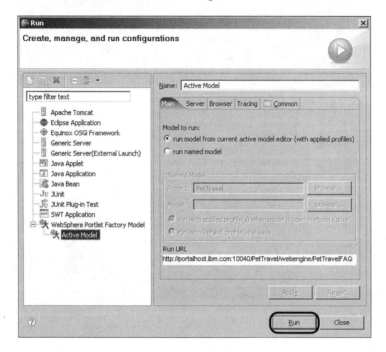

Figure 7.49   Run setup

c. Your model should run successfully. The page you provided HTML content for is shown in a browser as in Figure 7.50.

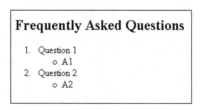

Figure 7.50   Main and page model successfully run

5. It is simple to make this model run as a portlet as well. Only one builder needs to be added.

a. In the outline window, click the Add a Builder Call to the Current Model icon as shown in Figure 7.51.

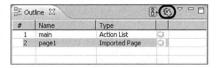

Figure 7.51 Add a builder call

b. In the Builder Picker window as shown in Figure 7.52, select Portal Integration for the category name and Portlet Adapter for the builder. Click OK.

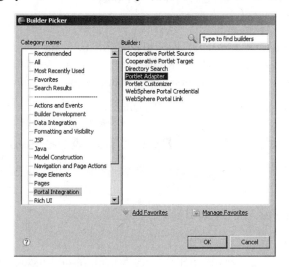

Figure 7.52 Select a builder to add to the model

c. Enter `PetTravelInfo` as the name and the portlet title. Enter `Pet Travel Information` as the portlet short title. Click Apply and then OK as shown in Figure 7.53.

Figure 7.53 Fill in information for the Portlet Adapter builder

    d. The Portlet Adapter builder has been added to the model as shown in Figure 7.54. Click File, Save.

Figure 7.54   The Portlet Adapter builder added to model

    6. You only need to do this step if you will not be doing the next section to create and test a portlet that accesses a database. Right-click `PetTravel` and click Portal Server WAR, Build Portlet WAR for Production Deployment. Keep the defaults. Click Finish.

You have created and tested the model. The model is used to generate the portlet.

Tutorial 7.2: Create and Test a Portlet That Accesses a Database

In this tutorial, you will create a service provider model to retrieve data from the database and create a service consumer model to present the data.

Step 1: Create a Service Provider Model

In this step, you will create a service provider model.

    1. Launch the WebSphere Portlet Factory Model Wizard to create a service provider model. It is one of the sample models provided by the IBM WebSphere Portlet Factory product. This sample model allows you to execute SQL statements against a database.

    a. Right-click `PetTravel` and click New, WebSphere Portlet Factory Model.

    b. Select `PetTravel` as the project. Click Next.

    c. Under Service Providers, select Database Service Provider as shown in Figure 7.55. Click Next.

    d. Enter `PetTravelServiceProvider` as the service name. Click Next.

    e. In step 1 of defining the service operation as shown in Figure 7.56, select `jdbc/PetDB` from the drop-down for SQL datasource and enter `Select * from Administrator.PetTravelCompany` as the SQL statement. Click Next.

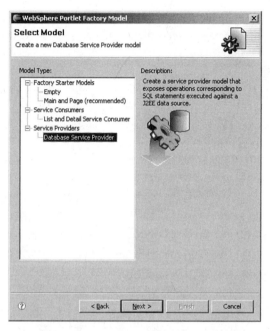

Figure 7.55   Select to create a Database Service Provider model

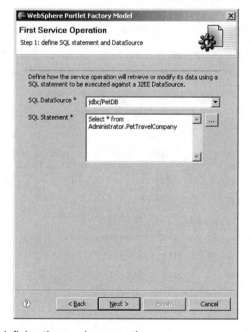

Figure 7.56   Step 1 of defining the service operation

f. In step 2 of defining the service operation as shown in Figure 7.57, enter `getCompany` as the operation name and keep all other defaults. Click Next.

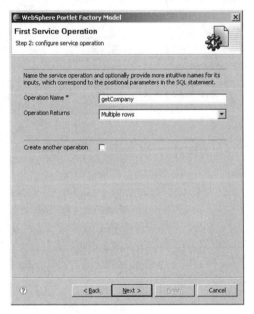

Figure 7.57   Step 2 of defining the service operation

g. Enter `PetTravelCompany` as the model name. Click Finish.

2. The `PetTravelCompany` model has been created successfully as shown in Figure 7.58. The outline window at the bottom shows the list of builders in this model.

Figure 7.58   Database Service Provider model created

3. Test the model.

   a. PetTravelCompany should be the selected model at this time. To test the model, click the Run Active Model icon.

   b. Your model should run successfully. You should see the `getCompany` operation you defined in the browser as shown in Figure 7.59. Click `getCompany`.

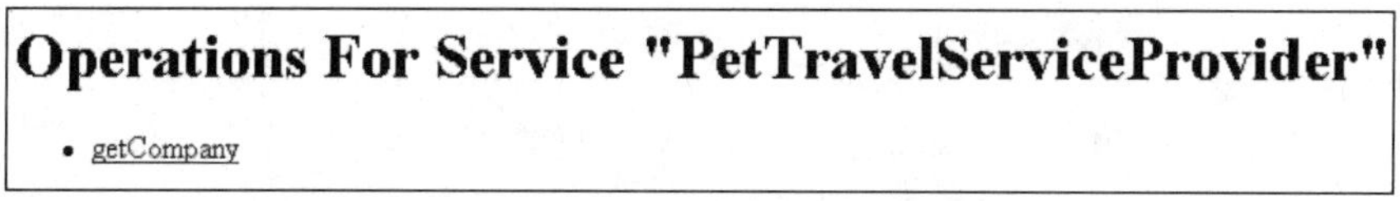

Operations For Service "PetTravelServiceProvider"

- getCompany

Figure 7.59   Database Service Provider model run successfully

   c. You should see the data from the database table `PetTravelCompany` displayed correctly as shown in Figure 7.60.

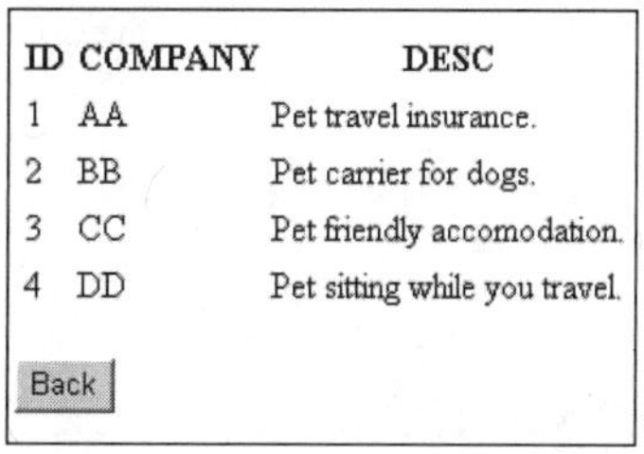

ID	COMPANY	DESC
1	AA	Pet travel insurance.
2	BB	Pet carrier for dogs.
3	CC	Pet friendly accomodation.
4	DD	Pet sitting while you travel.

Back

Figure 7.60   Data from database retrieved and displayed

In this step, you created a service provider model. You should see that the pieces are starting to come together. The service provider retrieves the data in the database table created in the "Tutorial Setup" section.

Step 2: Create a Service Consumer Model

In this step, you will create a service consumer model that will use a simple table to display the results from the provider model.

1. Launch the WebSphere Portlet Factory Model Wizard to create a service consumer model. It is one of the sample models provided by the IBM WebSphere Portlet Factory product. This sample model displays data from a database.

   a. Right-click `PetTravel` and click New, WebSphere Portlet Factory Model.

   b. Select `PetTravel` as the project. Click Next.

   c. Under Service Consumers, select List and Detail Service Consumer as shown in Figure 7.61. Click Next.

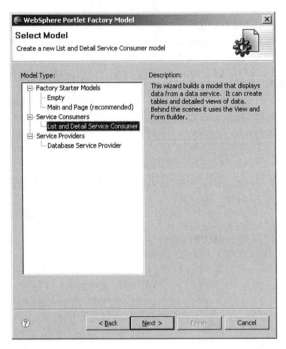

Figure 7.61   Select to create a List and Detail Service Consumer model

   d. Enter `PetTravelCompanySimpleTable` as the name and select `PetTravelCompany` as the provider model as shown in Figure 7.62. Recall that you created the `PetTravel-Company` model in the previous step. Click Next.

   e. Select `getCompany` from the drop-down for view data operation to provide the view data as shown in Figure 7.63. Recall that you defined the service operation `getCompany` to retrieve data from the database table `PetTravelCompany`. Click Next.

   f. Select `COMPANY` from the drop-down for details link column and keep all other defaults as shown in Figure 7.64. Recall that you created the database table `PetTravelCompany` with `ID`, `Company`, and `Desc` as the three columns. This is why `Company` appears as a choice in the drop-down. Click Next.

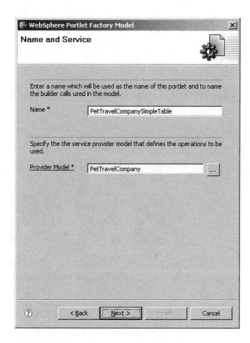

Figure 7.62   Enter name and service

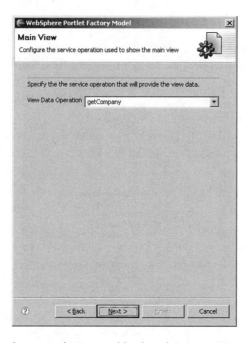

Figure 7.63   Specify service operation to provide view data

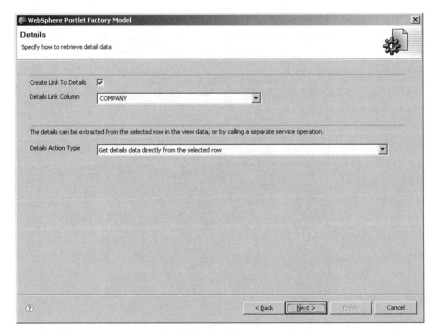

Figure 7.64   Specify how to get detail data

    g. Enter `ListPetTravelCompany` as the model name. Click Finish.

2. The `ListPetTravelCompany` model has been created successfully as shown in Figure 7.65. The outline window at the bottom shows the list of builders in this model.

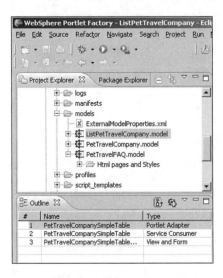

Figure 7.65   List and Detail Service Consumer model created

3. Test the model.

   a. `ListPetTravelCompany` should be the selected model at this time. To test the model, click the Run Active Model icon.

   b. You should see the data from the database table `PetTravelCompany` displayed correctly in a simple table with the Details link using the `Company` column as shown in Figure 7.66.

ID	COMPANY	DESC
1	AA	Pet travel insurance.
2	BB	Pet carrier for dogs.
3	CC	Pet friendly accomodation.
4	DD	Pet sitting while you travel.

Figure 7.66   List and Detail Service Consumer model run successfully

4. Build a portlet WAR file for deploying in production. IBM WebSphere Portal is the production server.

   a. Right-click `PetTravel` and click Portal Server WAR, Build Portlet WAR for Production Deployment as shown in Figure 7.67.

Figure 7.67   Build portlet WAR for production

   b. Keep the defaults as shown in Figure 7.68. Click Finish.

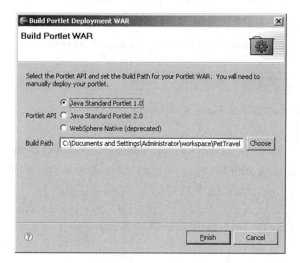

Figure 7.68   Select portlet API and build path

    c. Go to the above build path. You should see the `PA_PetTravel.war` WAR file.

You have created a service consumer model to present data in a simple table.

Tutorial 7.3: Deploy a Portlet

In this tutorial, you will install the portlets you built in Tutorials 7.1 and 7.2 in IBM Web-Sphere Portal. You will then add the portlets to portal pages and set permissions for the portlets.

    Step 1 shows you how to install a portlet in a production machine/environment performed by an administrator. If you want to do additional testing in a test machine/environment first with WebSphere Portal installed, you can deploy directly from WebSphere Portlet factory using a deployment configuration. Remaining steps on adding a portlet to a portal page or setting access permissions are the same.

Step 1: Install a Portlet in IBM WebSphere Portal

In this step, you will install the portlets to WebSphere Portal.

   1. Log in to WebSphere Portal.

     a. Start the WebSphere_Portal server if it is not already running.

     b. Open a browser and enter the URL `http://<hostname>:<port_number>/wps/portal`, where *`<hostname>` is the fully qualified host name of the machine that is running your WebSphere Portal, and* `<port_number>` *is the port number displayed on the confirmation panel during your install.*

For example, enter `http://portalhost.ibm.com:10040/wps/portal`

     c. Log in using your WebSphere Portal administrator user ID and password.

   2. Install the portlets.

     a. Click Administration at the top of the page as shown in Figure 7.69.

Figure 7.69   Select WebSphere Portal administration

     b. In the left pane, click Portlet Management, Web Modules as shown in Figure 7.70.

     c. On the Manage Web Modules page, click Install as shown in Figure 7.71.

     d. The Installing a Web Module Wizard appears. In step 1 of the wizard as shown in Figure 7.72, browse to the build path that you specified when you built the portlet WAR. Select `PA_PetTravel.war`. Click Next.

Figure 7.70   Portlet management

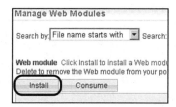

Figure 7.71   Manage Web modules

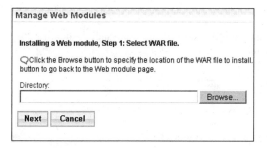

Figure 7.72   Step 1 of Installing a Web Module Wizard

For example: browse to `C:\Documents and Settings\Administrator\workspace\Pet-Travel\PA_PetTravel.war`.

e. In Step 2 of the wizard as shown in Figure 7.73, review the portlets that are going to be installed. You should see the two portlets that you created. Click Finish.

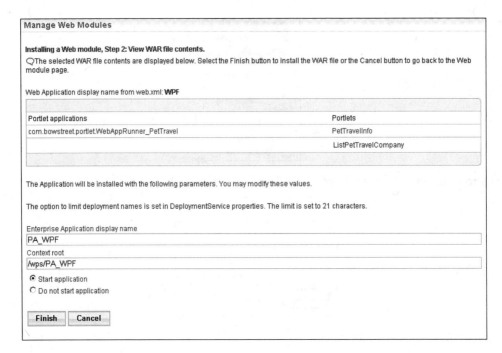

Figure 7.73   Step 2 of Installing a Web Module Wizard

   f. Once the installation is complete, a message indicating that the installation was successful is shown at the top of the page as in Figure 7.74.

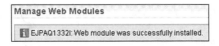

Figure 7.74   Portlet successfully installed

3. To verify the installation, search by File Name Contains and enter `PetTravel` as the
   search criteria. You should see `PA_PetTravel.war` in the list of Web modules as shown
   in Figure 7.75.

   In this step, you have installed the portlet application that was developed using WebSphere
Portlet Factory.

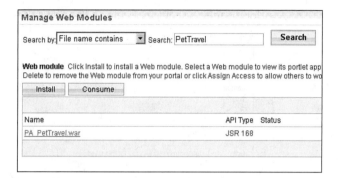

Figure 7.75   Verify portlet installation

Step 2: Add a Portlet to a WebSphere Portal Page

In the previous step, you installed the portlets. They will not appear in the portal site yet. They need to be added to portal pages. In this step, you will create a portal page and add the two portlets to the portal page.

1. Create a portal page.

    a. You should still be in the Administration page. In the left pane, click Portal User Interface, Manage Pages as shown in Figure 7.76.

Figure 7.76   Manage pages

    b. On the Manage Pages page, click Content Root. When you are at Content Root, click Home. Click New Page to create a new page under Home as shown in Figure 7.77.

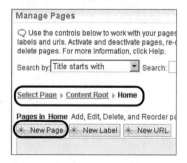

Figure 7.77   Create new page

   c. Enter `Pet Travel` for the title as shown in Figure 7.78. Click OK.

Figure 7.78   Page properties for new page

   d. You should see `Pet Travel` in the list of pages as shown in Figure 7.79.

Figure 7.79   Verify page creation

e. Select Home, and you will see the `Pet Travel` page.

2. Add portlets to a portal page.

   a. Click the Page Menu icon and click Edit Page Layout as shown in Figure 7.80.

Figure 7.80   Launch page menu

b. Click Add Portlets in the left column in the layout as shown in Figure 7.81.

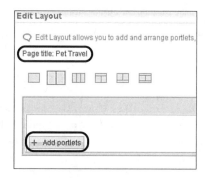

Figure 7.81   Edit layout

c. A search screen renders on the page to let you search for the portlet you want to add. Search by Title Contains and enter `PetTravel` as the search criteria as shown in Figure 7.82.

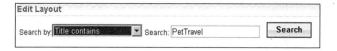

Figure 7.82   Search for portlet

d. In the search results, select the check box for both `ListPetTravelCompany` and `PetTravelInfo` as shown in Figure 7.83. Click OK.

e. `ListPetTravelCompany` and `PetTravelInfo` appear in the left column of the layout page as shown in Figure 7.84. Click the down arrow to the right of `ListPetTravelCompany` to move it below `PetTravelInfo`. Click Done.

Edit Layout
Search by: Title contains
Search: PetTravel
Search
Page 1 of 1
Portlet Title
Description
Unique name
Remote portlet
ListPetTravelCompany
ListPetTravelCompany
PetTravelInfo
PetTravelFAQ
Page 1 of 1
OK
Cancel

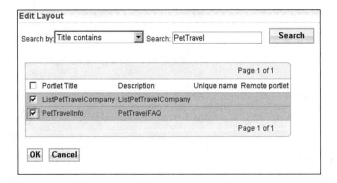

Figure 7.83 Select portlet

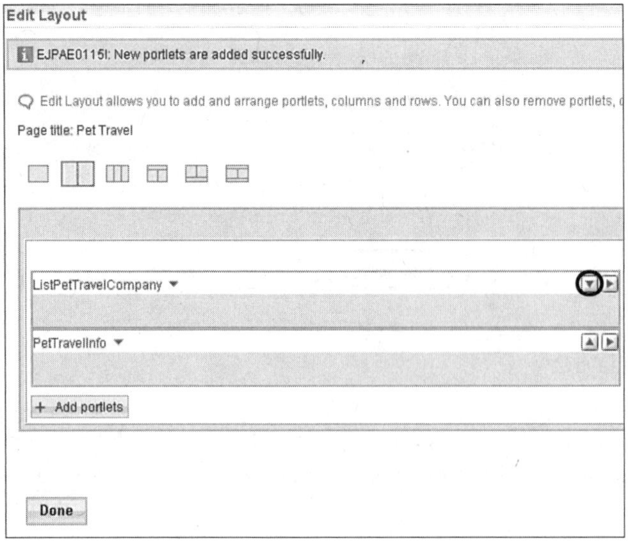

Edit Layout
EJPAE0115I: New portlets are added successfully.
Edit Layout allows you to add and arrange portlets, columns and rows. You can also remove portlets,
Page title: Pet Travel
ListPetTravelCompany
PetTravelInfo
+ Add portlets
Done

Figure 7.84 Portlet added

3. Your two portlets appear in the portal site as shown in Figure 7.85.

In this step, you have added the two portlets to a portal page. They now appear in the portal site.

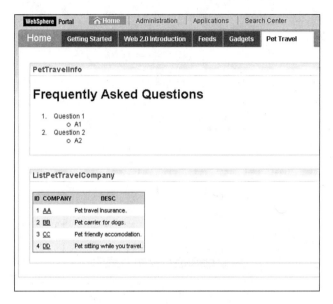

Figure 7.85   Portlets added to home page

Step 3: Access a Portlet as a New User

In this step, enroll in WebSphere Portal as a new user by filling out your own profile information; then log into Portal using the new ID.

1. Sign up as a new WebSphere Portal user.

    a. Open a browser and enter the URL `http://<hostname>:<port_number>/wps/portal` where `<hostname>` is the fully qualified host name of the machine that is running your WebSphere Portal, and `<port_number>` is the port number.

    For example, enter `http://portalhost.ibm.com:10040/wps/portal`.

    b. Click the Sign Up link above the Log In button.

    c. Fill in your user profile information to enroll in WebSphere Portal. You can choose your own user ID in Portal. In the example that follows as shown in Figure 7.86, the User ID registered is Mary. Click OK.

    d. A message is displayed saying the user was created successfully.

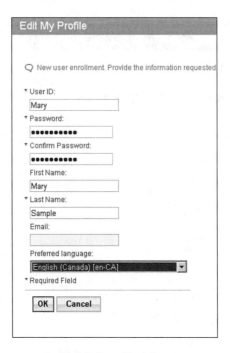

Figure 7.86   Sign up as new user in WebSphere Portal

2. Log in to Portal using the newly created user Mary.

3. Do you see the two portlets on the Pet Travel page? The portlets are not on user Mary's Pet Travel page. When you installed the portlets in WebSphere Portal, you did not grant users with access permission to the portlets. That is why you can only view the portlets as the administrator. No other users can view them at this point.

4. Exit WebSphere Portal by clicking Log Out in the upper-right corner.

   In this step, you logged in as a new user and were not able to access the portlets because you have not been granted access yet.

Step 4: Set Access Permissions for a Portlet

In this step, all authenticated portal users will be granted access to the portlets.

1. Go to the administrative function for setting permissions for portlets. Grant users access to the newly installed portlets.

   a. Log in to the WebSphere Portal as the Administrator again.

   b. Click Administration at the top of the page.

   c. Click Access, Resource Permissions.

2. Grant users access to the newly installed portlets.

    a. In the Resource Permissions page, as shown next in Figure 7.87, click Portlets.

Figure 7.87   Resource Permissions page

    b. Search by Title Contains and enter `PetTravel` as the search criteria.

    c. Click the Assign Access icon displayed beside the `PetTravelInfo` resource as shown in Figure 7.88.

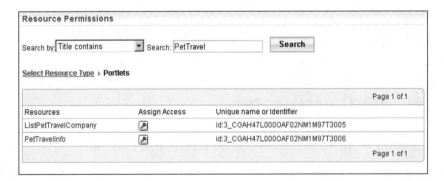

Figure 7.88   Assign Access

    d. Click the Edit Role icon beside the User role as shown in Figure 7.89.

    e. There are currently no members in this role, as shown next in Figure 7.90. This explains why you weren't able to see the `PetTravelInfo` portlet when you logged in as a user who is not an administrator (for example, Mary). Click Add to add members to this role.

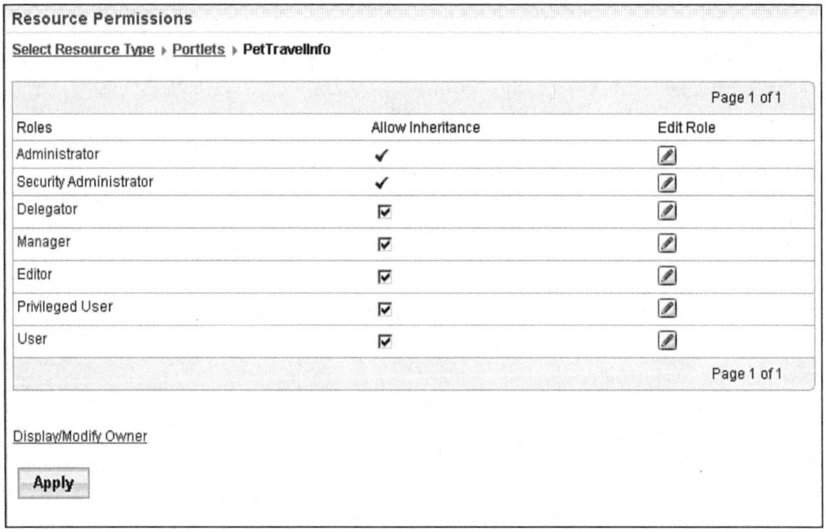

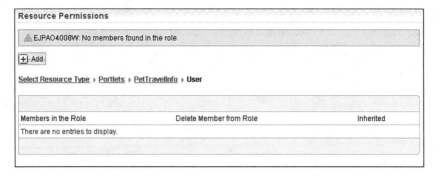

Figure 7.89   Modify access for a role

Figure 7.90   Members with access are shown

      f. Select the All Authenticated Portal Users check box. Click OK.

3. Log out of Portal, and log in as a user who is not an administrator. For example, log in as Mary.

4. What do you see in the `Pet Travel` page? You should see `PetTravelInfo` but not `ListPetTravelCompany` as shown in Figure 7.91. You have granted users access to the PetTravelInfo portlet but have not done that for the ListPetTravelCompany portlet yet.

In this step, you set access permissions to the portlet PetTravelInfo and confirmed that all portal users now have access to the portlet.

Figure 7.91   PetTravelInfo accessible by all users

Summary

In this chapter, you were introduced to the software IBM WebSphere Portlet Factory for developing portlets and the IBM WebSphere Portal for building, managing, and hosting portals.

First, as an overview, the chapter described key concepts and features. Then the tutorial was used to give you hands-on experience and reinforce the material introduced.

In the three-part tutorial, you developed and tested a simple portlet that displays information and a portlet that returns data from a database. You also deployed the portlets and saw them working in a production environment.

Tutorial summary:

- Tutorial 7.1: Create and Test a Simple Portlet
  - Create a project
  - Create a model
  - Add a builder
  - Create a portlet
  - Test a model
  - Build a WAR file for production deployment
- Tutorial 7.2: Create and Test a Portlet That Accesses a Database
  - Create a service provider model
  - Create a service consumer model

- Tutorial 7.3: Deploy a Portlet
  - Install a portlet
  - Create a portal page
  - Add a portlet to a portal page
  - Edit portal page layout
  - Give access to users on new portlets
  - Illustrate single login to portal website rather than to individual application

Service Security with IBM Tivoli Federated Identity Manager

Product Overview

A *federation* refers to two or more organizations establishing trust relationships to facilitate direct integration of business. With a federated relationship, identity information and entitlements are shared and provisioned in a trusted fashion across partners. An authenticated user of one organization, called the *identity provider*, can access other federation partners, called *service providers*, seamlessly. Several forms of inter-organization interaction may occur in a service-oriented deployment. Regardless of the form of the interaction, establishing a trust relationship between the organizations is a key step in allowing inter-organization cooperation. This involves establishing rules around the interaction, such as defining identity information that should be propagated between organizations. It is unlikely that user identities will be the same in all of the service components in a business process flow that spans different organizations. Identity services, therefore, will be required to validate the identity of the requesting users, confirm that they are authorized to perform the requested operation, and map their identity to one that the target service can understand and use to identify the users or services making the request. IBM Tivoli Federated Identity Manager (TFIM), as part of IBM SOA (service-oriented architecture) Foundation, can act as the identity service in the infrastructure. It helps increase the responsiveness to new business opportunities by providing security integration with heterogeneous types of service consumers.

TFIM provides functionality for federated single sign-on, identity provisioning, and Web services security management. This chapter focuses on the Web services security management functionality provided by TFIM. It establishes and manages federation relationships for Web services applications that use WS-Security tokens. Web services security management provides a WS-Trust approach to the management of WS-Security tokens that are sent within Web services requests. TFIM acting as the identity services in the infrastructure ensures Web services communications are managed in a secured and trusted manner.

What Are WS-Security and WS-Trust?

WS-Security (Web Services Security) was first released by the Organization for the Advancement of Structured Information Standards (OASIS) in April 2004. It is a communication protocol that specifies how to provide integrity, confidentiality, and security to Web services messages. It defines how to attach a security token to messages to ensure end-to-end security. Several supported token types can be used for Web services transactions, such as Security Assertion Markup Language (SAML), Lightweight Third-Party Authentication (LTPA), and Username.

Listing 8.1 shows a snippet of a Simple Object Access Protocol (SOAP) message that has a SAML security token attached. (SOAP is a protocol specification for applications to exchange information over the Web).

Listing 8.1   WS-Security Message Snippet

```
<env:Envelope xmlns:env="...">
<env:Header>
     <wsse:Security
          xmlns:wsse="http://docs.oasis-open.org/wss/2004/01/oasis-200401-wss-
wssecurity-secext-1.0.xsd">
                    <saml:Assertion ...>
                    :
                    </saml:Assertion>
          </wsse:Security>
     </env:Header>
     <soapenv:Body>
     :
     </soapenv:Body>
</env:Envelope>
```

WS-Trust (Web Services Trust Language) was approved by OASIS as a standard in March 2007. It provides extensions to WS-Security and specifies how to validate, renew, and issue security tokens. WS-Trust defines the concept of a *Security Token Service* (STS), a Web service that responds to WS-Trust requests and issues security tokens. TFIM provides an STS as one of its core components.

Listing 8.2 is a snippet of a WS-Trust message that requests security tokens.

Listing 8.2   RequestSecurityToken WS-Trust Message Snippet

```
<wst:RequestSecurityToken xmlns:wst="...">
```

```
    :
    <wst:Issuer xmlns:was="..." xmlns:wst="...">
          <wsa:Address>urn:itfim:wssm:tokenconsumer</wsa:Address>
    </wst:Issuer>
    <wsp:AppliesTo xmlns:wst="...">
          <wsa:EndpointReference>
                <wsa:Address>http://example.com/</wsa:Address>
          </wsa:EndpointReference>
    </wsp:AppliesTo>
    <wst:Base>
          <wss:BinarySecurityToken ..>
          :
          </wss:BinarySecurityToken>
    </wst:Base>
    :
<wst:RequestType>http://schemas.xmlsoap.org/ws/2005/02/trust/Validate</wst:Reque
stType>
</wst:RequestSecurityToken>
```

The `<wst:RequestSecurityToken>` element is used to send a request. `<wst:Issuer>` spec-ifies the issuer of the security token that is presented in the message. `<wst:AppliesTo>` defines the scope of the security token, `<wst:Base>` contains the security token, and `<wst:RequestType>` specifies the type of the request. In the example, the message requests validating the embedded binary security token.

Listing 8.3 shows a snippet of a WS-Trust message that responds to a `RequestSecurityToken`.

Listing 8.3   RequestSecurityTokenResponse WS-Trust Message Snippet

```
<wst:RequestSecurityTokenResponse xmlns:wst="...">
      <wst:Status>

<wst:Code>http://schemas.xmlsoap.org/ws/2005/02/trust/status/valid</wst:Code>
      </wst:Status>
      <wst:RequestedSecurityToken>
            <saml:Assertion ... >
            :
            </saml:Assertion>
      </wst:RequestedSecurityToken>
      :
</wst:RequestSecurityTokenResponse>
```

The `<wst:RequestSecurityTokenResponse>` element is used to return a security token or response to a request. `<wst:Status>` is used specifically for responding to a validation request to indicate the validation result. `<wst:RequestedSecurityToken>` returns the requested token. In the example, the message indicates that the received token was valid and has returned a SAML token.

What Are Security Token Service (STS) and Web Services Security Management (WSSM)?

Security Token Service (STS) and Web services security management (WSSM) are two key components of TFIM. Together, they allow the establishment and management of trust relationships between applications. STS is a Web service that responds to WS-Trust requests. It uses trust service chains to validate, transform, and issue security tokens. STS enables the management of security tokens across trust boundaries. The WSSM component provides functions for service requesters to create outbound security tokens using a token generator, and for service providers to process inbound security tokens using a token consumer. It enhances the WS-Security support provided by IBM WebSphere Application Server and provides a WS-Trust approach to the management of security tokens that STS supports.

Figure 8.1 and Figure 8.2 illustrate how these two components work together to securely send a service request at the requester side and to securely process a service request at the provider side. The tutorials in this chapter will illustrate step by step how to configure the WSSM and STS for Web services security management. We will show you how to enable security for a service provider, how to configure a service requester to access a protected provider, and how to test the service.

Generating a Security Token for a Web Services Request

Figure 8.1 shows how the WSSM and STS work together to include a security token in a service request.

1. When a service request is created at the requester side, the token generator is called as part of the WebSphere Application Server WS-Security authentication processing.

2. It works with the callback handler to generate a security token.

3. If the service requester is configured to call STS, the token generator then creates a `RequestSecurityToken` WS-Trust message with the security token included along with an AppliesTo and an Issuer.

4. The AppliesTo and Issuer are elements of a WS-Trust message. STS uses these two values to uniquely locate the right trust service chain, which then validates, maps, authorizes, and issues a security token.

5. Once processed, STS responds with a `RequestSecurityTokenResponse` WS-Trust message with a security token issued.

6. The token generator includes the security token from STS in the security header of the Web services request message, which is then sent to the service provider.

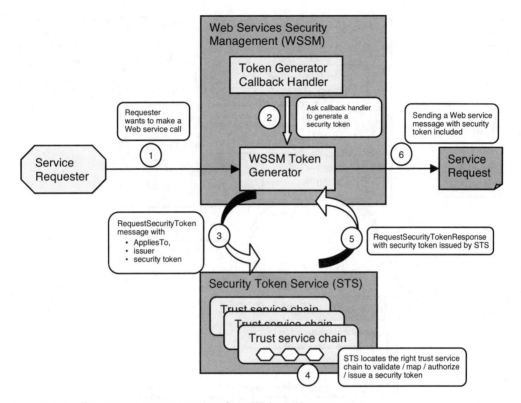

Figure 8.1 Generating a security token for a Web services request

Consuming a Security Token from a Web Services Request

Figure 8.2 illustrates how to consume the security token that is included in a service request.

1. When a service request is received at the provider side, the token consumer is called as part of the WebSphere Application Server WS-Security authentication processing.

2. If the service provider is configured to call STS, the token consumer then creates a `RequestSecurityToken` WS-Trust message with the security token included along with the AppliesTo and Issuer values.

3. STS uses these two values to uniquely locate the right trust service chain, which then validates, maps, authorizes, and issues a security token.

4. Once processed, STS responds with a `RequestSecurityTokenResponse` WS-Trust message with a security token issued.

5. The token consumer then works with the callback handler, which passes the security token to the appropriate login module for authentication.

6. Once the credential within the security token is validated, the service provider is accessed.

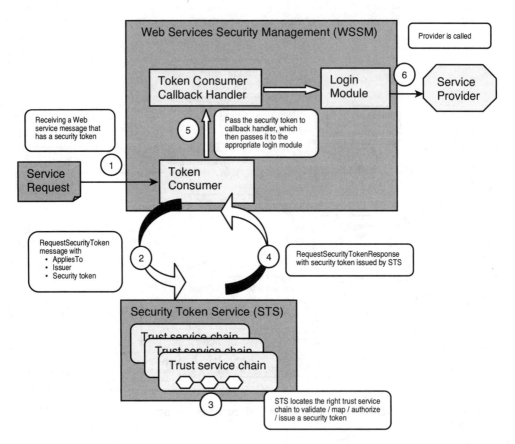

Figure 8.2   Consuming a security token from a Web services request

How Does It Support SOA?

Service orientation aims to provide services that can be interconnected and reused as appropriate to fulfill a particular business process. These services must be connected and implemented in a secure and auditable manner, according to a defined security policy. However, the loose coupling of services and their operations across trust boundaries create challenges in service security and identity federation. TFIM, as part of the IBM SOA Foundation, gives companies the tools needed to support **service security and manage security identities across SOA**. It, along with IBM Tivoli Access Manager and IBM Directory Server, provides security infrastructure services, which include secure token services, authorization services, authentication services, and directory services for the information technology (IT) infrastructure as illustrated in Figure 8.3.

The STS and WSSM of TFIM play a key role in an SOA scenario. STS enables the management of trust relationship between security domains; and WSSM adds the ability for message-level authentication and authorization. They together facilitate businesses to seamlessly and dynamically interact with each other in a secured, trusted and federated context. It helps increase the responsiveness to new business opportunities by providing security integration with heterogeneous types of service consumers.

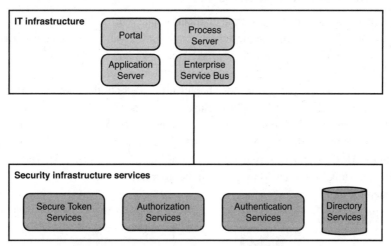

Figure 8.3   Security infrastructure services for the IT infrastructure

Besides, TFIM supports integration with IBM enterprise service bus (ESB) offerings, which include IBM WebSphere Message Broker, IBM WebSphere ESB, and IBM WebSphere DataPower and provides secure token services while connecting various services. A security token is like a security-pass or an identity card that you are required to show if you want to enter a restricted access area. There are several types of electronic security tokens. In a heterogeneous environment, it is likely that different token types will be supported by different middleware infrastructure components, thus requiring the need to transform token types. In many cases, service implementations may restrict the options and formats available for propagating a user's identity to/from the service. Identity services are therefore required in the infrastructure, as shown in Figure 8.4, to deal with these identity mediation issues so that services can be easily interconnected without worrying about how to map and propagate user identity from one service to the next.

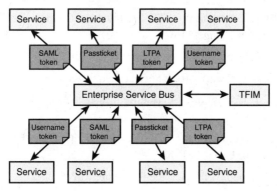

Figure 8.4   Integrating TFIM with an ESB to support token transformation

Tutorial Overview—Enable Security for a Calculator Service Provider and a Service Requester

This calculator service provider is a simple application that returns the sum of two numbers. You will enable security for it so that requesters must provide a valid Username security token for access. Then you will develop a calculator service requester and enable its security so that it will generate a valid security token for accessing the calculator provider.

The tutorials that are featured in this chapter illustrate both the token generator and token consumer functionalities of TFIM. And for illustrative purpose, the application is being configured so that transformation is required both at the requester side and at the provider side. As illustrated in Figure 8.5, the calculator service requester needs to work with the TFIM token generator to transform a SAML token to Username token before sending out a request. The calculator service provider then talks to the TFIM token consumer to transform the received Username token to a SAML token for login.

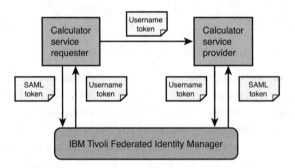

Figure 8.5   Tutorial overview

- Tutorial 8.1: Enable Security for a Service Provider
  - Tutorial 8.1.1: Configure a Service Provider to Use WSSM for Token Consumption Using RAD
  - Tutorial 8.1.2: Configure the STS Trust Service Chain to Be Invoked by the WSSM Token Consumer Using TFIM
  - Tutorial 8.1.3: Deploy the Service Provider to WAS
- Tutorial 8.2: Enable Security for a Service Requester
  - Tutorial 8.2.1: Configure a Service Requester to Use WSSM for Token Generation Using RAD
  - Tutorial 8.2.2: Configure the STS Trust Service Chain to Be Invoked by the WSSM Token Generator Using TFIM
  - Tutorial 8.2.3: Deploy the Service Requester to WAS
- Tutorial 8.3: Test the Service

System Requirements

The tutorial has been developed with the following products and environment, as illustrated in Figure 8.6.

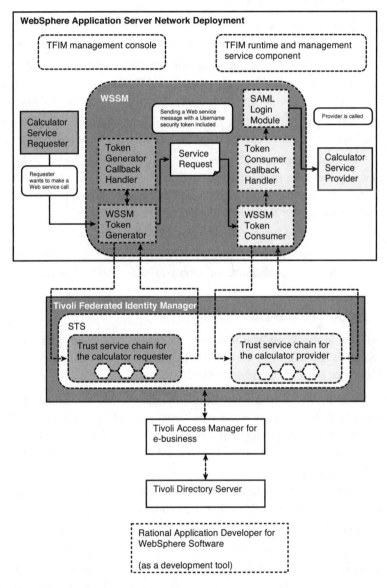

Figure 8.6   Tutorial overview

- IBM Federated Identity Manager version 6.2

- The Web services security management deployment scenario must be installed and configured properly. The software prerequisites for this scenario are as follows:
  - WebSphere Application Server
  - Tivoli Access Manager
  - Tivoli Federated Identity Manager runtime and management service component
  - Tivoli Federated Identity Manager management console component
- The out-of-the-box Echo demonstration application that is included by the product should be used to verify the installation and configuration. You will reuse the user configuration that is set up for the Echo demonstration application in our tutorial.

- IBM Tivoli Access Manager for e-business 6.1 is a prerequisite for the Web services security management deployment scenario of IBM Federated Identity Manager version 6.2.
- IBM WebSphere Application Server 6.1.0.17 is a prerequisite for the Web services security management deployment scenario IBM Federated Identity Manager version 6.2. Besides using it as prerequisite, you will use this IBM WebSphere Application Server for hosting the service requester and service provider in the tutorial.
- IBM Tivoli Directory Server 6.1 is the chosen user registry for this tutorial scenario.
- IBM Rational Application Developer for WebSphere Software 7.5 is used to configure the service requester application and service provider application before deployment.

What Is Included in the CD-ROM?

In the CD included in this book, you will find a completed and configured calculator service requester application and calculator service provider application. All of the tutorials covered in this chapter have been recorded as videos in the CD-ROM.

1. **chapter 8/tutorial 8.1/tutorial files/Setup.zip**—A project interchange archive that contains two initial projects: a calculator service provider project called MyProvider and a calculator service requester project called MyRequester. Security has not been enabled yet for these two projects. They will be used as the starting point of Tutorial 8.1 and Tutorial 8.2.

2. **chapter 8/tutorial 8.1/solution/MyProvider.zip**—A project interchange archive that contains a configured calculator service provider project called MyProvider.

3. **chapter 8/tutorial 8.1/solution/MyProviderEAR.ear**—The configured calculator service provider project exported as an Enterprise Archive (EAR) file.

4. **chapter 8/tutorial 8.2/solution/MyRequester.zip**—A project interchange archive that contains a configured calculator service requester project called MyRequester.

5. **chapter 8/tutorial 8.2/solution/MyRequesterEAR.ear**—The configured calculator service requester project exported as an EAR file.

6. **chapter 8/tutorial 8.x/video**—Contains the video files for all the tutorials discussed in this chapter. Open the Hypertext Markup Language (HTML) file in any browser to watch the video.

Tutorial 8.1: Enable Security for a Service Provider

This tutorial, as shown in Figure 8.7, enables the security for the calculator service provider so that requesters must provide a valid Username security token for access.

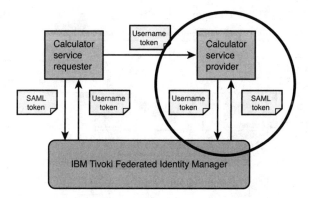

Figure 8.7   Focus of Tutorial 8.1

Figure 8.8 gives a deeper dive and illustrates how the calculator service provider consumes the Username security token that the service requester sends.

1. When a service request is received at the provider side, the token consumer is called as part of the WebSphere Application Server WS-Security authentication processing.

2. The token consumer calls the STS by default. It always sets the Issuer to `urn:itfim:wssm:tokenconsumer` and the AppliesTo to the URL of the Web service, such as `http://localhost:9080/MyProvider/services/Calculator`.

3. Trust service chains in TFIM can perform various actions such as authentication, authorization, identity mapping, and others. For simplicity, you will just configure a trust service chain that will validate a Username security token and issue a SAML 2.0 security token.

4. Once processed, STS responds with a `RequestSecurityTokenResponse` WS-Trust message with a security token issued.

5. You will configure the service provider to use the SAML assertion login module.

6. Once the credential within the security token is validated, the calculator service provider is accessed.

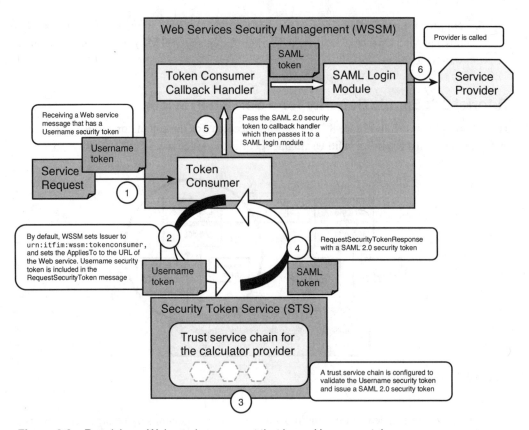

Figure 8.8   Receiving a Web services request that has a Username token

This tutorial is divided into three sections:

- Tutorial 8.1.1: Configure a Service Provider to Use WSSM for Token Consumption Using RAD
- Tutorial 8.1.2: Configure the STS Trust Service Chain to Be Invoked by the WSSM Token Consumer Using TFIM
- Tutorial 8.1.3: Deploy the Service Provider to WAS

Tutorial 8.1.1: Configure a Service Provider to Use WSSM for Token Consumption Using RAD

When a service provider is invoked, WebSphere Application Server invokes the WS-Security infrastructure on behalf of the application to consume the security token. In this tutorial, a Username security token is expected. The WS-Security infrastructure delegates the security token processing to the WSSM token consumer, which calls TFIM STS by default (unless a property of sts.call is added with a value of false). The WSSM token consumer class name is com.tivoli.am.fim.wssm.tokenconsumers.WSSMTokenConsumer, which must be specified in the Web services security binding configuration. Once STS receives a returned token, the WSSM token consumer passes the token to the callback handler, which then sends it to a login module. In this tutorial, a SAML login module is used.

To configure a service provider to expect a Username security token, to invoke WSSM for token consumption, to call STS for token exchange, and to use the SAML login module, you need to update the Web services deployment descriptor of the service provider. You can do this using RAD.

After completing this exercise, you will be able to configure a service provider to use WSSM for token consumption.

1. Import the setup files from the CD to RAD. Setup.zip is a project interchange archive which contains two projects: a calculator service provider project called MyProvider and a calculator service requester project called MyRequester. Security has not been enabled yet for these two projects. They will be used as starting points for Tutorial 8.1 and Tutorial 8.2.

   a. Click File, Import.

   b. Expand the Other folder.

   c. Click Project Interchange.

   d. Click Next.

   e. Click Browse to locate the file chapter 8/tutorial 8.1/tutorial files/Setup.zip from the CD. Then click Open.

   f. Click Select All to import the four projects, as shown in Figure 8.9.

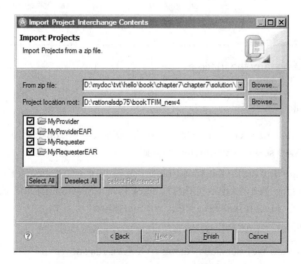

Figure 8.9   Importing the provider and the requester projects

    g. Click Finish.

2. Look at the service provider.

    a. Right-click `MyProvider`.

    b. Click Properties on the pop-up menu.

    c. Click Targeted Runtimes. Figure 8.10 shows that this tutorial deploys the applications onto WebSphere Application Server v6.1. As mentioned in the "System Requirements" section, the IBM WebSphere Application Server 6.1.0.17 that has been used as a prerequisite for TFIM is also used for hosting the service requester and service provider in this tutorial.

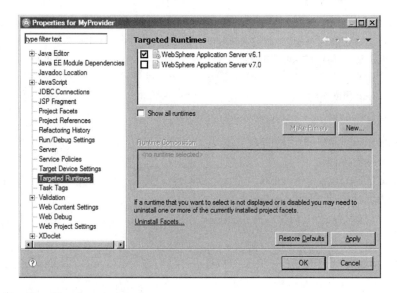

Figure 8.10   Checking targeted runtime

    d. Click OK.

3. To configure a service provider to use WSSM for token consumption, you need to update its Web services deployment descriptor.

    a. Make sure you are in the Java Enterprise Edition (EE) perspective. If not, click Windows, Open Perspective, Other. Select Java EE (default) and click OK. Select the Show All check box if Java EE is not in the list.

    b. Open the file MyProvider, WebContent, `WEB-INF`, `webservices.xml`.

    c. Note that the Web service is using JAX-RPC, as shown in Figure 8.11. JAX-RPC has a successor called JAX-WS that uses policy sets to enable security for Web services applications. However, TFIM 6.2 WSSM does not support JAX-WS or policy sets yet. So JAX-RPC is used here. By default, Web services created by RAD 7.5 are configured to use JAX-WS. When generating your Web services applications, make sure you override the default and choose JAX-RPC if you plan to configure it to use identity service from TFIM.

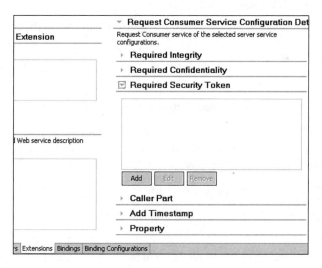

Figure 8.11 JAX_RPC is used

   d. Click the Extensions tab of the Web Services Editor.

   e. Expand Request Consumer Service Configuration Details.

4. Configure the security provider to only accept the Username security token.

   a. Expand Required Security Token.

   b. The page should look like Figure 8.12. Click Add.

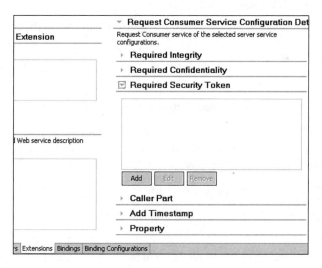

Figure 8.12 Adding a security token

   c. In the Name field, type `Username`.

   d. In the Token Type list, specify Username Token.

   e. The Local Part and Usage Type are automatically filled in. The page should look like Figure 8.13.

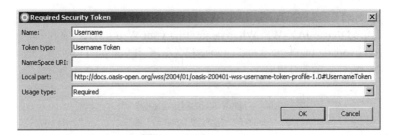

Figure 8.13   Specifying a security token

    f. Click OK.

5. Configure the *caller part* of the service provider. The caller configuration defines which token type is used by the WebSphere security runtime to create the WebSphere credentials.

    a. Expand Caller Part.

    b. Click Add.

    c. In the Name field, type `Username`.

    d. In the Namespace URI field, type `urn:oasis:names:tc:SAML:2.0:assertion`.

    e. In the Local Part field, type `Assertion`.

    f. Click Add under Property to add the following property. (Note: The Value field is blank.)

      • Name: `com.ibm.wsspi.wssecurity.caller.tokenConsumerNS`

      • Value:

    g. Click Add again under Property to add the following property.

      • Name: `com.ibm.wsspi.wssecurity.caller.tokenConsumerLN`

      • Value: http://docs.oasis-open.org/wss/2004/01/oasis-200401-wss-username-token-profile-1.0#UsernameToken

    h. The page should look like Figure 8.14.

    i. Click OK.

6. Add a token consumer.

    a. Click the Binding Configurations tab of the Web Services Editor.

    b. Expand Request Consumer Binding Configuration Details.

    c. Expand Token Consumer.

    d. The page should look like Figure 8.15. Click Add.

7. Configure the token consumer to use TFIM WSSM classes and the SAML login module.

    a. In the Token Consumer Name field, type `Username`.

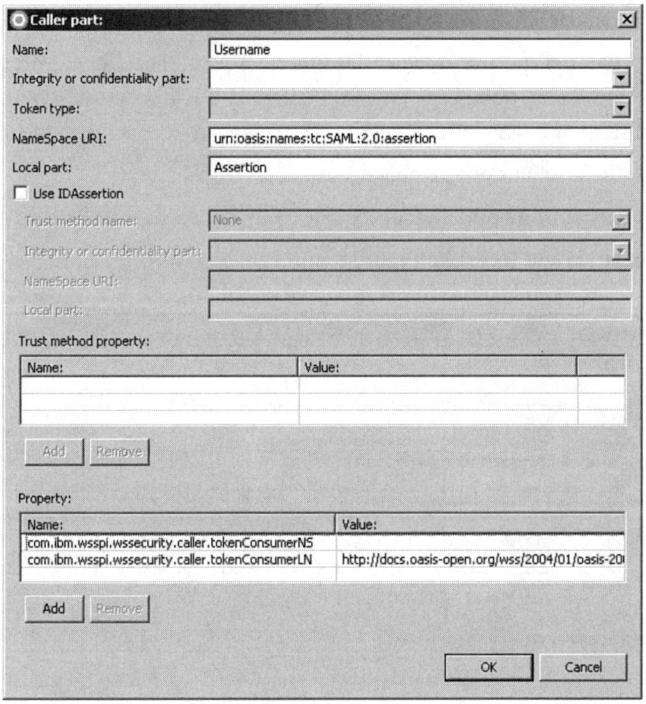

Figure 8.14 Adding a caller part

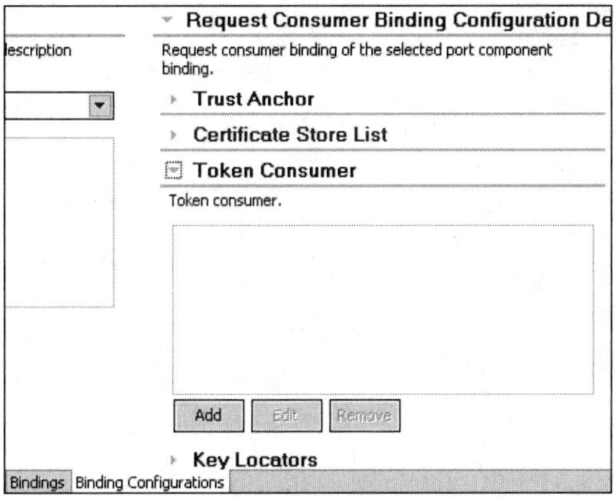

Figure 8.15 Adding a token consumer

  b. In the Token Consumer Class field, type com.tivoli.am.fim.wssm.tokenconsumers.
  WSSMTokenConsumer. Note: This class name is not available from the drop-down list.
  You have to type it in manually.

  c. In the Security Token list, specify Username.

    d. Select the Use Value Type check box.

    e. In the Value Type list, specify Username Token. The Local Part is populated with http://docs.oasis-open.org/wss/2004/01/oasis-200401-wss-Username-token-profile-1.0#UsernameToken after selecting Username Token as the value type.

    f. Check the Use jaas.config check box.

    g. In the jaas.config.name field, type `system.itfim.wssm.samla`.

    h. The page should look like Figure 8.16.

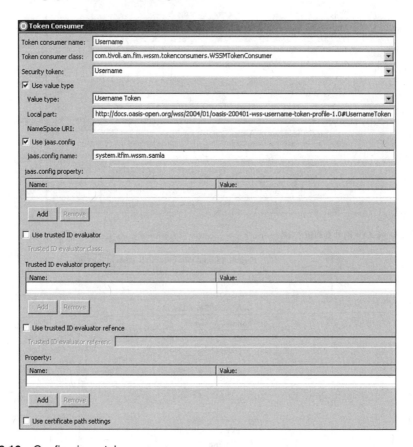

Figure 8.16 Configuring a token consumer

    i. Click OK.

8. Click File, Save All to save all the changes. The service provider is now configured to accept a Username token, call TFIM trust service, and then call the SAML login module.

9. Export the application as an EAR file.

    a. Right-click the project `MyProviderEAR`.

    b. Click Export, EAR File on the pop-up menu.

    c. Click Browse to specify the target location of the EAR file. Use the default name `MyProviderEAR`. Click Save.

    d. Click Finish.

You have configured a service provider to expect a Username token from its requesters. The service provider is now ready for deployment. You will deploy this EAR file in Tutorial 8.1.3.

Tutorial 8.1.2: Configure the STS Module Chain to Be Invoked by the WSSM Token Consumer Using TFIM

In Tutorial 8.1.1, you have configured the service provider to expect a Username token and then use the SAML login module. The WSSM token consumer calls STS by default. STS can be used to perform various functions such as authentication, authorization, identity mapping, and others. For simplicity, you will just configure an STS trust service chain to validate a Username token and issue a SAML 2.0 token.

After completing this exercise, you will be able to create a trust service chain to transform a Username token to a SAML token.

1. Create a trust service chain. STS uses trust service chains to validate, transform, and issue security tokens.

    a. Log on to the WAS Administrative console (`https://localhost:9043/ibm/console/logon.jsp`), where the TFIM management console component is installed.

    b. Expand Tivoli Federated Identity Manager.

    c. Expand Configure Trust Service.

    d. Click Trust Service Chains.

    e. Click Create to create a new trust service chain.

    f. After reading the introduction material, click Next.

    g. In the Chain Mapping Name field on the Chain Mapping Identification page, type `Calculator service provider module chain`.

    h. In the Description field, type `Generate SAML 20 from Username`.

    i. The page should look like Figure 8.17. Click Next.

2. Specify AppliesTo and Issuer. STS uses these two values to uniquely locate the right trust service chain. By default, WSSM sets Issuer to `urn:itfim:wssm:tokenconsumer` and sets AppliesTo to the URL of the Web service. Configure the trust service with these two values.

    a. In the AppliesTo Address field on the Chain Mapping Lookup page, type `REGEXP:(.*/MyProvider/services/Calculator)`.

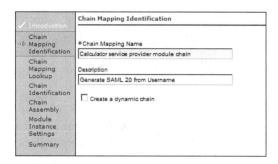

Figure 8.17   Naming the new trust service chain

b. In the Issuer Address field, type `urn:itfim:wssm:tokenconsumer` as shown in Figure 8.18.

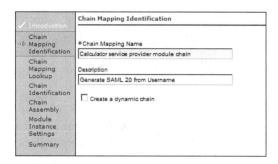

Figure 8.18   Specifying chain mapping lookup values

c. Click Next.

d. Keep the default chain name, `Calculator service provider module chain`.

e. Click Next.

3. Add module instances to the trust service chain. A *trust service chain* is composed of a group of module instances that are being executed in sequential order. Each module instance performs a specific function such as validating an incoming token, converting the data into a token-neutral format, mapping and modifying the user identity data within the token-neutral format to reflect application-specific requirements, and issuing the new token instance by converting the token-neutral data into a different token module type. For this tutorial, you will add two module instances to the trust service chain. One is to validate a Username security token; another is to issue a SAML 2.0 security token.

    a. For the Module Instance list on the Chain Assembly page, specify Default Username Token.

    b. For the Mode list, specify Validate.

    c. Click Add Selected Module Instance to Chain.

    d. Similarly, add the module instance Default SAML 2.0 Token with an Issue mode to the chain.

    e. The trust service chain should look something like Figure 8.19. TFIM supports other actions such as authentication, authorization, identity mapping, and others. You could do identity mapping and retrieve additional attributes to include in the assertion by adding a "map" mode module between the validate and issue modules. For simplicity, you just configure it to validate a Username security token and issue a SAML 2.0 security token.

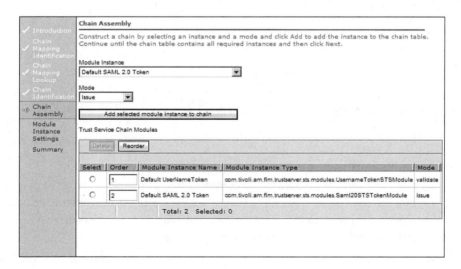

Figure 8.19   Creating a trust service chain

    f. Click Next.

    g. Click Continue in the message box that says that the trust service chain you have assembled does not meet the recommended Trust Service trust service chain structure, which suggests Validate, Map, Issue.

4. Configure the Username module.

    a. Select the Skip Password Validation check box on the Username Module configuration page.

    b. For the Amount of Time the Token Is Valid after Being Issued (Seconds) field, type `-1`. Certain identity providers may not include the creation time in their identity; set the amount of time to –1 to skip the creation time validation.

    c. Leave other fields as default, similar to Figure 8.20. Click Next.

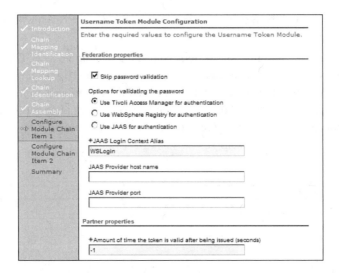

Figure 8.20   Specifying the Username module information

5. Configure the SAML 2.0 module.

    a. For The Name of the Organization Issuing the Assertions field on the SAML 2.0 Module Configuration page, type `Calculator Company` as the company name. Note: This field cannot be left blank; otherwise, you will get a runtime exception saying the generated security token does not comply to standard.

    b. Clear the Sign SAML Assertions check box. To sign an assertion, you need a keystore with keys or certificates. For simplicity, you do not sign assertions in this tutorial.

c. Leave other fields as default. The page should look like Figure 8.21. Click Next.

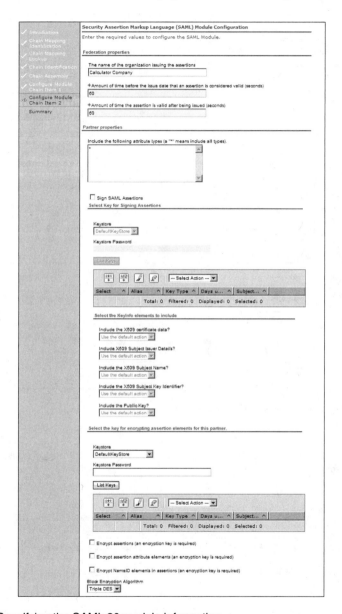

Figure 8.21 Specifying the SAML 20 module information

6. Review the summary information which should look similar to Figure 8.22 and click Finish.

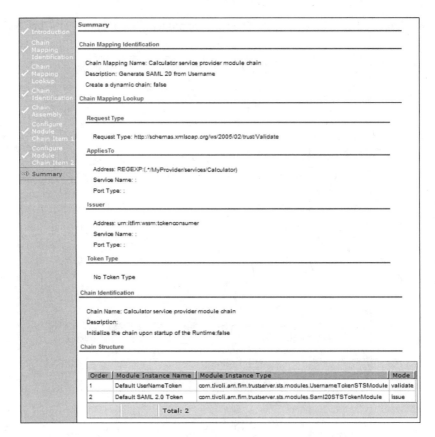

Figure 8.22   Reviewing the summary information

7. Click Load Configuration Changes to Tivoli Federated Identity Manager Runtime like Figure 8.23 to save the changes.

Figure 8.23   Loading configuration changes to TFIM

8. A trust service chain for generating a SAML 2.0 security token from a Username security token is now created for the service provider, as shown in Figure 8.24.

You have created a trust service chain in TFIM to transform a Username token to a SAML token.

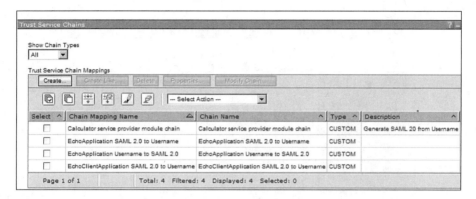

Figure 8.24   The calculator service provider module chain

Tutorial 8.1.3: Deploy the Service Provider to WAS

In Tutorial 8.1.1, you created an EAR file for the calculator service provider. Let's deploy it to WAS. As mentioned in the "System Requirements" section, the IBM WebSphere Application Server 6.1.0.17 that has been used as a prerequisite for TFIM is also used for hosting the service requester and service provider in this tutorial.

1.   Install the service provider EAR file, `MyProviderEAR.ear`, that was created in Tutorial 8.1.1.

   a.   Log on to the WAS Administrative console (https://localhost:9043/ibm/console/logon.jsp), where the TFIM management console component is installed.

   b.   Expand Applications.

   c.   Click Install New Application.

   d.   Click Browse to specify the location of the EAR file.

   e.   Click Next.

   f.   Keep clicking Next. Accept all the default values.

   g.   The installation summary should look like Figure 8.25. Click Finish.

   h.   Once the application is deployed successfully, click Save to save the changes like Figure 8.26

2.   Start the application.

   a.   Expand Applications.

   b.   Click Enterprise Applications.

   c.   Select the MyProviderEAR application check box, as shown in Figure 8.27.

   d.   Click Start to start the calculator service provider. The application status should turn from red-cross to green-arrow upon a successful start.

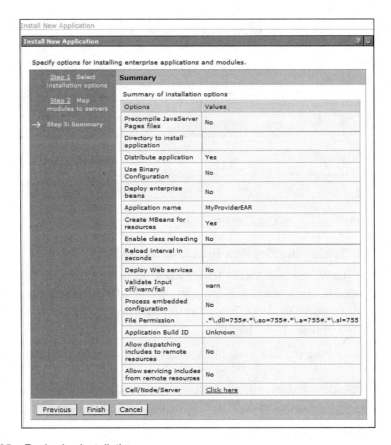

Figure 8.25 Reviewing installation summary

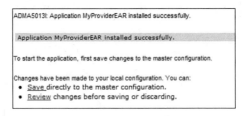

Figure 8.26 Saving the changes

The service provider is now deployed to an application server and is ready to process service requests.

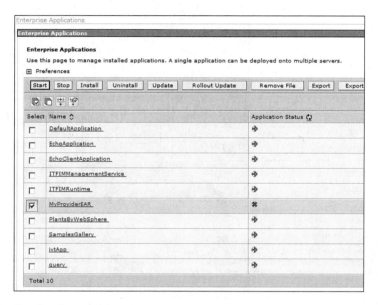

Figure 8.27   Starting the provider

Tutorial 8.2: Enable Security for a Service Requester

This tutorial, as illustrated in Figure 8.28, enables the security for the calculator service requester so that it will generate a valid security token for accessing the calculator provider.

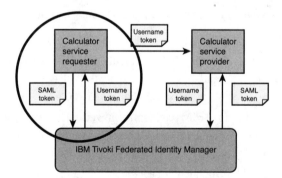

Figure 8.28   Sending out a Web services request that contains a Username token

Figure 8.29 gives a deeper dive and illustrates how the calculator service requester generates a Username security token.

1. The calculator service requester makes a service request to the calculator service provider.

2. The WSSM token generator works with the callback handler to generate a security token. You will configure the service requester to use the JAAS subject credential XML callback handler. By default, this callback handler returns the JAAS subject in a SAML 2.0 assertion.

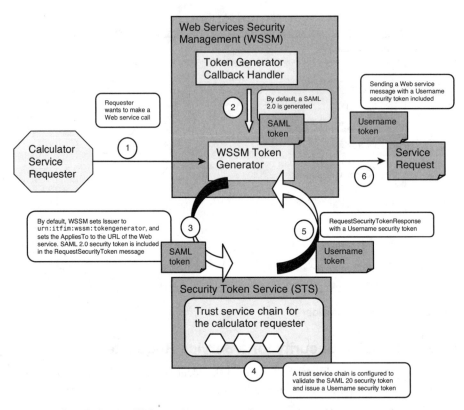

Figure 8.29   Sending out a Web services request that contains a Username token

3. The token generator calls the STS by default. It always sets the Issuer to `urn:itfim:wssm:tokengenerator` and the AppliesTo to the URL of the Web service, such as `http://localhost:9080/MyProvider/services/Calculator`.

4. Trust service chains in TFIM can perform various actions such as authentication, authorization, identity mapping, and others. For simplicity, you will just configure it to validate a SAML 2.0 security token and issue a Username security token.

5. Once processed, STS responds with a `RequestSecurityTokenResponse` WS-Trust message with a Username security token issued.

6. You will configure the service requester to use the WebSphere Application Server callback handler, Username callback handler, which will insert the Username security token into the security header of the Web services request message.

This tutorial is divided into three sections:

• Tutorial 8.2.1: Configure a Service Requester to Use WSSM for Token Generation Using RAD

- Tutorial 8.2.2: Configure the STS Trust Service Chain to Be Invoked by the WSSM Token Generator Using TFIM
- Tutorial 8.2.3: Deploy the Service Requester to WAS

Tutorial 8.2.1: Configure a Service Requester to Use WSSM for Token Generation Using RAD

The WSSM token generator works with the callback handler to generate a security token. The WSSM token generator class name is `com.tivoli.am.fim.wssm.tokengenerators.WSSMToken Generator`, which must be specified in the Web services security binding configuration. You will configure the service requester to use the JAAS subject credential XML callback handler and the Username WebSphere Application Server callback handler, which will insert the Username security token in the security header of the Web services request message.

To configure a service requester to use WSSM for token generation, you need to update the WS-Binding and WS-Extension of its Web deployment descriptor. You can do this using RAD. You will also enable security for the service requester by creating a security constraint in the descriptor.

Do this exercise using the same RAD workbench as Tutorial 8.1.1. After completing this exercise, you will be able to configure a service requester to use WSSM for token generation.

1. Edit the Web Deployment descriptor to enable security for the service requester so that only authorized users can access it.

   a. Continue from the RAD workbench that you used in Tutorial 8.1.1 which has the four projects from the setup files imported. Make sure you are in the Java EE perspective. If not, click Windows, Open Perspective, Other. Select Java EE (default) and click OK. Select the Show All check box if Java EE is not in the list.

   b. Open the file `MyRequester`, `WebContent`, `WEB-INF`, `web.xml`.

   c. Click the Security tab of the Web Deployment Descriptor Editor.

2. Add a security role. A *security role* defines a group of people who can access the client.

   a. Click Add under the Security Roles section.

   b. In the Name field, type `MySecurityRole`.

   c. Click Finish.

   d. A security called `MySecurityRole` is added, as illustrated in Figure 8.30.

Figure 8.30   Adding a security role

3. Add a security constraint. A *security constraint* prescribes access policies for specific Web resources.

   a. Click Add under the Security Constraint section.

   b. In the Constraint Name field, type `MyConstraints`.

   c. Click Next.

   d. In the Resource Name field on the Add Web Resource page, type `MyResource`.

   e. Click Add beside the Pattern section.

   f. In the Name field, type `/*` as shown in Figure 8.31, and click OK to dismiss the page. This declares to which URL pattern this security constraint applies.

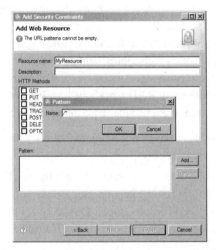

Figure 8.31   Defining a pattern for the Web resource of a security constraint

   g. Click Finish to dismiss the Add Security Constraints page. The page should look like Figure 8.32.

Figure 8.32   Adding a security constraint

4. Add an *authorization constraint*. This defines which security roles have access to the collection of Web resources defined in this security constraint.

a. Click Add beside Authorized Roles.

b. In the Description field on the Define Authorization Constraint page, type `MyAuthConstraint`.

c. Select the `MySecurityRole` check box listed in the Role Name section.

d. Click Finish.

e. The security information should look like Figure 8.33. You have defined a security constraint, `MyConstraints`. It allows the security role, `MySecurityRole`, to access all the Web resources of the `MyRequester` (because the URL pattern is `/*`).

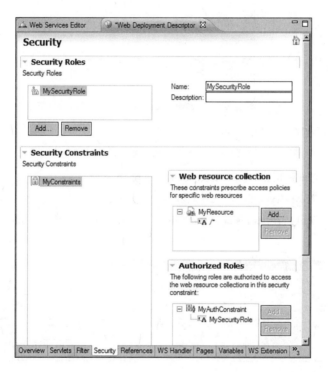

Figure 8.33 Adding security information

5. Define what type of security token should be generated by this client when making a service request. This client intends to access the Calculator service provider, which accepts the Username token only.

a. Click the WS Extension tab of the Web Deployment Descriptor Editor.

b. Expand Request Generator Configuration.

c. Expand Security Token.

d. The page should look like Figure 8.34. Click Add.

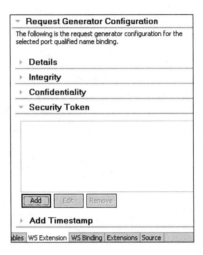

Figure 8.34   Adding a security token

e. In the Name field on the Security Token page, type `Username`.

f. In the Token Type field, type `Username Token`.

g. The Local Part field is automatically filled in. The page should look like Figure 8.35.

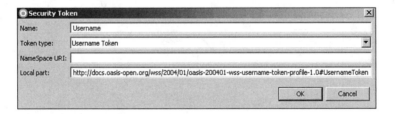

Figure 8.35   Adding a security token for request generator

h. Click OK.

6. Add a token generator.

   a. Click the WS Binding tab of the Web Deployment Descriptor Editor.

   b. Expand Service Request Generator Binding Configuration Details.

   c. Expand Token Generator.

   d. The page should look like Figure 8.36. Click Add.

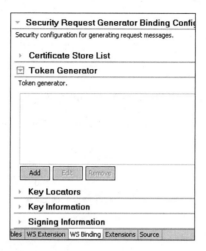

Figure 8.36   Adding a token generator

7. Configure the token generator to use WSSM and call the right callback handler.

  a. In the Token Generator Name field, type `Username`.

  b. In the Token Generator Class field, type `com.tivoli.am.fim.wssm.tokengenerators.` `WSSMTokenGenerator`. Note: This class name is not available from the drop-down list. You have to type it in manually.

  c. In the Security Token list, specify Username. This is to generate a Username security token for accessing the calculator provider.

  d. Select the Use Value Type check box.

  e. In the Value Type list, specify Username Token. The Local Part is populated with http://docs.oasis-open.org/wss/2004/01/oasis-200401-wss-Username-token-profile-1.0#UsernameToken after selecting Username Token as the value type.

  f. In the Callback Handler field, type `com.tivoli.am.fim.wssm.callbackhandlers.` `WSSMTokenGeneratorCallbackHandler`. Note: This handler name is not available from the drop-down list. You have to type it in manually. The WSSM token generator works with the callback handler to generate a security token.

  g. Click Add under Callback Handler Property to add the following property. This is to configure the service requester to use the JAAS subject credential callback handler.

    • Name: `xml.callback.handler.class.name`

    • Value: `com.tivoli.am.fim.wssm.callbackhandlers.JAASSubjectCallbackHandler`

  h. Click Add again under Callback Handler Property to add the following property. This is to call the Username callback handler, which will insert the Username security token in the security header of the Web services request message.

- Name: `token.callback.handler.class.name`
- Value: `com.tivoli.am.fim.wssm.callbackhandlers.UsernameCallbackHandler`

i. The page should look like Figure 8.37.

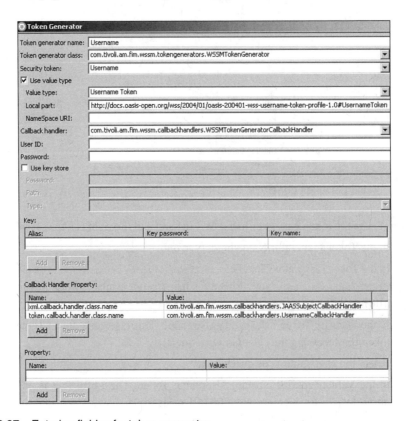

Figure 8.37   Entering fields of a token generator

j. Click OK.

8. Click File, Save All to save all the changes. The service requester is now configured to generate a Username token, and its security is enabled.

9. Export the application as an EAR file.

a. Right-click the project `MyRequesterEAR`.

b. Click Export, EAR file on the pop-up menu.

c. Click Browse to specify the target location of the EAR file. Use the default name `MyRequesterEAR`. Click Save.

d. Click Finish.

You have enabled security for a service requester and configured it to include a Username token in a service request. The service requester is now ready for deployment. You will deploy this EAR file in Tutorial 8.2.3.

Tutorial 8.2.2: Configure the STS Module Chain to Be Invoked by the WSSM Token Generator Using TFIM

In Tutorial 8.2.1, you configured the service requester to use the JAAS subject credential XML callback handler. By default, this callback handler returns the JAAS subject in a SAML 2.0 assertion. You will use TFIM management console to create an STS trust service chain that validates a SAML 2.0 security token and issues a Username security token. Once processed, STS responds with a `RequestSecurityTokenResponse` WS-Trust message with a Username security token issued.

After completing this exercise, you will be able to create a trust service chain that transforms a SAML token to a Username token.

1. Create a trust service chain. STS uses trust service chains to validate, transform, and issue security tokens.

   a. Log on to the WAS Administrative console (`https://localhost:9043/ibm/console/logon.jsp`), where the TFIM management console component is installed.

   b. Expand Tivoli Federated Identity Manager.

   c. Expand Configure Trust Service.

   d. Click Trust Service Chains.

   e. Click Create to create a new trust service chain.

   f. After reading the introduction material, click Next.

   g. In the Chain Mapping Name field on the Chain Mapping Identification page, type `Calculator service requester module chain`.

   h. In the Description field, type `Generate Username token from SAML 20`.

   i. The page should look like Figure 8.38. Click Next.

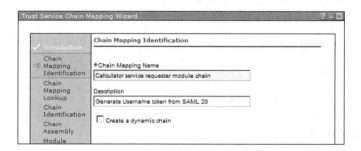

Figure 8.38   Naming the new trust service chain

2. Specify AppliesTo and Issuer. STS uses these two values to uniquely locate the right trust ser-
    vice chain. By default, WSSM sets Issuer to `urn:itfim:wssm:tokengenerator`, and it sets
    AppliesTo to the URL of the Web service. Use these two values for the trust service chain.

    a. In the AppliesTo Address field on the Chain Mapping Lookup page, type
        `REGEXP:(.*/MyProvider/services/Calculator)`.

    b. In the Issuer Address field, type `urn:itfim:wssm:tokengenerator` as illustrated in
        Figure 8.39.

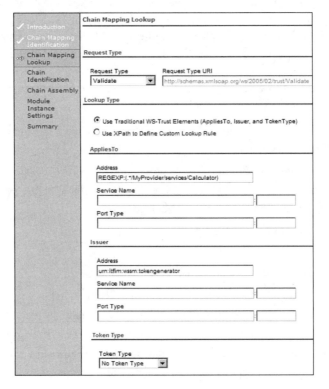

Figure 8.39   Specifying chain mapping lookup values

    c. Click Next.

    d. Keep the default chain name, `Calculator service requester module chain`.

    e. Click Next.

3. Add module instances to the trust service chain. For this tutorial, you will add two mod-
    ule instances to the trust service chain. One is to validate a SAML 2.0 security token;
    another is to issue a Username security token.

    a. For the Module Instance list on the Chain Assembly page, specify Default SAML
        2.0 Token.

b. For the Mode list, specify Validate.

c. Click Add Selected Module Instance to Chain.

d. Similarly, add the module instance Default Username Token with an Issue mode to the chain.

e. The trust service chain should look something like Figure 8.40. TFIM supports other actions such as authentication, authorization, identity mapping, and others. You could do identity mapping and retrieve additional attributes to include in the assertion by adding a "map" mode module between the validate and issue modules. For simplicity, just configure it to validate a SAML 2.0 security token and issue a User-name security token.

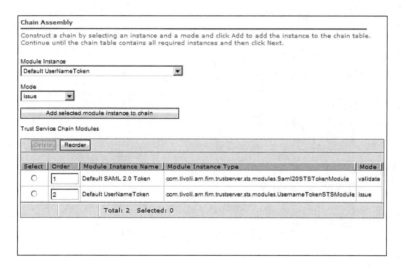

Figure 8.40   Creating a trust service chain

f. Click Next.

g. Click Continue in the message box that says that the trust service chain you have assembled does not meet the recommended Trust Service trust service chain structure, which suggests Validate, Map, Issue.

4. Configure the SAML 2.0 module.

a. Clear the Enable One-Time Assertion Use Enforcement check box.

b. Clear the Enable Signature Validation check box. To validate a signature, you need a keystore with keys or certificates. For simplicity, you do not sign assertions in this tutorial.

c. Leave other fields as default. The page should look like Figure 8.41. Click Next.

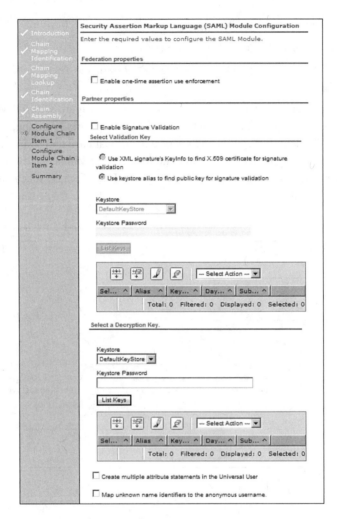

Figure 8.41   Specifying the SAML 20 module information

5. Configure the Username module.

    a. On the Username Token Module Configuration page, use the default values. The page should look like Figure 8.42. Click Next.

6. Review the summary information. The page should look similar to Figure 8.43. Click Finish.

7. Click Load Configuration Changes to Tivoli Federated Identity Manager Runtime to save the changes.

8. A trust service chain for generating a Username token from a SAML 2.0 is now created for the service requester, as shown in Figure 8.44.

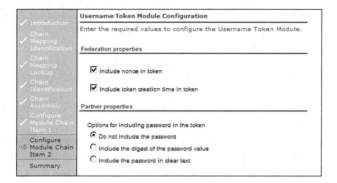

Figure 8.42 Specifying the Username module information

Summary

Chain Mapping Identification

Chain Mapping Name: Calculator service requester module chain
Description: Generate Username token from SAML 20
Create a dynamic chain: false

Chain Mapping Lookup

Request Type

Request Type: http://schemas.xmlsoap.org/ws/2005/02/trust/Validate

AppliesTo

Address: REGEXP:(.*/MyProvider/services/Calculator)
Service Name: :
Port Type: :

Issuer

Address: urn:itfim:wssm:tokengenerator
Service Name: :
Port Type: :

Token Type

No Token Type

Chain Identification

Chain Name: Calculator service requester module chain
Description:
Initialize the chain upon startup of the Runtime:false

Chain Identification

Chain Name: Calculator service requester module chain
Description:
Initialize the chain upon startup of the Runtime:false

Chain Structure

Order	Module Instance Name	Module Instance Type	Mode
1	Default SAML 2.0 Token	com.tivoli.am.fim.trustserver.sts.modules.Saml20STSTokenModule	validate
2	Default UserNameToken	com.tivoli.am.fim.trustserver.sts.modules.UsernameTokenSTSModule	issue
	Total: 2		

Figure 8.43 Reviewing the summary information

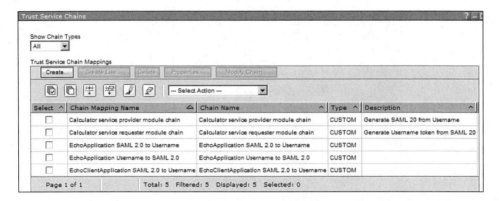

Figure 8.44   The calculator service requester module chain

You have created a trust service chain that transforms a SAML token to a Username token.

Tutorial 8.2.3: Deploy the Service Requester to WAS

In Tutorial 8.2.1, you created an EAR file for the calculator service requester. Let's deploy it to WAS. As mentioned in the "System Requirements" section, the IBM WebSphere Application Server 6.1.0.17 that has been used as a prerequisite for TFIM is also used for hosting the service requester and service provider in this tutorial.

1.   Install the service requester EAR file, `MyRequesterEAR.ear`, that was created in Tutorial 8.2.1.

   a.   Log on to the WAS Administrative console (`https://localhost:9043/ibm/console/logon.jsp`) where the TFIM management console component is installed.

   b.   Expand Applications.

   c.   Click `Install New Application`.

   d.   Click Browse to specify the location of the EAR file.

   e.   Click Next.

   f.   Keep clicking Next. Accept all the default values.

   g.   The installation summary should look like Figure 8.45. Click Finish.

   h.   Once the application is deployed successfully, click Save to save the changes.

2.   Start the application.

   a.   Expand Applications.

   b.   Click Enterprise Applications.

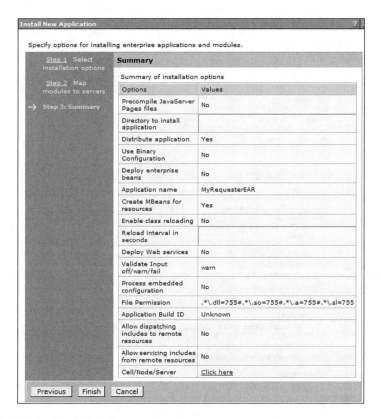

Figure 8.45   Reviewing installation summary

    c.   Select the `MyRequesterEAR` application check box.

    d.   Click Start to start the calculator service provider. The application status should turn from red-cross to green-arrow upon a successful start, similar to Figure 8.46.

Figure 8.46   Starting the requester

    3.   Configure the security role mapping. In Tutorial 8.2.1, you created a security role `MySecurityRole`, which defines a group of people who can access the client. You will map this role to all authenticated users in the application server.

    a.   Click `MyRequesterEAR`.

b. Click Security Role to User/Group Mapping under the Detail Properties section, as illustrated in Figure 8.47.

Figure 8.47   Setting the security role to user/group mapping

c. As shown in Figure 8.48, select the All Authenticated check box for the `MySecurityRole` role.

d. Click OK.

4. Click Save to save the changes, like Figure 8.49.

You have deployed the service requester to an application server. You can now test the service.

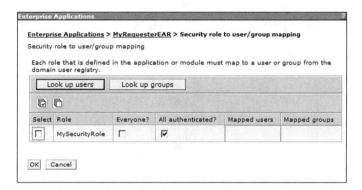

Figure 8.48   Mapping the MyRequesterSecurityRole

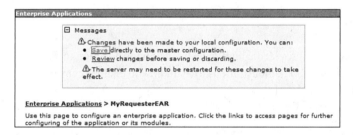

Figure 8.49   Saving the changes

Tutorial 8.3: Test the Service

Now both the calculator service requester and the calculator service provider have been deployed and secured. To run the application, the service provider and the service requester have to share a federated identity. Configuring the user registry is out of scope for this chapter. However, if you have correctly installed and configured the sample Echo application that comes with TFIM, a user named `wssm-testuser` with a password of `testonly123` should have been created. Let's use it to test our application.

1. Invoke the calculator service.

    a. Open any browser and access the calculator client (`http://localhost:9080/MyRequester/sampleCalculatorProxy/TestClient.jsp`).

    b. Log on as `wssm-testuser`, which should have a password of `testonly123`.

    c. Click the `getEndpoint()` link.

    d. Click Invoke to check the endpoint of the service provider. Something like `http://localhost:9080/MyProvider/services/Calculator` should be returned. If your system has a different port number, click the link `setEndpoint(java.lang.String)`. Enter a correct endpoint and click Invoke to change it.

    e. Click the `getSum(double, double)` link.

    f. Enter any numbers like Figure 8.50, and test the result.

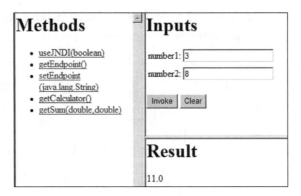

Figure 8.50   Testing the calculator

Summary

The preceding tutorials provided a high-level hands-on introduction to TFIM. You have followed step-by-step exercises and demonstrations to learn how to enable security for a service requester and a service provider.

Tutorial summary:

- Tutorial 8.1: Enable Security for a Service Provider
  - Tutorial 8.1.1: Configure a Service Provider to Use WSSM for Token Consumption Using RAD
    - Configure the caller part of a service provider
    - Configure the token consumer to use TFIM WSSM classes and SAML login module
  - Tutorial 8.1.2: Configure the STS Trust Service Chain to Be Invoked by the WSSM Token Consumer Using TFIM
    - Create a trust service chain
    - Specify the AppliesTo and Issuer of a service chain
    - Add a validate module instance to validate a Username token
    - Add an issue module instance to generate a SAML token
  - Tutorial 8.1.3: Deploy the Service Provider to WAS
- Tutorial 8.2: Enable Security for a Service Requester
  - Tutorial 8.2.1: Configure a Service Requester to Use WSSM for Token Generation Using RAD
    - Add a security role
    - Add a security constraint

- Add an authorization constraint
- Configure the token generator to use WSSM and call the right callback handler
- Tutorial 8.2.2: Configure the STS Trust Service Chain to Be Invoked by the WSSM Token Generator Using TFIM
  - Create a trust service chain
  - Specify the AppliesTo and Issuer of a service chain
  - Add a validate module instance to validate a SAML token
  - Add an issue module instance to generate a Username token
- Tutorial 8.2.3: Deploy the Service Requester to WAS
- Tutorial 8.3: Test the Service

Conclusion

Congratulations on completing the book *Understanding IBM SOA Foundation Suite: Learning Visually with Examples.*

This book provides one starting point for you to learn and build a good knowledge base on IBM SOA products. It covers products overview, key concepts and features, the products' support of SOA, and step-by-step tutorials. The tutorials are also recorded as videos to provide another effective learning mechanism.

Either by doing them hands-on or watching the videos on the accompanying CD-ROM, you have come a long way by finishing 26 tutorials on 10 IBM products from the IBM SOA Foundation suite. We hope that you find the tutorials useful.

Following are the products that you have learned:

1. IBM Rational Software Architect
2. IBM Rational Application Developer
3. IBM WebSphere Application Server
4. IBM WebSphere Service Registry and Repository
5. IBM WebSphere Integration Developer
6. IBM WebSphere Process Server
7. IBM WebSphere Message Broker
8. IBM WebSphere Portlet Factory
9. IBM WebSphere Portal
10. IBM Tivoli Federated Identity Manager

Although the products featured in this book are not a complete list from the IBM SOA Foundation suite, they represent a solid collection of products in various aspects of SOA that will be valuable to you in a SOA project. To find out more about the IBM SOA Foundation suite, the following URL is a good starting point for your reference:

- www-01.ibm.com/software/solutions/soa/offerings.html

As your next step, IBM Software Library, IBM developerWorks, and IBM Redbooks offer many useful technical resources and literature for advance reading:

- www-01.ibm.com/software/sw-library/
- www.ibm.com/developerworks/
- www.redbooks.ibm.com/

We would like to congratulate you once again on the successful completion of this book. We hope that the knowledge you have gained through the book will be helpful for your current and future SOA projects. Thank you for joining us on this wonderful journey.

Index

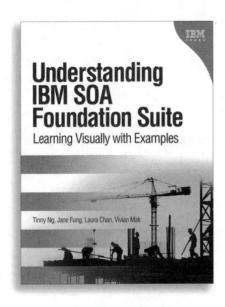

FREE Online Edition

Your purchase of **Understanding IBM SOA Foundation Suite** includes access to a free online edition for 45 days through the Safari Books Online subscription service. Nearly every IBM Press book is available online through Safari Books Online, along with more than 5,000 other technical books and videos from publishers such as Addison-Wesley Professional, Cisco Press, Exam Cram, O'Reilly, Prentice Hall, Que, and Sams.

SAFARI BOOKS ONLINE allows you to search for a specific answer, cut and paste code, download chapters, and stay current with emerging technologies.

Activate your FREE Online Edition at
www.informit.com/safarifree

> **STEP 1:** Enter the coupon code: DQWPFDB.

> **STEP 2:** New Safari users, complete the brief registration form.
> Safari subscribers, just log in.

If you have difficulty registering on Safari or accessing the online edition, please e-mail customer-service@safaribooksonline.com

About the CD

In the CD included in this book, you will find completed solutions for all the exercises discussed in this book. All of the tutorials have been recorded as videos so you can learn the operational concepts of the products.

The CD is organized as follows:

```
readme.htmlchapter x
readme.html
  /setup
  /tutorial x.y
    /solution
    /tutorial files
    /video
```

There is a readme file that can be opened in any browser. It provides a table of links to the readme file of each chapter.

Each chapter folder has the following structure:

A readme file that can be opened in any browser. It gives you a brief introduction to what to expect in the folder underneath. It also provides a table of links to the videos that can be clicked and run directly.

A setup folder that contains the files, if any, that are needed to set up the tutorials.

A set of tutorial x.y folders. Each has

A solution folder that contains a completed solution, if any, for the subject tutorial.

A tutorial files folder that contains the files, if any, that are needed when exercising the subject tutorial.

A video folder that contains the video files for the subject tutorial allowing readers to watch the step-by-step instructions. Open the HTML file in any browser to watch the video.

System Requirements:

System Requirements: Operating System: Mac OS® X v10.4 or higher or Windows® XP or Windows Vista®.

Adobe® Flash® Player plug-in is required to view the videos.

License Agreement

Use of the contents on the CD accompanying *Understanding IBM® SOA Foundation Suite: Learning Visually with Examples* is subject to the Terms of Use and Warranty Disclaimer found on the media sleeve.

Technical Support

Pearson Education does not offer technical support for any of the programs on the CD.

However, if the CD is damaged, you may obtain a replacement copy by describing the problem through http://www.ibmpressbooks.com/about/contact_us.